The
Math Teacher's
BOOK OF LISTS

PRENTICE HALL

The
Math Teacher's
BOOK OF LISTS

Judith A. Muschla
Gary Robert Muschla

PRENTICE HALL

Library of Congress Cataloging-in-Publication Data

Muschla, Gary Robert.
    The math teacher's book of lists / Gary Robert Muschla, Judith Muschla.
      p.   cm.
    ISBN 0-13-180357-3 : Spiral—ISBN 0-13-255910-2 : Paper
    1. Mathematics—Study and teaching.   I. Muschla, Judith.   II. Title.
QA11.M76   1995   94-36753
510′.71′2—dc20   CIP

Many thanks to Dover Publications for allowing us to use the illustrations.

Printed in the United States of America

10   9   8   7   6   5   4 (S)   10   9   8   7   6   5   4   (P)

ISBN 0-13-180357-3 (S)   ISBN 0-13-255910-2 (P)

PRENTICE HALL
Paramus, NJ 07652

On the World Wide Web at http://www.phdirect.com

For Erin . . .

ABOUT THE AUTHORS

Gary Robert Muschla received his B.A. and M.A.T. from Trenton State College, and teaches at Appleby School in Spotswood, New Jersey. He has spent much of his 20 years in the classroom teaching mathematics at the elementary level. He has also taught reading and writing.

Along with his math experience in the classroom, Mr. Muschla has been a successful freelance writer, editor and ghostwriter. He is a member of the Authors Guild, the National Writers Club, and the Associated Business Writers of America, and has conducted writing workshops for teachers and students, and edited magazines of students' writing.

Mr. Muschla has also authored four other resources for teachers: the *Writing Workshop Activities Kit: Ready-to-Use Worksheets and Enrichment Lessons for Grades 4-9* (The Center for Applied Research in Education, 1989), *The Writing Teacher's Book of Lists* (Prentice Hall, 1991), the *Writing Workshop Survival Kit* (The Center for Applied Research in Education, 1993), and the *English Teacher's Great Books Activities Kit* (The Center for Applied Research in Education, 1994).

Judith Muschla received her B.A. in Mathematics from Douglass College at Rutgers University and is certified K–12. She has taught mathematics at both the middle school and high school in South River, New Jersey, for the last 20 years, and was the recipient of the 1990–91 Governor's Teacher Recognition Program Award in New Jersey.

In addition, she has served as a Team Leader at South River Middle School where she worked on revision of the mathematics curriculum to implement the standards of the NCTM, coordinated interdisciplinary units, and conducted mathematics workshops for both teachers and parents. This is her first venture at collaborating with her husband.

ACKNOWLEDGEMENTS

We'd like to thank James Pope, principal at South River High School for his support of our efforts. Our appreciation also to Richard Kwiatkowski, the Math Department Chairman at South River High, for his comments and helpful suggestions, and our colleagues whose support and encouragement are more valuable than they can ever guess.

Also thanks to Sonia Helton, Professor of Education at the University of South Florida, whose comments on our manuscript were very helpful.

Our thanks to Donna Cooper, our typist, who ensured that the final version of the manuscript was updated and accurate.

We also greatly appreciate the efforts and advice of Susan Kolwicz, our editor, who was always there to answer our questions and offer suggestions to improve the usefulness of this book.

Finally, we'd like to thank our students, who are, in the end, what teaching is all about.

ABOUT MATHEMATICS INSTRUCTION

Mathematics is an extremely broad field that permeates our entire society. Balance your checkbook, read a plane schedule, or plot the orbital path of a satellite and you will be using mathematics. Mathematics is everywhere and its use will only increase in the future.

To ensure that the mathematics taught in school are relevant to the needs of our students, mathematics curriculums across the country are changing. Increasingly, the purpose of mathematics instruction is to help students apply math to solve real-life problems and understand their world. More than ever students in math classes are actively involved in investigating meaningful problems, working in groups and sharing ideas and insights, examining models, using calculators and computers in problem-solving, writing about their observations and conclusions, and connecting math with other subject areas.

As a mathematics teacher, you work side-by-side with your students, encouraging and supporting their efforts in mastering math, and helping them acquire the skills that will serve them well in the years to come. To those ends, we trust that this book will be an important resource.

Our best wishes to you as you teach the crucial skills of mathematics that will prepare your students for their future success.

HOW TO USE THIS RESOURCE

The *Mathematics Teacher's Book of Lists* is divided into two parts. Part I contains eight sections of reproducible lists and offers specific information on over 300 topics. Part II contains an assortment of handy reproducible teaching aids that you can use as needed in your program. All of the lists and reproducibles of the book can be adapted to various methods of instructions, giving you great flexibility.

Part I provides lists that can be used as handouts to students and references for you. For examples, suppose you are teaching rounding to sixth graders. You might distribute copies of List 35, "Rules for Rounding Numbers." If you are teaching problem-solving skills to a ninth-grade class, you might hand out copies of List 46, "Problem-Solving Strategies, II." (List 45, "Problem-Solving Strategies, I," is for elementary students.)

Because each list contains specific information about a particular skill or topic, the lists may be used to introduce lessons, reinforce concepts, synthesize related topics, or as reviews before tests or quizzes. If you wish, you might instruct students to file, for future reference, the lists you distribute to them in folders according to general topic. Not only will they be able to refer to the lists as needed, but the saved lists will build an impressive reference collection over the year.

Sections I through V of Part I focus on specific topics in mathematics, including: "Numbers: Theory and Operation," "Measurement," "Geometry," "Algebra," and "Trigonometry and Calculus." Section VI, "Math in Other Areas," and Section VII, "Potpourri," offer many interesting lists that you can use to show your students the broad applications of math. The lists of these sections also provide you with an assortment of subjects and facts that you, or your students, can use to create stimulating and exciting word problems, or use as data bases for math projects.

Section VIII, "Lists for Teacher's Reference," offers lists designed to make your teaching easier and more efficient. For example, List 283, "The Math Teacher's Management Strategies," provides information that will help you to handle your workload more smoothly. List 285, "How to Run a Cooperative Math Class," offers concise information how to set up an environment where students work together. Some of these lists lend themselves well to interdisciplinary cooperation. For example, List 295, "How to Start a Math Magazine," is ideal for working together with the English teacher. You can focus on the math, while the English teacher handles the language and writing skills students need to produce a high-quality magazine. When students take part in activities like this, they quickly see how knowledge in math and other subjects is essential to a real-world project's successful completion.

We suggest that you use this book as a resource, pulling the lists you need to supplement your curriculum and teaching methods. The more than 300 lists throughout this resource provide a wealth of interesting material and information you can share with your students. They will enable your students to see the broad range of mathematics, recognize its relevance to today's world, and help them to master the mathematics essential to their courses of study, which will help to make your teaching easier and more effective.

TABLE OF CONTENTS

PART I
Ready-to-Use Lists   1

SECTION I—NUMBERS: THEORY AND OPERATION

SECTION II—MEASUREMENT

SECTION III—GEOMETRY

SECTION IV—ALGEBRA

SECTION V—TRIGONOMETRY AND CALCULUS

SECTION VI—MATH IN OTHER AREAS

SECTION VII—POTPOURRI

SECTION VIII—LISTS FOR TEACHER'S REFERENCES

PART II
Reproducibles   375

PART I

Ready-to-Use Lists

NUMBERS: THEORY AND OPERATION

LIST 1   THE REAL NUMBERS

Numbers and the operations we can perform with them are the basis of our numerical system. Each set of numbers listed below is a part or subset of the Real Numbers.

- *Natural Numbers*—the set of the counting numbers. They can be classified as odd or even. {1, 2, 3, 4, 5 . . .}
- *Whole Numbers*—the set of the natural numbers and zero. {0, 1, 2, 3, 4, 5 . . .}
- *Integers*—the set of the natural numbers, their opposites, and zero. {. . . −3, −2, −1, 0, 1, 2, 3 . . .}
- *Rational Numbers*—the set of all the numbers that can be expressed in the form a/b where a and b are integers, b ≠ 0. Examples: integers, finite decimals and their opposites, and repeating decimals and their opposites.
- *Irrational Numbers*—the set of the numbers that cannot be written as terminating or repeating decimals. Examples: $\sqrt{2}$, $\sqrt{3}$, π, and e.

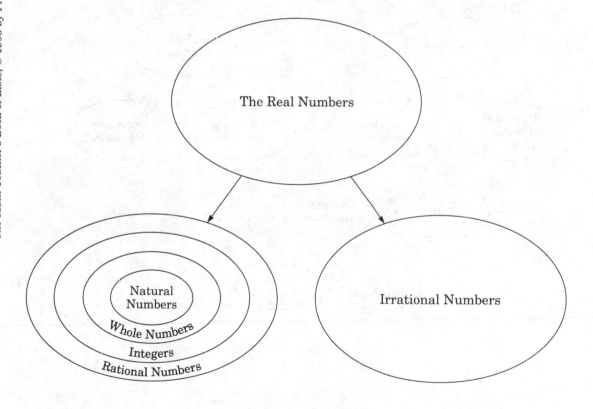

LIST 2   CLASSIFICATION OF REAL NUMBERS

In math and science, it is common to classify things that have common characteristics. In math we can classify real numbers according to the following chart.

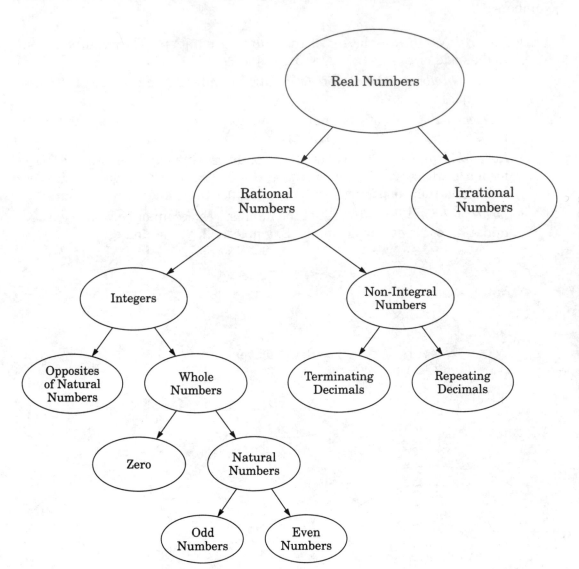

LIST 3   CARDINAL AND ORDINAL NUMBERS

When we count, or specify a total number of items, we are using cardinal numbers. *Ten* is a cardinal number. Ordinal numbers are used to show order. *Tenth* is an ordinal number. Several examples of cardinal and ordinal numbers appear below.

Cardinal Number	Ordinal Number	Shortened Form
1	First	1st
2	Second	2nd
3	Third	3rd
4	Fourth	4th
5	Fifth	5th
6	Sixth	6th
7	Seventh	7th
8	Eighth	8th
9	Ninth	9th
10	Tenth	10th
11	Eleventh	11th
12	Twelfth	12th
13	Thirteenth	13th
14	Fourteenth	14th
15	Fifteenth	15th
16	Sixteenth	16th
17	Seventeenth	17th
18	Eighteenth	18th
19	Nineteenth	19th
20	Twentieth	20th
21	Twenty-First	21st
22	Twenty-Second	22nd
23	Twenty-Third	23rd
24	Twenty-Fourth	24th
25	Twenty-Fifth	25th
26	Twenty-Sixth	26th
27	Twenty-Seventh	27th
28	Twenty-Eighth	28th
29	Twenty-Ninth	29th
30	Thirtieth	30th

Successive Numbers repeat in the same pattern.

100	One Hundredth	100th
101	One Hundred First	101st
102	One Hundred Second	102nd
103	One Hundred Third	103rd
104	One Hundred Fourth	104th
105	One Hundred Fifth	105th

LIST 4   PRIME NUMBERS

A prime number is an integer greater than 1 whose only whole number factors are itself and 1. For example, 2 is a prime number because its only factors are 2 and 1. The number 383 is prime for the same reason. Its only factors are 383 and 1. Following is a list of the first 100 prime numbers.

2	101	233	383
3	103	239	389
5	107	241	397
7	109	251	401
11	113	257	409
13	127	263	419
17	131	269	421
19	137	271	431
23	139	277	433
29	149	281	439
31	151	283	443
37	157	293	449
41	163	307	457
43	167	311	461
47	173	313	463
53	179	317	467
59	181	331	479
61	191	337	487
67	193	347	491
71	197	349	499
73	199	353	503
79	211	359	509
83	223	367	521
89	227	373	523
97	229	379	541

The Math Teacher's Book of Lists, © 1995 by Prentice Hall

LIST 5 TYPES OF PRIME NUMBERS

Prime numbers are natural numbers that have only two factors, 1 and the number. Certain types of primes have common characteristics, and are grouped together and have special names.

Twin primes are a set of two consecutive odd primes, which differ by only two. Below is a list of twin primes less than 100.

3, 5	29, 31
5, 7	41, 43
11, 13	59, 61
17, 19	71, 73

Symmetric primes, also called Euler primes, are a pair of prime numbers that are the same distance from a given number on a number line. There are no symmetric primes for 1, 2, or 3. It has not been proven if all natural numbers greater than 3 have symmetric primes. The following list shows the symmetric primes for the numbers 1 through 20.

Number	Symmetric Primes
1	None
2	None
3	None
4	3,5
5	3,7
6	5,7
7	3,11
8	5,11; 3,13
9	7,11; 5,13
10	7,13; 3,17
11	5,17; 3,19
12	11,13; 7,17; 5,19
13	7,19; 3,23
14	11,17; 5,23
15	13,17; 11,19; 7,23
16	15,17; 13,19; 3,29
17	11,23; 5,29; 3,31
18	17,19; 13,23; 7,29; 5,31
19	9,29; 7,31
20	17,23; 11,29; 3,37

LIST 5   (Continued)

An *emirp* is a prime number that remains a prime when its digits are reversed. Think of it like this: if the palindrome of a prime number is a prime, then the prime number is an emirp. "Emirp" of course is "prime" spelled backwards. Following are the emirps of less than 200.

11	31	73	101	131	157	181
13	37	79	107	149	167	191
17	71	97	113	151	179	199

Relatively prime numbers are numbers whose greatest common factor is 1. If two numbers are relatively prime, they are said to be relatively prime in pairs. Notice that the numbers of the following list are not limited to primes. Numbers that are relatively prime don't have to be prime numbers. They must not have any common factors other than 1. Below is a list of the numbers from 1 through 10 which are relatively prime in pairs.

1,2	4,5
1,3	4,7
1,4	4,9
1,5	
1,6	5,6
1,7	5,7
1,8	5,8
1,9	5,9
1,10	
2,3	6,7
2,5	
2,7	7,8
2,9	7,9
	7,10
3,4	
3,5	
3,7	8,9
3,8	
3,10	9,10

LIST 6   COMPOSITE NUMBERS

Composite numbers are positive integers that have more than two positive whole number factors. The number 6 is a composite number because its factors are 1, 2, 3, and 6. The first 100 composite numbers follow. Note that the number 1 is the only natural number that is neither prime nor composite.

4	39	72	104
6	40	74	105
8	42	75	106
9	44	76	108
10	45	77	110
12	46	78	111
14	48	80	112
15	49	81	114
16	50	82	115
18	51	84	116
20	52	85	117
21	54	86	118
22	55	87	119
24	56	88	120
25	57	90	121
26	58	91	122
27	60	92	123
28	62	93	124
30	63	94	125
32	64	95	126
33	65	96	128
34	66	98	129
35	68	99	130
36	69	100	132
38	70	102	133

LIST 7   PERFECT SQUARES AND CUBES

To square a number, multiply it by itself. For example, $4 \times 4 = 16$. Thus we say 4 squared is 16.

To cube a number, multiply it by itself twice. $4 \times 4 \times 4 = 64$, and we say that 4 cubed is 64.

The following list contains squares and cubes of numbers 1 to 25.

Number	Squared	Cubed
1	1	1
2	4	8
3	9	27
4	16	64
5	25	125
6	36	216
7	49	343
8	64	512
9	81	729
10	100	1,000
11	121	1,331
12	144	1,728
13	169	2,197
14	196	2,744
15	225	3,375
16	256	4,096
17	289	4,913
18	324	5,832
19	361	6,859
20	400	8,000
21	441	9,261
22	484	10,648
23	529	12,167
24	576	13,824
25	625	15,625

The Math Teacher's Book of Lists, © 1995 by Prentice Hall

LIST 8   ABUNDANT, DEFICIENT, AND PERFECT NUMBERS

The ancient Greeks were thinkers of the first order. They enjoyed mathematics, and categorized all the natural numbers as being abundant, deficient, or perfect.

Abundant—a number that is less than the sum of its factors, excluding itself.

Deficient—a number that is greater than the sum of its factors, excluding itself.

Perfect—a number that is equal to the sum of its factors, excluding itself.

The following list groups the first 50 numbers as the ancient Greeks would have. After that is a separate sublist of perfect numbers.

Number	Factors Excluding Itself	Sum	Type
1		0	Deficient
2	1	1	Deficient
3	1	1	Deficient
4	1,2	3	Deficient
5	1	1	Deficient
6	1,2,3	6	Perfect
7	1	1	Deficient
8	1,2,4	7	Deficient
9	1,3	4	Deficient
10	1,2,5	8	Deficient
11	1	1	Deficient
12	1,2,3,4,6	16	Abundant
13	1	1	Deficient
14	1,2,7	10	Deficient
15	1,3,5	9	Deficient
16	1,2,4,8	15	Deficient
17	1	1	Deficient
18	1,2,3,6,9	21	Abundant
19	1	1	Deficient
20	1,2,4,5,10	22	Abundant
21	1,3,7	11	Deficient
22	1,2,11	14	Deficient
23	1	1	Deficient
24	1,2,3,4,6,8,12	36	Abundant
25	1,5	6	Deficient
26	1,2,13	16	Deficient
27	1,3,9	13	Deficient
28	1,2,4,7,14	28	Perfect
29	1	1	Deficient

The Math Teacher's Book of Lists, © 1995 by Prentice Hall

LIST 8 (Continued)

Number	Factors Excluding Itself	Sum	Type
30	1,2,3,5,6,10,15	42	Abundant
31	1	1	Deficient
32	1,2,4,8,16	31	Deficient
33	1,3,11	15	Deficient
34	1,2,17	20	Deficient
35	1,5,7	13	Deficient
36	1,2,3,4,6,9,12,18	55	Abundant
37	1	1	Deficient
38	1,2,19	22	Deficient
39	1,3,13	17	Deficient
40	1,2,4,5,8,10,20	50	Abundant
41	1	1	Deficient
42	1,2,3,6,7,14,21	54	Abundant
43	1	1	Deficient
44	1,2,4,11,22	40	Deficient
45	1,3,5,9,15	33	Deficient
46	1,2,23	26	Deficient
47	1	1	Deficient
48	1,2,3,4,6,8,12,16,24	76	Abundant
49	1,7	8	Deficient
50	1,2,5,10,25	43	Deficient

The Math Teacher's Book of Lists, © 1995 by Prentice Hall

Perfect Numbers

Perfect numbers are mathematical rarities that have no practical use. Still, mathematicians have found them challenging, and have even worked out a formula to find them: $2^{p-1}(2^p - 1)$ where p and $(2^p - 1)$ are prime numbers. No one has found an odd perfect number, nor has anyone proven whether or not odd perfect numbers even exist. Even with the help of supercomputers, only 30 perfect numbers have been discovered. The thirtieth perfect number has 130,099 digits, too many to fit on this page (or any other for that matter). Below is a list of the first eight perfect numbers and their formulas. After that the numbers simply become too large.

Perfect Number	Formula
6	$2^1(2^2 - 1)$
28	$2^2(2^3 - 1)$
496	$2^4(2^5 - 1)$
8,128	$2^6(2^7 - 1)$
33,550,336	$2^{12}(2^{13} - 1)$
8,589,869,056	$2^{16}(2^{17} - 1)$
137,438,691,328	$2^{18}(2^{19} - 1)$
2,305,843,008,139,952,128	$2^{30}(2^{31} - 1)$

LIST 9 AMICABLE NUMBERS

Amicable numbers come in pairs. They are quite special, because each number of the pair has factors that (excluding itself) add up to equal the other number of the pair.

For example, 220 and 284 are the first pair of amicable numbers. The factors of 220, excluding itself, are 1, 2, 4, 5, 10, 11, 20, 22, 24, 55, and 110. Their sum equals 284. The factors of 284, excluding itself, are 1, 2, 4, 71, and 142, which add up to 220.

More than 1,000 pairs of amicable numbers have been found. This list offers the 10 smallest pairs.

220 and 284
1,184 and 1,210
2,620 and 2,924
5,020 and 5,564
6,232 and 6,368
10,744 and 10,856
12,285 and 14,595
17,296 and 18,416
63,020 and 76,084
66,928 and 66,992

LIST 10 SOME LESSER KNOWN TYPES OF NUMBERS

Mathematicians often group numbers according to their properties. While most students of math are familiar with the types of numbers found in List 1, "The Real Numbers," there are many others that are not as well known.

Algebraic Numbers—numbers that are the solution of an algebraic equation. Example: $2 + x = 9$. The answer is 7, which is an algebraic number.

Almost Perfect Numbers—numbers that are one more or one less than the sum of all of their factors, except themselves. Example: 4 is almost perfect because $1 + 2 = 3$, which is one less than 4. (All powers of 2 are almost perfect.)

Automorphic Numbers—numbers that when raised to a power end in the original number. Example: $5^2 = 25$; $5^3 = 125$; $6^2 = 36$; $25^2 = 625$.

Complex Numbers—numbers in the form of $a + bi$ where where a and b stand for real numbers and $i^2 = -1$ or $(i = \sqrt{-1})$. Example: $-2 + \sqrt{-2}$ can be written as $-2 + i\sqrt{2}$.

Crowd—a chain of three sociable numbers. No one has yet found such a chain, but no one has proven that such chains don't exist either.

Cute Numbers—numbers that have exactly four factors. Example: 6, whose factors are 1, 2, 3, and 6; 8, whose factors are 1, 2, 4, and 8.

Cyclic Numbers—an integer of n digits with the following characteristic: When multiplied by a number from 1 to n, the product has the same digits as the original number, in the same cycle. Example: 142,857 is the smallest cyclic number, other than one.

$$1 \times 142{,}857 = 142{,}857$$
$$2 \times 142{,}857 = 285{,}714$$
$$3 \times 142{,}857 = 428{,}571$$
$$4 \times 142{,}857 = 571{,}428$$
$$5 \times 142{,}857 = 714{,}285$$
$$6 \times 142{,}857 = 857{,}142$$

Denominate Numbers—numbers whose unit represents a unit of measure such as 3 pounds, 7 inches, 2 quarts, etc.

Fibonacci Numbers—numbers of the sequence 1, 1, 2, 3, 5 . . . where successive numbers are the sum of the two preceding numbers. Examples: $1 + 1 = 2$; $1 + 2 = 3$; $2 + 3 = 5$, etc.

Imaginary Numbers—numbers involving the imaginary unit i, where $i^2 = -1$ or $(i = \sqrt{-1})$. Example: $\sqrt{-2} = i\sqrt{2}$.

Lucas Numbers—numbers of the sequence 1, 3, 4, 7, 11, 18 . . . where successive numbers are the sum of the two preceding numbers. Examples: $1 + 3 = 4$; $3 + 4 = 7$; $4 + 7 = 11$; $7 + 11 = 18$, etc.

LIST 10   (Continued)

Mersenne Primes—primes of the form $2^p - 1$ where p is prime. Examples: 3, 7, 31, 127.

Random Numbers—numbers that are obtained without any pattern and can only be described by listing the digits. Examples: Picking numbers from a hat, such as 8, 3, 7, 0, 1, 2, 9, 9, 8, 1, 2, 6.

Repunit Numbers—an abbreviated form of "repeated unit" of the digit "1," but excluding the number one. Examples: 11, 111, 1111, etc.

Sociable Numbers—one of a chain of numbers whose factors add up to the next number in the chain. Example of a five-link chain: 12496, 14288, 15472, 14536, 14264.

> The sum of the factors of 12496 = 14288
> The sum of the factors of 14288 = 15472
> The sum of the factors of 15472 = 14536
> The sum of the factors of 14536 = 14264
> The sum of the factors of 14264 = 12496

Note that the chain is completed with the last number.

Surds—algebraic numbers that cannot be written as an exact ratio of two integers. A surd is one type of irrational number. (The other type of irrational number is the transcendental number.) Examples: $\sqrt{2}$, $\sqrt{3}$.

Transcendental Numbers—any irrational numbers that are not algebraic numbers. Examples: π, e.

Unit Number—the number 1.

Untouchable Numbers—numbers that are never the sum of the factors of any other number. Examples: 2, 5, 52, 88, 96, 120.

Weird Numbers—a special type of abundant number that does not represent the sum of any of its factors. Examples: 70; 836; 4,030; 5,830; 7,192.

LIST 11   MULTIPLICATION TABLE

Even in this day of computers and calculators, a basic knowledge of multiplication facts is important to understand some of the relationships between numbers. Knowing your multiplication tables is necessary for any problem that requires multiplying or dividing, especially when a calculator isn't handy.

X	1	2	3	4	5	6	7	8	9	10	11	12
1	1	2	3	4	5	6	7	8	9	10	11	12
2	2	4	6	8	10	12	14	16	18	20	22	24
3	3	6	9	12	15	18	21	24	27	30	33	36
4	4	8	12	16	20	24	28	32	36	40	44	48
5	5	10	15	20	25	30	35	40	45	50	55	60
6	6	12	18	24	30	36	42	48	54	60	66	72
7	7	14	21	28	35	42	49	56	63	70	77	84
8	8	16	24	32	40	48	56	64	72	80	88	96
9	9	18	27	36	45	54	63	72	81	90	99	108
10	10	20	30	40	50	60	70	80	90	100	110	120
11	11	22	33	44	55	66	77	88	99	110	121	132
12	12	24	36	48	60	72	84	96	108	120	132	144

The Math Teacher's Book of Lists, © 1995 by Prentice Hall

LIST 12 RULES FOR FINDING DIVISIBILITY

Understanding divisibility is useful in many mathematical applications. Two of the most obvious are reducing fractions and finding common denominators. In advanced mathematics, divisibility tests and common factors are useful in factoring polynomials.

For a number to be divisible by

2, it must be an even number, ending in 2, 4, 6, 8, 0.

3, the sum of the digits of the number must be divisible by 3.

4, the number must be even and the last two digits of the number are divisible by 4.

5, the number must end in 0 or 5.

6, it must be even and the sum of its digits must be divisible by 3.

7, you must be able to drop the ones' digit, and subtract 2 times the ones' digit from the remaining number. If that answer can be divided by 7, the original number can be divided by 7 too.

8, the number formed by the last 3 digits of the number can be divided by 8.

9, the sum of the digits must be divisible by 9.

10, the number must end in 0.

11, you must first add the alternate digits, beginning with the first digit. Next you must add the alternate digits, beginning with the second. Subtract the smaller sum from the larger. If the difference is divisible by 11, the original number is divisible by 11.

12, the number must be divisible by both 3 and 4.

The Math Teacher's Book of Lists, © 1995 by Prentice Hall

LIST 13 RULES FOR FINDING THE GREATEST COMMON FACTOR (GCF)

A factor is a number that divides into a larger number evenly. The greatest common factor is the largest number that divides into two or more numbers evenly. Being able to find the greatest common factor is an important skill for reducing fractions. It is also helpful in algebra, in factoring polynomials.

Listing Factors

- List all the numbers that divide evenly into the first given number. These are its factors.
- List all the factors of the second given number.
- Circle the largest factor that appears in both lists. This is the greatest common factor.

Find the greatest common factor of 24 and 36.

The factors of 24 are 1, 2, 3, 4, 6, 8, (12), 24

The factors of 36 are 1, 2, 3, 4, 6, 9, (12), 18, 36

12 is the greatest common factor of 24 and 36.

Expressing Each Number as the Product of Primes

- Factor each number into its primes.
- Circle those factors (by pairs) common to each.
- The greatest common factor is the product of the numbers which are circled.

Find the greatest common factor of 24 and 36.

$$24 = 2 \times 2 \times 2 \times 3$$
$$36 = 2 \times 2 \times 3 \times 3$$
$$2 \times 2 \times 3 = 12$$

12 is the greatest common factor of 24 and 36.

LIST 14 RULES FOR FINDING LEAST COMMON MULTIPLE (LCM)

A common multiple is a number that two other numbers will divide into evenly. The least common multiple is the lowest multiple of two numbers. It is most useful for finding common denominators.

Strategy One

- Start with the bigger number.
- List its multiples by multiplying the number by 1, 2, 3, 4, 5, etc.
- After each multiplication, check to see if the multiple of the larger number is also a multiple of the smaller number. If it is, you have found the least common multiple.

Find the least common multiple of 10 and 15

15 is the larger number

Multiples of 15: 15, 30 . . .

Is 15 a multiple of 10? No

Is 30 a multiple of 10? Yes

30 is the least common multiple of 10 and 15.

Strategy Two

- Find the product of the two numbers. Divide this product by the greatest common factor of the numbers.

Find the least common multiple of 10 and 15

The product of 10 and 15 is 150

The greatest common factor of 10 and 15 is 5.

$\dfrac{150}{5} = 30$ 30 is the least common multiple of 10 and 15

Strategy Three

- Factor each number into its primes.

- Write each product using exponents.

- Write each base.

- If the base is a factor of only one number, write the base and the exponent in exponential form.

- If the base is a factor of more than 1 number, write the base in exponential form using the larger (or largest) exponents of the bases. If the exponents of a given base are the same, write the base and exponent in exponential form.

- The least common multiple is the product of these numbers.

Find the least common multiple of 24 and 36.

$24 = 2 \times 2 \times 2 \times 3$
$36 = 2 \times 2 \times 3 \times 3$
$24 = 2^3 \times 3$
$36 = 2^2 \times 3^2$

The bases are 2 and 3.

$2^3 \times 3^2$

$2^3 \times 3^2 = 72$
The least common multiple of 24 and 36 is 72.

LIST 15   TYPES OF FRACTIONS

A fraction is a part of a whole. There are many types of fractions.

Simple Fraction—a fraction in which the numerator and denominator are both integers. Also known as a common fraction.

Examples: $\dfrac{2}{3}$, $\dfrac{7}{3}$, $-\dfrac{6}{7}$, $\dfrac{5}{1}$

Proper Fraction—a fraction in which the numerator is less than the denominator.

Examples: $\dfrac{1}{4}$, $\dfrac{2}{7}$, $-\dfrac{1}{8}$

Improper Fraction—a fraction in which the numerator is equal to or greater than the denominator. Improper fractions are usually changed to whole or mixed numbers.

Examples: $\dfrac{5}{3}$, $\dfrac{7}{7}$, $-\dfrac{11}{8}$

Mixed Number—a number that is a combination of an integer and a proper fraction. Thus, it is "mixed."

Examples: $2\dfrac{2}{3}$, $5\dfrac{7}{8}$, $-2\dfrac{1}{2}$

Unit Fraction—a fraction in which the numerator is one.

Examples: $\dfrac{1}{5}$, $\dfrac{1}{14}$

An Integer Represented as a Fraction—a fraction in which the denominator is one.

Examples: $\dfrac{2}{1}$, $-\dfrac{3}{1}$

Complex Fraction—a fraction in which the numerator or the denominator, or both numerator and denominator, are fractions.

Examples: $\dfrac{\frac{3}{5}}{\frac{7}{8}}$, $\dfrac{\frac{7}{9}}{4}$, $\dfrac{5}{\frac{1}{3}}$

Reciprocal—the fraction that results from dividing one by that number.

Example: 4 is the reciprocal of $\dfrac{1}{4}$.

LIST 15   (Continued)

Zero Fraction—a fraction in which the numerator is zero. A zero fraction equals zero.

Example: $\dfrac{0}{3} = 0$

Undefined Fraction—a fraction with a denominator of zero. (7/0 means 7 divided by 0, which is an impossibility because nothing can be divided by 0. Therefore, the fraction remains undefined.)

Indeterminate Form—an expression having no quantitative meaning.

Example: $\dfrac{0}{0}$

The Math Teacher's Book of Lists, © 1995 by Prentice Hall

LIST 16   RULES FOR SIMPLIFYING FRACTIONS

You can simplify fractions by dividing numerators and denominators by common factors.

- Find the biggest number that will divide into the numerator and denominator of the fraction evenly. This number is the greatest common factor between the numerator and denominator. (If you didn't find the greatest common factor the first time, you can simplify further by finding another common factor.)

- Divide both the numerator and denominator by the greatest common factor.

Simplify $\dfrac{18}{24}$

6 is the greatest common factor of 18 and 24.

$$\dfrac{18 \div 6}{24 \div 6} = \dfrac{3}{4}$$

or

$$\dfrac{18 \div 2}{24 \div 2} = \dfrac{9 \div 3}{12 \div 3} = \dfrac{3}{4}$$

$$\dfrac{18}{24} = \dfrac{3}{4}$$

For Renaming Improper Fractions as Mixed Numbers

- Divide the denominator of the fraction into the numerator.

- Write the mixed number. If there is no remainder, you will write a whole number.

- Simplify the remaining fraction according to the rules above.

Simplify $\dfrac{7}{5}$ $\dfrac{7}{5} = 1\dfrac{2}{5}$

Simplify $\dfrac{8}{4}$ $\dfrac{8}{4} = 2$

Simplify $\dfrac{18}{4}$ $\dfrac{18}{4} = 4\dfrac{2}{4} = 4\dfrac{1}{2}$

LIST 17   RULES FOR OPERATIONS
WITH FRACTIONS

The following rules cover addition and subtraction of fractions with *like* and *unlike* denominators, multiplication, and division.

Addition of Fractions with Like Denominators

- Add the numerators.

- Write the sum over the common denominator. (Do not add the denominators.)

- Simplify if possible.

$$\begin{array}{r} \dfrac{3}{4} \\ +\dfrac{2}{4} \\ \hline \dfrac{5}{4} = 1\dfrac{1}{4} \end{array}$$

Subtraction of Fractions with Like Denominators

- Subtract the numerators.

- Write the difference over the common denominator. (Do not subtract the denominators.)

- Simplify if possible.

$$\begin{array}{r} \dfrac{5}{6} \\ -\dfrac{1}{6} \\ \hline \dfrac{4}{6} = \dfrac{2}{3} \end{array}$$

Addition of Fractions with Unlike Denominators

- Find the lowest common denominator by finding the least common multiple of the denominators. In the example to the right, the least common multiple of the denominators is 20. Twenty is therefore the lowest common denominator.

- Write equivalent fractions with the common denominator.

- Add the numerators. (Do not add the denominators.)

- Simplify if possible.

$$\dfrac{4}{5} = \dfrac{}{20}$$
$$+\dfrac{3}{4} = \dfrac{}{20}$$

$$\dfrac{4}{5} \times \dfrac{4}{4} = \dfrac{16}{20}$$
$$+\dfrac{3}{4} \times \dfrac{5}{5} = \dfrac{15}{20}$$
$$\dfrac{31}{20}$$

$$\dfrac{31}{20} = 1\dfrac{11}{20}$$

Subtraction of Fractions with Unlike Denominators

- Find the lowest common denominator by finding the least common multiple of the denominators.

- Write equivalent fractions with the common denominator.

- Subtract the numerators. (Do not subtract the denominators.)

- Simplify if possible.

$$\dfrac{4}{5} = \dfrac{}{20}$$
$$-\dfrac{3}{4} = \dfrac{}{20}$$

$$\dfrac{4}{5} \times \dfrac{4}{4} = \dfrac{16}{20}$$
$$-\dfrac{3}{4} \times \dfrac{5}{5} = \dfrac{15}{20}$$
$$\dfrac{1}{20}$$

LIST 17 (Continued)

Multiplication of Fractions

- Multiply the numerators.
- Multiply the denominators.
- Simplify if possible.

$$\frac{3}{4} \times \frac{2}{3} = \frac{6}{12} = \frac{1}{2}$$

Division of Fractions

- After setting up the problem write the reciprocal of the divisor. (The divisor is the fraction after the division sign.)
- Rewrite the division sign as multiplication.
- Multiply the numerators.
- Multiply the denominators.
- Simplify if possible.

$$\frac{3}{4} \div \frac{2}{3}$$

The reciprocal of $\frac{2}{3}$ is $\frac{3}{2}$

$$\frac{3}{4} \div \frac{2}{3} = \frac{3}{4} \times \frac{3}{2} = \frac{9}{8} = 1\frac{1}{8}$$

The Math Teacher's Book of Lists, © 1995 by Prentice Hall

LIST 18 RULES FOR OPERATIONS WITH MIXED NUMBERS

A mixed number is just what its name implies: a whole number combined with a fraction. The two are mixed together to express a value that lies somewhere between two whole numbers. While working with mixed numbers is much like working with fractions, there are a few additional skills you'll need to know.

Adding Mixed Numbers (Like Denominators)

- Add the numerators of the fractions. (Do not add the denominators.)

- Add the whole numbers.

- Simplify if possible.

$$3\frac{1}{5}$$
$$+2\frac{3}{5}$$
$$\overline{5\frac{4}{5}}$$

Subtracting Mixed Numbers (Like Denominators) without Regrouping

- If the numerator after the minus sign is smaller than the first numerator, subtract the numerators. (Do not subtract the denominators.)
- Subtract the whole numbers.
- Simplify if possible.

$$5\frac{6}{7}$$
$$-3\frac{2}{7}$$
$$\overline{2\frac{4}{7}}$$

Subtracting Mixed Numbers (Like Denominators) with Regrouping

- If the numerator after the minus sign is larger than the first numerator, you must regroup one from the whole number. Rewrite the one as a fraction with the same denominator, and add it to the first fraction.

$$8\frac{1}{4}$$
$$-3\frac{3}{4}$$

$$8 = 7\frac{4}{4}$$

- Subtract the numerators. (Do not subtract the denominators.)

- Subtract the whole numbers.

- Simplify if possible.

$$8\frac{1}{4} = 7\frac{4}{4} + \frac{1}{4} = 7\frac{5}{4}$$
$$-3\frac{3}{4} \qquad\qquad = 3\frac{3}{4}$$
$$\overline{\qquad\qquad\qquad 4\frac{2}{4} = 4\frac{1}{2}}$$

Adding Mixed Numbers (Unlike Denominators)

- Write equivalent fractions with the same denominators.
- Add the numerators. (Do not add the denominators.)
- Add the whole numbers.
- Simplify if possible.

$$3\frac{1}{3} = 3\frac{5}{15}$$
$$+2\frac{4}{5} = 2\frac{12}{15}$$
$$\overline{5\frac{17}{15} = 6\frac{2}{15}}$$

LIST 18   (Continued)

Subtracting Mixed Numbers (Unlike Denominators) without Regrouping

- Write equivalent fractions with the same denominators.
- Subtract the numerators. (Do not subtract the denominators.)
- Subtract the whole numbers.
- Simplify if possible.

$$3\frac{4}{5} = 3\frac{8}{10}$$
$$-2\frac{1}{10} = 2\frac{1}{10}$$
$$\underline{\hphantom{-2\frac{1}{10} = }\;}$$
$$1\frac{7}{10}$$

Subtracting Mixed Numbers (Unlike Denominators) with Regrouping

- Write equivalent fractions with the same denominators.

- If necessary, rename one from the whole number and rewrite it as a fraction with the same denominator. Add it to the first fraction.

- Subtract the numerators. (Do not subtract the denominators.)

- Subtract the whole numbers.

- Simplify if possible.

$$4\frac{1}{8} = 4\frac{3}{24}$$
$$-2\frac{2}{3} = 2\frac{16}{24}$$

$$4 = 3\frac{24}{24}$$

$$4\frac{3}{24} = 3\frac{24}{24} + \frac{3}{24} = 3\frac{27}{24}$$
$$-2\frac{16}{24} = \hphantom{3\frac{24}{24} + \frac{3}{24} = } 2\frac{16}{24}$$
$$\underline{\hphantom{-2\frac{16}{24} = }\;}$$
$$1\frac{11}{24}$$

Multiplying Mixed Numbers

- Change the mixed numbers to improper fractions. (To change a mixed number to an improper fraction, multiply the denominator times the whole number and add the numerator.)

- If possible, simplify the fractions before multiplying.

- Multiply the fractions.

- Be sure the fraction is simplified to lowest terms.

$$3\frac{1}{2} \times 2\frac{4}{7} = \frac{7}{2} \times \frac{18}{7}$$

$$\frac{7}{2}^{\,1} \times \frac{18}{7}^{\,9} = \frac{9}{1} = 9$$

Dividing Mixed Numbers

- Change the mixed numbers to improper fractions. (To change a mixed number to an improper fraction, multiply the denominator times the whole number and add the numerator.)

$$4\frac{2}{3} \div 1\frac{1}{3} = \frac{14}{3} \div \frac{4}{3} =$$

LIST 18   (Continued)

- Change the divisor to its reciprocal, and rewrite the division sign as multiplication.

$$\frac{14}{3} \times \frac{3}{4} =$$

- If possible, simplify the fractions before multiplying.

$$\frac{\overset{7}{\cancel{14}}}{\underset{1}{\cancel{3}}} \times \frac{\overset{1}{\cancel{3}}}{\underset{2}{\cancel{4}}} = \frac{7}{2} = 3\frac{1}{2}$$

- Multiply the fractions.
- Be sure the fraction is simplified to lowest terms.

LIST 19   PLACE VALUE CHART

Understanding place value causes some students (and their teachers) big-time headaches. Since the value of any digit depends upon its "place," understanding place value is an important skill. In the example below, 5 represents 5 ten thousands and also 5 ten-millionths. The digits are the same, but the values are quite different.

trillions	hundred billions	ten billions	billions	hundred millions	ten millions	millions	hundred thousands	ten thousands	thousands	hundreds	tens	ones		tenths	hundredths	thousandths	ten-thousandths	hundred-thousandths	millionths	ten-millionths
3,	2	8	7,	3	8	4,	6	5	1,	2	9	6	.	3	7	8	2	6	1	5

LIST 20 TYPES OF DECIMALS

In the broadest sense, a decimal is any numeral in the base ten number system. Following are several types of decimals.

Decimal Fraction—a number that has no digits other than zeros to the left of the decimal point.

    Examples: 0.349, .84, 0.3001

Mixed Decimal—an integer and a decimal fraction.

    Examples: 8.341, 27.1, 341.7

Similar Decimals—decimals which have the same number of places to the right of the decimal point.

    Examples: 3.87 and .12, 14.015 and 3.396

Decimal Equivalent of a Proper Fraction—the decimal fraction that equals the proper fraction.

    Examples: $.25 = \frac{1}{4}$, $.3 = \frac{3}{10}$

Finite (or Terminating) Decimal—a decimal that has a finite number of digits.

    Examples: .3, .2765, .38412

Infinite (or Nonterminating) Decimal—a decimal that has an unending number of digits to the right of the decimal point.

    Examples: π, $\sqrt{3}$, $.\overline{33}$, $.\overline{37}$, 34.12794 . . .

Repeating (Or Periodic) Decimal—Nonterminating decimals in which the same digit or group of digits repeats. A bar is used to show that a digit or group of digits repeats. The repeating set is called the period or repetend. All rational numbers can be written as finite or repeating decimals.

    Examples: $.\overline{3}$, $.\overline{37}$

Nonrepeating (or Nonperiodic) Decimal—decimals that are nonterminating and nonrepeating. Such decimals are irrational numbers.

    Examples: π, $\sqrt{3}$

LIST 21   RULES FOR OPERATIONS
WITH DECIMALS

Adding, subtracting, multiplying, and dividing decimals isn't as hard as it may seem. Use the following as guides.

Adding Decimals

- Line up the numbers according to decimal points before adding. Keep columns straight and the digits in their proper places.

$$2.73 + .145 =$$
$$\begin{array}{r} 2.73 \\ +\ .145 \\ \hline \end{array}$$

- Add zeros for placeholders if necessary.

- After setting up the problem, bring the decimal point straight down.

$$\begin{array}{r} 2.730 \\ +\ .145 \\ \hline 2.875 \end{array} \quad \text{or} \quad \begin{array}{r} 2.730 \\ +0.145 \\ \hline 2.875 \end{array}$$

- Remember that a whole number is placed to the left of the decimal point. For example, the whole number 5 is written 5.0 as a decimal.

$$7.4 + 5 =$$
$$\begin{array}{r} 7.4 \\ +5.0 \\ \hline 12.4 \end{array}$$

- Add as you would with whole numbers.

- If you carry, carry to the next place.

Subtracting Decimals

- Line up the numbers according to decimal points before subtracting. Keep columns straight and the digits in their proper places.

$$2.75 - .042$$
$$\begin{array}{r} 2.75 \\ -\ .042 \\ \hline \end{array}$$

- Add zeros for placeholders if necessary.

- After setting up the problem bring the decimal point straight down.

$$\begin{array}{r} 2.750 \\ -\ .042 \\ \hline 2.708 \end{array} \quad \text{or} \quad \begin{array}{r} 2.750 \\ -0.042 \\ \hline 2.708 \end{array}$$

- Remember that a whole number is placed to the left of the decimal point. The whole number 8 is written 8.0 as a decimal.

$$9.34 - 8$$
$$\begin{array}{r} 9.34 \\ -8.00 \\ \hline 1.34 \end{array}$$

- Borrow as you would for whole number subtraction.

- Subtract as you would with whole numbers.

LIST 21 (Continued)

Multiplying Decimals

- Line up the numbers by columns, not according to decimal points.

- Multiply as you would with whole numbers.

- Count the places held by digits to the right of the decimal points in the numbers you multiply.

- Start to the right of your answer and count the same number of places to the left. Place the decimal point there.

4.32×0.7

$$
\begin{array}{rl}
4.32 & \text{(2 places)} \\
\times\, 0.7 & +\text{(1 place)} \\
\hline
3.024 & \text{(3 places)}
\end{array}
$$

Dividing Decimals

- When dividing by a whole number, bring the decimal point straight up. Divide as you would with whole numbers.

$$
\begin{array}{r}
.41 \\
8\overline{)3.28} \\
\underline{32} \\
8 \\
\underline{8}
\end{array}
$$

- When dividing by a decimal, move the decimal point to the right, making the divisor a whole number.

$$
\begin{array}{r}
4.1 \\
.8\overline{)3.28}
\end{array}
$$

- Move the decimal point to the right in the dividend the same number of places.

- Bring the decimal point straight up.

$$
\begin{array}{r}
410. \\
.8\overline{)328.0} \\
\underline{32} \\
8 \\
\underline{8} \\
0 \\
\underline{0}
\end{array}
$$
Add zero as a placeholder

- Divide as you would with whole numbers.

- If necessary, add a zero or zeros to the dividend to finish dividing. (The problem might work out evenly, end as a repeating decimal, or you might need to round off your answer.)

$$
\begin{array}{r}
2.925 \\
.8\overline{)2.3400} \\
\underline{16} \\
74 \\
\underline{72} \\
20 \\
\underline{16} \\
40 \\
\underline{40}
\end{array}
$$
Add zeros to finish dividing

LIST 22   RULES FOR CHANGING DECIMALS TO FRACTIONS

Decimals can easily be converted to fractions. The key is understanding the place value of the decimal.

- Read the decimal. Here are some examples:
  - —One place to the right of the decimal point is tenths.
  - —Two places to the right of the decimal point are hundredths.
  - —Three places to the right of the decimal point are thousandths.
  - —Four places to the right of the decimal point are ten-thousandths.
- Write the decimal as a fraction with a denominator that is the same value of the decimal.
- Simplify if possible.

Change each decimal listed below to a fraction.

.5

.23

.143

.7625

$.5 = \dfrac{5}{10} = \dfrac{1}{2}$

$.23 = \dfrac{23}{100}$

$.145 = \dfrac{145}{1000} = \dfrac{29}{200}$

$.7625 = \dfrac{7625}{10000} = \dfrac{1525}{2000} = \dfrac{305}{400} = \dfrac{61}{80}$

If the Decimal Is a Mixed Decimal

- Multiply by 1/10, 1/100, 1/1000, etc. Here are some examples:
  - —Multiply by 1/10 if the decimal has only 1 digit to the right of the decimal point.
  - —Multiply by 1/100 if the decimal has 2 digits to the right of the decimal point.
  - —Multiply by 1/1000 if the decimal has 3 digits to the right of the decimal point.
- Remember to rewrite the mixed number as an improper fraction.
- If possible, simplify, either before or after you multiply.

Change each mixed decimal listed below to a fraction.

$.3\dfrac{1}{3} = 3\dfrac{1}{3} \times \dfrac{1}{10} = \dfrac{\overset{1}{10}}{3} \times \dfrac{1}{\underset{1}{10}} = \dfrac{1}{3}$

$.87\dfrac{1}{2} = 87\dfrac{1}{2} \times \dfrac{1}{100} = \dfrac{\overset{7}{175}}{2} \times \dfrac{1}{\underset{4}{100}} = \dfrac{7}{8}$

$.666\dfrac{2}{3} = \dfrac{\overset{2}{2000}}{3} \times \dfrac{1}{\underset{1}{1000}} = \dfrac{2}{3}$

LIST 22   (Continued)

If the Decimal Repeats

- Multiply by 10, 100, 1000, etc. Here are some examples:

  —Multiply by 10 if 1 digit repeats.

  —Multiply by 100 if 2 digits repeat.

  —Multiply by 1000 if 3 digits repeat.

Change each repeating decimal to a fraction.

$.\overline{3}, .\overline{34}, .\overline{371}$

$n = .\overline{3}$ so $10n = 3.\overline{3}$

$n = .\overline{34}$ so $100n = 34.\overline{34}$

$n = .\overline{371}$ so $1000n = 371.\overline{371}$

- Subtract.

$$
\begin{array}{ll}
10n = & 3.\overline{3} \\
- n = & -.\overline{3} \\
\hline
\dfrac{9n}{9} & \dfrac{3}{9}
\end{array}
\qquad
\begin{array}{ll}
100n = & 34.\overline{34} \\
- n = & -.\overline{34} \\
\hline
\dfrac{99n}{99} & \dfrac{34}{99}
\end{array}
\qquad
\begin{array}{ll}
1000n = & 371.\overline{371} \\
- n = & -.\overline{371} \\
\hline
\dfrac{999n}{999} & \dfrac{371}{999}
\end{array}
$$

- Divide by the coefficient of the variable.

$$n = \frac{1}{3} \qquad n = \frac{34}{99} \qquad n = \frac{371}{999}$$

- Simplify, if possible.

Therefore:

$$.\overline{3} = \frac{1}{3}$$

$$.\overline{34} = \frac{34}{99}$$

$$.\overline{371} = \frac{371}{999}$$

LIST 23   RULES FOR CHANGING FRACTIONS TO DECIMALS

There are two methods for changing fractions to decimals. The first is to rewrite the fraction to make the denominator a decimal equivalent in the form of tenths, hundredths, or thousandths. The second is to divide the denominator of the fraction into its numerator. Both methods are detailed below.

Rewriting the Fraction

- Multiply the numerator and denominator of the fraction by the same number so that the denominator is equal to tenths, hundredths, or thousandths.

- A simple way to see if this method will work is to divide the denominator into tenths, hundredths, or thousandths. If the denominator divides evenly, multiply the numerator and denominator by the same number to find the equivalent fraction.

- Change the fraction to an equivalent decimal.

Change $\dfrac{1}{2}$ to a decimal.

$$\frac{1}{2} \times \frac{5}{5} = \frac{5}{10} = .5$$

$$\frac{1}{2} = .5$$

Change $\dfrac{3}{4}$ to a decimal.

$$\frac{3}{4} \times \frac{25}{25} = \frac{75}{100} = .75$$

$$\frac{3}{4} = .75$$

Dividing the Numerator by the Denominator

- For fractions whose denominators are not equivalent to tenths, hundredths, or thousandths, divide the numerator by the denominator.

- Add a decimal point after the numerator, and add two zeros. (Add more zeros only if instructed to do so, or if you are trying to find repeating decimals. For repeating decimals, be sure to indicate the digits that repeat by putting a bar over them. In this case omit the next step.)

- Write the remainder as a fraction.

Change $\dfrac{1}{3}$ to a decimal.

$$3\overline{)1}$$

$$\begin{array}{r} .33\frac{1}{3} \\ 3\overline{)1.00} \\ \underline{9} \\ 10 \\ \underline{9} \\ 1 \end{array} \quad = .\overline{3}$$

$$\frac{1}{3} = .\overline{3}$$

The Math Teacher's Book of Lists, © 1995 by Prentice Hall

LIST 24   RULES FOR CHANGING DECIMALS TO PERCENTS

Percent means part of a hundred, or hundredths. Changing a decimal to a percent requires that you change the decimal to hundredths first. You may do this in one of two ways. The first is to change the decimal to an equivalent fraction. The other is to change the decimal to a percent directly. Both methods are shown below. Choose the one you prefer.

Changing the Decimal to a Fraction, Then to a Percent

- Write the decimal as a fraction.

- If necessary, change the fraction to an equivalent fraction with a denominator of 100.

- Change the fraction to a percent.

Change .7 to a percent.

$$.7 = \frac{7}{10}$$

$$\frac{7}{10} \times \frac{10}{10} = \frac{70}{100}$$

$$\frac{70}{100} = 70\%$$

Changing the Decimal Directly to a Percent

- Move the decimal point two places to the right, and include the percent sign. (This shortcut is the same as multiplying the decimal by a hundred.)

Change .7 to a percent.

$$.70 = 70\%$$

LIST 25   RULES FOR CHANGING PERCENTS TO DECIMALS

Since percent means a part of a hundred, percents can be converted directly to decimals. You can also convert percents to decimals by writing equivalent fractions. Both methods are shown below. Use the one you like best.

Changing the Percent Directly to a Decimal

- Since percents equal parts of a hundred, change the percent directly to a decimal by moving the decimal point two places to the left. (This is the same as dividing by a hundred. Note that in 58%, for example, the decimal point is not shown, but it is located after the eight. 58% therefore becomes .58 after moving the decimal point two spaces to the left.)

Change each percent listed below to a decimal.

$$58\% = .58$$
$$125\% = 1.25$$
$$2\% = .02$$
$$33\tfrac{1}{3}\% = .33\tfrac{1}{3}$$

Changing the Percent to a Decimal by Writing an Equivalent Fraction

- Write the percent as a fraction with a denominator of 100.
- Write a decimal with the same name. (The numerator of the fraction becomes the decimal.)

Change each percent listed below to a decimal.

$$29\% = \frac{29}{100} = .29$$
$$150\% = \frac{150}{100} = 1.5$$
$$33\tfrac{1}{3}\% = \frac{33\tfrac{1}{3}}{100} = .33\tfrac{1}{3}$$

LIST 26   RULES FOR CHANGING FRACTIONS TO PERCENTS

There are two methods for changing fractions to percents. The first is to change the fraction to an equivalent fraction with a denominator of 100. The second, used for fractions that cannot be changed to equivalent fractions with denominators of 100, is to change the fraction first to a decimal, and then change the decimal to a percent.

Changing Fractions to Percents Using Equivalent Fractions

- If the denominator of the fraction is a factor of 100, change the fraction to an equivalent fraction with a denominator of 100. Do that by multiplying the numerator and denominator by the same number.

- Change the new fraction to a percent.

Change each fraction to a percent.

$$\frac{2}{5} \times \frac{20}{20} = \frac{40}{100} = 40\%$$

$$\frac{3}{4} \times \frac{25}{25} = \frac{75}{100} = 75\%$$

Changing Fractions to Percents Using the Decimal Method

- For fractions whose denominators are not factors of 100, divide the numerator of the fraction by its denominator.

- Add a decimal point and two zeros. (The two zeros are necessary to change to a percent, because percent means part of a hundred.)

- Divide. Write any remainder as a fraction.

- Change the decimal to a percent.

Change $\frac{4}{9}$ to a percent.

$9\overline{)4.00}$

$$9\overline{)4.00} \quad .44\frac{4}{9} = 44\frac{4}{9}\%$$
$$\underline{36}$$
$$40$$
$$\underline{36}$$
$$4$$

The Math Teacher's Book of Lists, © 1995 by Prentice Hall

LIST 27   RULES FOR CHANGING PERCENTS TO FRACTIONS

The word "percent" and the symbol "%" are so commonly used in magazines, newspapers, and TV that they are sometimes taken for granted. Percent means hundredth. In general, n% means $n \times \frac{1}{100}$ or $n \times .01$. When changing percents to fractions use the meaning expressed as a fraction.

Percents can easily be changed to fractions as the following two methods show.

Changing the Percent Directly to a Fraction

- Change the percent directly to a fraction with a denominator of 100. The number of the percent becomes the numerator of the fraction. (Remember, percent means a part of a hundred.)
- Simplify if possible.

Change each percent below to a fraction.

$$50\% = \frac{50}{100} = \frac{1}{2}$$

$$125\% = \frac{125}{100} = 1\frac{25}{100} = 1\frac{1}{4}$$

Changing the Percent When It Is a Mixed Number

- Multiply the percent by 1/100. Remember to change the mixed number to an improper fraction.
- Simplify if possible, either before you multiply or after.

Change $87\frac{1}{2}\%$ to a fraction.

$$87\frac{1}{2}\% = 87\frac{1}{2} \times \frac{1}{100} = \frac{175}{2} \times \frac{1}{100}$$

$$\frac{\overset{7}{\cancel{175}}}{2} \times \frac{1}{\underset{4}{\cancel{100}}} = \frac{7}{8}$$

$$87\frac{1}{2}\% = \frac{7}{8}$$

LIST 28   PERCENT EQUIVALENTS

The following chart shows the relationships between fractions, decimals, and percents.

Word Name	Fraction	Decimal	Percent
One-half	1/2	.50	50%
One-fourth	1/4	.25	25%
Three-fourths	3/4	.75	75%
One-third	1/3	$.33\frac{1}{3}$ or $.\overline{3}$	$33\frac{1}{3}\%$ or $33.\overline{3}\%$
Two-thirds	2/3	$.66\frac{2}{3}$ or $.\overline{6}$	$66\frac{2}{3}\%$ or $66.\overline{6}\%$
One-fifth	1/5	.20	20%
Two-fifths	2/5	.40	40%
Three-fifths	3/5	.60	60%
Four-fifths	4/5	.80	80%
One-sixth	1/6	$.16\frac{2}{3}$ or $.1\overline{6}$	$16\frac{2}{3}\%$ or $16.\overline{6}\%$
Five-sixths	5/6	$.83\frac{1}{3}$ or $.8\overline{3}$	$83\frac{1}{3}\%$ or $83.\overline{3}\%$
One-eighth	1/8	$.12\frac{1}{2}$ or $.125$	$12\frac{1}{2}\%$ or 12.5%
Three-eighths	3/8	$.37\frac{1}{2}$ or $.375$	$37\frac{1}{2}\%$ or 37.5%
Five-eighths	5/8	$.62\frac{1}{2}$ or $.625$	$62\frac{1}{2}\%$ or 62.5%
Seven-eighths	7/8	$.87\frac{1}{2}$ or $.875$	$87\frac{1}{2}\%$ or 87.5%
One-ninth	1/9	$.11\frac{1}{9}$ or $.\overline{1}$	$11\frac{1}{9}\%$ or $11.\overline{1}\%$
Two-ninths	2/9	$.22\frac{2}{9}$ or $.\overline{2}$	$22\frac{2}{9}\%$ or $22.\overline{2}\%$
Four-ninths	4/9	$.44\frac{4}{9}$ or $.\overline{4}$	$44\frac{4}{9}\%$ or $44.\overline{4}\%$
Five-ninths	5/9	$.55\frac{5}{9}$ or $.\overline{5}$	$55\frac{5}{9}\%$ or $55.\overline{5}\%$
Seven-ninths	7/9	$.77\frac{7}{9}$ or $.\overline{7}$	$77\frac{7}{9}\%$ or $77.\overline{7}\%$
Eight-ninths	8/9	$.88\frac{8}{9}$ or $.\overline{8}$	$88\frac{8}{9}\%$ or $88.\overline{8}\%$
One-tenth	1/10	.10	10%
Three-tenths	3/10	.30	30%
Seven-tenths	7/10	.70	70%
Nine-tenths	9/10	.90	90%
One whole	1	1.00	100%

LIST 29   RULES FOR SOLVING PROPORTIONS

A proportion is a statement that two ratios are equal. Proportions can be helpful in solving word problems, particularly those involving percents.

- Set up the proportion.
- Show the cross products of the proportion.
- Find the products.
- Divide both sides of the equation by the coefficient of N.

Solve for N

$$\frac{N}{8} = \frac{10}{13}$$

$$8 \times 10 = 13 \times N$$

$$80 = 13$$

$$\frac{80}{13} = \frac{\cancel{13}N}{\cancel{13}}$$

$$6\frac{2}{13} = N$$

LIST 30   RULES FOR FINDING PERCENTS OF NUMBERS

There are several ways you can find the percent of a number, for example, 20% of 80.

The Decimal Method

- Change the percent to an equivalent decimal.
- Multiply the decimal by the number. Be sure to count off your decimal points.

Find 20% of 80.

$20\% = .2$

$$\begin{array}{r} 80 \\ \times\ .2 \\ \hline 16.0 \end{array}$$ 20% of 80 = 16

The Fraction Method

- Change the percent to an equivalent fraction.
- Simplify.
- Multiply the fraction by the number.
- Simplify if possible.

Find 20% of 80.

$20\% = \dfrac{20}{100} = \dfrac{1}{5}$

$\dfrac{1}{\cancel{5}_1} \times \dfrac{\cancel{80}^{16}}{1} = \dfrac{16}{1} = 16$ 20% of 80 = 16

The Proportion Method

- Set up the problem in the form of a percent proportion, using this form:

$$\frac{\text{Part}}{\text{Base}} = \frac{\text{Percent}}{100}$$

Note that the number after the word "of" is the base.

- Show the cross products of the equation.
- Find the products.
- Divide both sides of the equation by the coefficient of N.

Find 20% of 80.

$$\frac{N}{80} = \frac{20}{100}$$

$80 \times 20 = 100 \times N$

$1600 = 100N$

$\dfrac{1600}{100} = \dfrac{100N}{100}$ 20% of 80 = 16

$16 = N$

LIST 31   RULES FOR FINDING PERCENT
AND THE BASE

Finding what percent a number is of another number, and finding what number is a certain percent of another number are confusing for many students. The following lists make the steps of each process clear.

Finding the Percent

- Set up a percent proportion, using this form:

$$\frac{\text{Part}}{\text{Base}} = \frac{\text{Percent}}{100}$$

  Note that the number after the word "of" is the base.

What percent of 64 is 16?

$$\frac{16}{64} = \frac{N}{100}$$

- Show the cross products of the proportion.

$$16 \times 100 = 64 \times N$$
$$1600 = 64N$$

- Find the products.

$$\frac{1600}{64} = \frac{64N}{64} \qquad \text{25\% of 64 is 16.}$$

- Divide both sides by the coefficient of N.

$$25 = N$$

Finding the Base

- Set up a percent proportion, using this form:

$$\frac{\text{Part}}{\text{Base}} = \frac{\text{Percent}}{100}$$

  Note that the phrase "what number" after the word "of" is the base.

15 is 25% of what number?

$$\frac{15}{N} = \frac{25}{100}$$

- Show the cross products of the proportion.

$$15 \times 100 = 25 \times N$$
$$1500 \times 25N \qquad \text{15 is 25\% of 60.}$$

- Find the products.

$$\frac{1500}{25} = \frac{25N}{25}$$

- Divide both sides by the coefficient of N.

$$60 = N$$

LIST 32   RULES FOR OPERATIONS WITH INTEGERS

Integers include all positive and negative whole numbers, and zero. Because negative numbers are the opposite of positives, special rules are needed for working with them.

Adding 2 Integers

- When the integers are positive, add them, and the sign remains positive.

$$^+4\ +\ ^+3\ =\ ^+7$$

- When the integers are negative, add the absolute values. The sign is negative. (The absolute value of any integer is its distance from 0 on the number line. The absolute value of both +4 and −4 is 4.)

$$^-4\ +\ ^-3\ =$$
$$|^-4| + |^-3| = 4 + 3 = 7$$
$$^-4\ +\ ^-3\ =\ ^-7$$

- When the signs of the integers are different, subtract the absolute values (the smaller from the larger), and keep the sign of the integer with the greater absolute value.

$$^-4 + ^+9 =$$
$$|9| - |^-4| = 9 - 4 = 5$$
$$^-4 + 9 = 5$$

- When the integers are opposites, the sum is 0.

$$^-4 + ^+4 = 0$$

Adding More Than 2 Integers

- **Method One:** Work from left to right and add integers two at a time, following the rules above.

$$^-4 + (^+6) + (^-7) + (^+2) =$$
$$2 \quad + (^-7) + (^+2) =$$
$$^-5 \quad + (^+2) = ^-3$$
$$^-4 + (^+6) + (^-7) + (^+2) = ^-3$$

- **Method Two:** Add all the positive integers, then all the negative integers, following the rules above. Find the sums of your answers.

$$^-4 + (^+6) + (^-7) + (^+2) =$$
$$^+6 + (^+2) + (^-4) + (^-7) =$$
$$^+8 + (^-11) = ^-3$$
$$^-4 + (^+6) + (^-7) + (^+2) = ^-3$$

Subtracting Integers

- Rewrite the problem by using the definition of subtraction:
$$(a - b) = a + (^-b)$$

$$3 - 6 = 3 + (^-6) = ^-3$$
$$^-2 - (^-5) = ^-2 + (^+5) = ^+3$$
$$12 - (^-4) = 12 + 4 = 16$$

- Follow the rules for adding integers.

Multiplying 2 Integers

- Find the product of the absolute values of the numbers.

$$|8| = |^-8| = 8 \qquad |7| = |^-7| = 7$$

LIST 32   (Continued)

- Use the correct sign:
  —If both integers are positive, the answer is positive.

  —If both integers are negative, the answer is positive.

  —If one number you multiplied is positive and the other is negative, the answer is negative.

  —If one of the numbers is 0, the answer is 0.

$^+8 \times {}^+7 = 56$

$^-8 \times {}^-7 = 56$

$^-8 \times (^+7) = {}^-56$

$^-8 \times 0 \ = 0$

Multiplying More Than 2 Integers

- **Method One:** Work from left to right and multiply the integers two at a time, following the rules above.

- **Method Two:** Find the product of the absolute values. If all the numbers you multiply are positive, the answer is positive. If there is an odd number of negative factors, the answer is negative. If there is an even number of negative factors, the answer is positive. (Of course if any one of the factors is 0, your answer is 0.)

$^-3 \times (^-7) \times (^+2) =$
$\quad 21 \quad \times \ 2 \ = 42$

$|3| = |^-3| = 3$
$|7| = |^-7| = 7$
$|2| = |^-2| = 2$
$^-3 \times (^-7) \times (^+2) = 42$
$\quad$ (There are 2 negative factors.)
$^-3 \times (^+7) \times (^+2) = {}^-42$
$\quad$ (There is 1 negative factor.)
$^-3 \times (^-7) \times (^-2) = {}^-42$
$\quad$ (There are 3 negative factors.)
$^-3 \times (^-7) \times 0 = 0$

Dividing Integers

- Find the quotient of the absolute values.

- Use the correct sign:
  —If both integers are positive, the quotient is positive.

  —If both integers are negative, the quotient is positive.

  —If the integers have different signs, the quotient is negative.

- If 0 is divided by an integer, the quotient is 0.

- If an integer is divided by 0, the quotient is undefined.

$|3| = |^-3| = 3$
$|21| = |^-21| = 21$

$^+21 \div (^+3) = {}^+7$

$^-21 \div (^-3) = {}^+7$

$^-21 \div (^+3) = {}^-7$

$0 \div (^-7) = 0$

$^-7 \div 0 = \varnothing$

The Math Teacher's Book of Lists, © 1995 by Prentice Hall

LIST 33   PROPERTIES OF INTEGERS

Integers have special properties. Understanding those properties can make computation easier. The commutative property, for example, allows you to change the order of adding or multiplying integers. The associative property allows you to change grouping.

In the chart below, a, b, and c are integers.

	Addition	*Multiplication*
Closure Property	a + b is an integer	(a)(b) is an integer
Commutative Property	a + b = b + a	ab = ba
Associative Property	(a + b) + c = a + (b + c)	(ab)c = a(bc)
Identity Property	a + 0 = a	1(a) = a
Inverse Property	a + −a = 0	
Multiplication Property of Zero		a(0) = 0
Distributive Property		a(b + c) = ab + bc

LIST 34   RULES FOR FINDING THE AVERAGE (MEAN)

Understanding what an average (also called the mean) is has many practical applications. There are batting averages in baseball, average incomes, and the average grade you maintain in your math class. The following list shows you how to find the average of just about anything.

- Add up all the items you need to average.
- Divide the sum by the total number of items you added.
- If necessary, add a decimal point and zeros. (It is usually not necessary to work out the problem past the hundredths place. Round it off to the nearest tenth.)

Find the average of 92, 84, and 87.

92 + 84 + 87 = 263

$$87.66 = 87.\overline{6} \approx 87.7$$

$$
\begin{array}{r}
3)\overline{263.00} \\
\underline{24} \\
23 \\
\underline{21} \\
2\,0 \\
\underline{1\,8} \\
20 \\
\underline{18} \\
2
\end{array}
$$

The Math Teacher's Book of Lists, © 1995 by Prentice Hall

LIST 35   RULES FOR ROUNDING NUMBERS

Rounding is an important estimation skill. When you go to the grocery store, for example, it can be helpful to round off and estimate the cost of the items you are buying.

Steps for Rounding Up

- Circle the digit that is to be rounded.

- If the digit to the right is 5 or greater, round the "circled" digit up by adding 1 to it.

- Change all digits to the right of the rounded digit to zeros.

- Delete any zeros which are not placeholders.

Round 3854 to the nearest thousand.

③854 ≈ 4000

Round 2.874 to the nearest tenth.

2.⑧74 ≈ 2.9̶0̶0̶

≈ 2.9

Steps for Rounding Down

- Circle the digit that is to be rounded.

- If the digit to the right is less than 5, the "circled" digit stays the same.

- Change all digits to the right of the rounded digit to zeros.

- Delete any zeros which are not placeholders.

Round 3512 to the nearest hundred.

3⑤12 ≈ 3500

Round 2.874 to the nearest hundredth.

2.8⑦4 ≈ 2.87̶0̶

≈ 2.87

When 9 Is in the Place You Are Rounding

- Circle the digit that is to be rounded, which in this case is 9.

- If the digit to the right is 5 or greater, round the "circled" 9 up by adding 1 to it. (If the digit to the right is less than 5, follow the steps for "rounding down.")

- Since 9 + 1 is 10, write 0 in the circle, carry 1, and add it to the digit to the left.

- Change all numbers to the right of the rounded number to zeros.

- Delete any zeros which are not placeholders.

Round 3985 to the nearest hundred.

3⑨85 ≈ 4000

Round 2.897 to the nearest hundredth.

2.8⑨7 ≈ 2.90̶0̶

≈ 2.90

The Math Teacher's Book of Lists, © 1995 by Prentice Hall

LIST 36   RULES FOR FINDING PRIME FACTORIZATIONS

The prime factorization of a number means expressing the number as a product of prime numbers. The following list is helpful to finding the prime factorization of a number.

Finding the Prime Factorization Through a Factor Tree

- Find any pair of factors of the number.

- Circle the prime factor(s).

- Find any other factors.

- Circle the prime factor(s).

- When you have found all the prime factors, write them out as a product.

- Write the product using exponents.

Find the prime factorization of 28.

$$28 \qquad or \qquad 28$$
$$②\times 14 \qquad\qquad 4\times⑦$$
$$②\times⑦ \qquad\qquad ②\times②$$

$$2\times 2\times 7 \qquad\qquad 2\times 2\times 7$$

$$2^2\times 7 \qquad\qquad 2^2\times 7$$

$2^2 \times 7$ is the prime factorization of 28.

Finding the Prime Factorization by Dividing by Primes

- Divide by 2 if possible, until the quotient is not divisible by 2.

- Divide by 3 if possible, until the quotient is not divisible by 3.

- Divide by 5 if possible, until the quotient is not divisible by 5.

- Continue this pattern, dividing by prime numbers only, until the quotient is prime.

- Write the product of the divisors and quotient using exponents.

Find the prime factorization of 140.

2 |140   Divide by 2
2 | 70   Divide by 2
5 | 35   Can't divide by 3 so divide by 5
   7   7 is prime

$2^2 \times 5 \times 7$ is the prime factorization of 140.

LIST 37   SCIENTIFIC NOTATION

Scientific notation is used to express very large or very small numbers. For example, the mean distance of Pluto from the sun is about 3,670,000,000 miles. That's a jawbreaker to say and even worse to write. Using scientific notation, though, the number can be expressed as 3.67×10^9.

In writing scientific notation for large numbers, follow these rules:

- The first factor is greater than or equal to 1 and is less than 10.
- The second factor is a power of 10 in exponential form.
- To write numbers with exponents, count the number of places to the right of the first nonzero number in standard form. That number becomes the exponent. In the case of 3,670,000,000, the first nonzero number is 3. There are 9 digits to the right of the 3 so 9 is the exponent. $3,670,000,000 = 3.67 \times 10^9$.

In writing very small numbers, follow these rules:

- The first factor is greater than or equal to 1 and is less than 10.
- The second factor is a negative power of 10 in exponential form.
- To write numbers with a negative exponent, count the number of places to the right of the decimal point, up to and *including* the first nonzero number. That number of places becomes the negative exponent. $.00079 = 7.9 \times 10^{-4}$. (The exponent must be negative because you are counting places to the right of the decimal point.)

The Math Teacher's Book of Lists, © 1995 by Prentice Hall

LIST 38 BASES

The base of any number system is the number of different symbols used. The Arabic system, which we use, is a base ten system because ten symbols are used in writing numerals—0, 1, 2, 3, 4, 5, 6, 7, 8, 9. It's thought that the base ten system reflects our eight fingers and two thumbs. Primitive people found it easier to count that way.

Number systems can be based on any amount of symbols, however. The binary system (base two), for example, only has two digits 0 and 1, and is base two. Computers perform their calculations in binary codes. Pulses of electrical energy representing 0 and 1 turn tiny switches on and off in the microprocessor.

Following is a comparison of the numerals of base ten, with those of base two, base five, and base eight.

Base Ten	Base Two	Base Five	Base Eight
1	1	1	1
2	10	2	2
3	11	3	3
4	100	4	4
5	101	10	5
6	110	11	6
7	111	12	7
8	1,000	13	10
9	1,001	14	11
10	1,010	20	12
11	1,011	21	13
12	1,100	22	14
13	1,101	23	15
14	1,110	24	16
15	1,111	30	17
16	10,000	31	20
17	10,001	32	21
18	10,010	33	22
19	10,011	34	23
20	10,100	40	24

LIST 39   BIG NUMBERS

Most of us can comprehend numbers up to around a hundred thousand. That's about how many people a big football stadium can seat. If we use our imaginations and envision five stadiums that large side by side, all filled, we can grasp a half-million. Ten filled stadiums is a million, but after that the numbers soon become too hard to imagine. The following list shows numbers up to a googolplex, which is big even for "big" numbers.

To eliminate the appearance of a page covered with zeros, we used exponents to express numbers after 1 decillion. One vigintillion, for example, can be expressed as 10^{63}. This means that the number would be written as a 1, followed by 63 zeros.

Word Name	*Digits*
One million	1,000,000
One billion	1,000,000,000
One trillion	1,000,000,000,000
One quadrillion	1,000,000,000,000,000
One quintillion	1,000,000,000,000,000,000
One sextillion	1,000,000,000,000,000,000,000
One septillion	1,000,000,000,000,000,000,000,000
One octillion	1,000,000,000,000,000,000,000,000,000
One nonillion	1,000,000,000,000,000,000,000,000,000,000
One decillion	1,000,000,000,000,000,000,000,000,000,000,000

*From here on we will use exponents in place of digits.

One undecillion	10^{36}
One duodecillion	10^{39}
One tredecillion	10^{42}
One quattuordillion	10^{45}
One quindecillion	10^{48}
One sexdecillion	10^{51}
One septendecillion	10^{54}
One octodecillion	10^{57}
One novemdecillion	10^{60}
One vigintillion	10^{63}
One googol	10^{100}
One googolplex	10^{googol}

Are numbers infinite? A simple test suggests that they are. Try imagining the biggest number you can. No matter how big it is, it's not the biggest. You can always add at least 1 to it.

The Math Teacher's Book of Lists, © 1995 by Prentice Hall

LIST 40   MATHEMATICAL SIGNS
AND SYMBOLS

The following list provides the signs and symbols used most often in mathematics.

+	addition, plus, positive
−	subtraction, minus, negative, opposite of
×	multiplication, multiply by, times
·	multiplication, multiply by, times
÷	division, divided by
$\frac{x}{y}$	division
=	is equal to, equals
≈	is approximately equal to
≠	is not equal to
>	is greater than
≥	is greater than or equal to
<	is less than
≤	is less than or equal to
∴	therefore
∞	infinity
$	dollar sign
¢	cent(s)
@	at
#	number or pounds
%	percent
:	is to
△	triangle
⊓	square
▭	rectangle
°	degree
∠ABC	angle ABC
^{m}∠ABC	measure of angle ABC
∟	right angle
$\overset{\frown}{AB}$	arc AB
‖	is parallel to
⊥	is perpendicular to
$\overrightarrow{AB}$	ray AB
$\overline{AB}$	segment AB

LIST 40   (Continued)

AB	measure of line segment AB
$\overleftrightarrow{AB}$	line AB
π	pi which is about 3.14
≅	is congruent to
~	is similar to
( )	parentheses, grouping symbol
[ ]	braces, grouping symbol
±	plus or minus
|n|	absolute value of n
(x,y)	ordered pair of numbers
x^a	x to the a power
$\sqrt{}$	positive square root
$^-\sqrt{}$	negative square root
f(x)	f of x, the value of f at x
{ }	indicates a set
∅	empty set
∈	is an element of
∩	intersection
∪	union
P(E)	probability of event E
n!	n factorial
nPr	number of permutations of n items, taken r at a time
nCr	number of combinations of n items, taken r at a time
SinA	sine of angle A
CosA	cosine of angle A
TanA	tangent of angle A
CotA	cotangent of angle A
SecA	secant of angle A
CscA	cosecant of angle A

The Math Teacher's Book of Lists, © 1995 by Prentice Hall

LIST 41 THE MATH STUDENT'S RESPONSIBILITIES

By accepting the following responsibilities, you will help to ensure your success in math this year.

✓ Come to class each day ready to work and learn.

✓ Bring the required materials to class. These might include textbooks, notebooks, binders, pencils, pens, and calculators.

✓ Be curious and inquisitive about numbers. Always look for relationships that will provide insight and understanding.

✓ Recognize that learning the basics is important to any worthwhile activity.

✓ Be diligent in the completion of homework.

✓ Be persistent and determined in your work.

✓ Be willing to try various strategies in solving problems.

✓ Ask questions when you don't understand something.

✓ Accept the challenge of working with classmates in the learning of mathematics skills and concepts.

✓ Be willing to share your understanding of math with others, as well as being open to the ideas of others.

✓ Behave properly, listen to and follow directions, and avoid disturbing others.

✓ Take pride in your work and never let yourself fall into the trap of believing you can't do math. Virtually everybody can, if he or she is willing to work hard enough.

LIST 42   OVERCOMING MATH ANXIETY

By the time they reach the middle grades, many students are convinced that math is hard. They believe that they don't have the "knack" for it, and they dread math class. These students worry so much about math that they almost guarantee themselves failure. If you're one of these students, there's much you can do to replace your math worries with math success.

- Realize that boys and girls can do math equally well. The same is true for people of various ethnic groups. There is no one type of person who is predestined for math greatness.

- Keep your mind open and your emotions down. If you let yourself think that math is hard or impossible, it will be.

- Be persistent in working on your math. Remember that everybody makes mistakes. Learn from your mistakes.

- Get in touch with your math feelings. When your mind starts to flood with math worries, stop, take a deep breath and clear your thoughts. If you're at home, get up and walk around. If you're in class, look out the window for a moment or two. Then redirect yourself to the problem you're working on and tell yourself that you can do it.

- Write down your math worries on a sheet of paper. (For example, "I can't do word problems.") Write down possible solutions. (For example, "I can take better notes, ask my teacher for help, work on more problems for practice.") Seeing your worries, and ways you can overcome them, helps put things in perspective. Every problem has a solution.

- Make a commitment to study. Being prepared is one of the best ways to reduce worry.

- View overcoming math anxiety as just another problem *you can solve.*

- When you don't understand something, don't be afraid or embarrassed to ask your teacher. Others probably have the same question.

- Keep notes and review your notes as necessary.

- Study with a friend. The companionship can make the worries easier to handle.

- Keep a sense of humor. So you missed a problem. It's not the end of the world. You'll try again tomorrow, and probably be successful.

LIST 43   STRATEGIES FOR TAKING MATH TESTS

When their teacher announces an upcoming math test, many students experience a rush of anxiety. For some, that anxiety can sabotage their performance and lower their scores. The following test-taking strategies can reduce your apprehension and boost your grades.

Before the Test

- Prepare by studying all the types of problems that might be on the test.

- Try to anticipate new or trick problems; create some examples for yourself and try working them out.

- If you are having trouble with some of the material, ask your teacher for help a few days before the test. This will give you time to master the problems.

- If you find it helpful, study with a friend. Working with a classmate gives you the chance to share insights and talk about specific problems. It also reduces the feeling of isolation, that you are the only one who finds some of the problems difficult.

- Think positively about the test. Don't let the comments of others about how hard the test will be affect you. It won't be hard if you're prepared.

- Recognize that most people are anxious or nervous about tests. Such feelings usually pass once the test starts.

- Employ mental imaging. Imagine yourself doing well on the test. Picture yourself solving the problems and getting a high score. Professional athletes often use mental imaging to improve their performance.

- Promise yourself a reward for doing well on the test. (After doing well be sure to give yourself your reward.)

- Prepare yourself physically. Get a restful night's sleep, eat a good breakfast, and get to class on time. Rushing to avoid being late will likely upset your concentration for the upcoming test. If your test is in the afternoon, remain calm throughout the day and eat a good lunch.

- Go to class ready to take the test. Be sure you have everything you need—pencils, erasers, calculator, etc. Don't forget your glasses or contacts. Bring plenty of tissues if you have the sniffles.

During the Test

- Listen carefully to any instructions. If you have any questions, or don't understand something, ask for clarification.

- If you are taking a standardized test, do the sample items. Not only are they examples of problems on the test, but they will help you to "warm up."

The Math Teacher's Book of Lists, © 1995 by Prentice Hall

LIST 43   (Continued)

- If you feel very nervous, take a few deep breaths and, for a few moments, think of a favorite place, or an activity you enjoy doing. Getting your mind off the test will help you to regain your composure.

- Read any directions carefully.

- If you are using a standardized answer sheet, make certain that you are putting your answers in the proper place. Use a notecard or your finger to help you stay in the right spot.

- Pace yourself. Work quickly but be accurate. Make sure that your answers are clear.

- Don't waste time on hard problems. Move on to easier ones, but remember to go back. Place a check by the numbers of questions you must return to.

- Budget your time; spend the most time on portions of the test that are worth the most points.

- On multiple choice tests—if you get stuck on an item, eliminate the answers that you know can't be right and work from there. If necessary, make an educated guess from the answers you can't eliminate.

- If time remains after completing the test, go over it and double-check your answers.

- If you run out of time, and if unanswered questions will be marked wrong, *guess*. Fill in an answer for the remaining questions. You have nothing to lose.

- For standardized tests, be sure you have filled in all the spaces neatly, and that you have not left any stray marks on the answer sheet.

After the Test

- If you did well, reward yourself.

- If you didn't do as well as you believe you could have, reward yourself for trying and learn from your mistakes. Resolve to do better next time.

The Math Teacher's Book of Lists, © 1995 by Prentice Hall

LIST 44   STEPS FOR SOLVING
WORD PROBLEMS

If you find solving word problems hard, the following suggestions can help you be more successful.

- ✓ Read the problem carefully. If necessary, read it again. A third time may even be needed.

- ✓ Focus your attention on the question. Identify the problem. What is it really asking? Look for key words like *sum, total, all together, about, difference,* and *how much more* (or *less*) *than.*

- ✓ Decide what operation or operations you will need to find the answer.

- ✓ Draw a picture of the problem.

- ✓ Go back through the problem and pick out the facts you'll need to solve the problem. Ignore any unnecessary information.

- ✓ Supply any missing facts.

- ✓ Work the problem out accurately.

- ✓ Double-check your work.

- ✓ Ask yourself if your answer satisfies the question. Is your answer logical? Does it make sense?

LIST 45 PROBLEM-SOLVING STRATEGIES, I
(FOR THE ELEMENTARY GRADES)

It's always easier to solve math problems when you have a plan. Following are some suggestions to help you solve these tough problems.

- Read the problem slowly and carefully. Reread it if you are not sure what it is asking.
- If necessary, rewrite the problem in your own words. This will help you to understand it.
- Circle the facts. Cross out any facts that are not needed to solve the problem.
- Draw or sketch a picture that will help you to visualize the problem. This is especially useful in geometry.
- Plan what to do. Decide what operation or operations you will use to solve the problem.
- Work the problem out, being careful that your calculations are accurate.
- Double-check your computations.
- As a final check, ask yourself if your answer is logical. Does it make sense?

LIST 46   PROBLEM-SOLVING STRATEGIES, II (FOR THE UPPER GRADES)

A student once asked her math teacher what was the best way to solve a particular problem. The teacher answered, "The way that works best for you." Many strategies can be used to solve math problems. When you feel that there is only one or two, you severely limit your options and reduce the chances of finding the correct answer. Following are some helpful problem-solving strategies.

Understand the Problem

- Read the problem carefully, two, three, or as many times as it takes.
- Decide what the question is asking.
- Find the important information.
- Eliminate any unnecessary information.
- Supply any missing facts.

Work Toward a Solution

- Decide on the operation or operations you'll need.
- Use trial and error (sometimes called guess and check).
- Write equations.
- Use estimation.
- Use logic.
- Design tables or charts to organize data.
- Sketch or draw a model.
- Make comparisons.
- Change your point of view. Look at the problem from different angles.
- Work backwards.
- Act out the problem.
- Substitute easier numbers. Replacing fractions with whole numbers often makes it easier to see which operation to use.
- Make notes of your attempted solutions in the margin. This will help you to keep track of your steps.
- Periodically review what you've done.
- Be patient and persistent.

After You Find a Solution, Check Your Work

- Make sure you used all the important information.
- Check your calculations.
- Make sure your answer makes sense. (No one pays $2,500.00 for a parking ticket; move the decimal point and $25.00 becomes a logical answer.)

LIST 47   CHARACTERISTICS OF GOOD PROBLEM-SOLVERS

Successful problem-solvers share many of the same characteristics, which they use in working out hard problems. How many do you possess? How many can you make a part of your "problem-solving" personality?

Good Problem-Solvers Do Many of the Following

- ✓ Work actively toward solutions.
- ✓ Search for key ideas.
- ✓ Identify important information.
- ✓ Ignore unimportant information.
- ✓ Can supply missing information.
- ✓ Recognize hidden questions.
- ✓ Work carefully.
- ✓ Follow a step-by-step method.
- ✓ Recognize relationships.
- ✓ Try various strategies.
- ✓ Look at a problem from various angles.
- ✓ Are open to new ideas.
- ✓ Keep notes of their attempts at solutions.
- ✓ Often recheck their facts.
- ✓ Use logic.
- ✓ Rely on past experience in solving problems.
- ✓ Are persistent.

The Math Teacher's Book of Lists, © 1995 by Prentice Hall

LIST 48   STEPS FOR WRITING
WORD PROBLEMS

You are probably familiar with reading and solving word problems. Writing word problems, which you can then share with classmates, is an excellent way to improve your own problem-solving skills. After all, when you construct your own word problems and see what goes in to them, you learn what to look for in the problems other people write.

When you are writing word problems, it is helpful to follow the steps of the *Writing Process:* prewriting, drafting, revising, editing, and publishing (sharing). You have likely learned about the writing process in your English classes. There are various activities in each stage. You might do some or all of them.

The Math Teacher's Book of Lists, © 1995 by Prentice Hall

1. *Prewriting.*
   - Think of a purpose.
   - Generate ideas for problems.
   - Gather the necessary facts.
   - Conduct research if necessary.
   - Analyze your ideas.
   - Organize your ideas.
   - Focus your topics.

2. *Drafting.*
   - Write.
   - Rearrange your information as needed.
   - Elaborate on your ideas.

3. *Revising.*
   - Polish your writing.
   - Rethink or rearrange your information.
   - Clarify your work.
   - Rewrite your material where necessary.
   - Eliminate any unnecessary information.
   - Check facts.
   - Conduct additional research.
   - Entertain the opinions or critiques of your peers.

4. *Editing.*
   - Proofread for accuracy.
   - Make the final polishing.
   - Correct any remaining mistakes in mechanics.

5. *Publishing or sharing.*
   - Share your work with classmates.
   - Produce copies of your problems and make them available to others.
   - Publish your word problems with the problems of other students in a class Word Problem Book.
   - Display your problems for others to review.

LIST 49   MATH JOURNAL GUIDELINES
FOR STUDENTS

Keeping a journal can be helpful in your study of mathematics. You can use a journal to note questions, insights, and reflections you may have about your math work. A journal can become a record of your progress, showing the growth of your understanding of math. Following are suggestions for keeping a math journal.

- Use a standard spiral notebook, or designate a section of a looseleaf binder for your journal. If you use a separate notebook and run out of space, simply start a new one and number it 2, 3, 4, etc.
- Use your math journal only for math.
- Date your entries. Some students find that writing the topic at the top of the page is useful if they need to look that topic up later.
- Be willing to write about topics and problems that interest you. Journals need not be kept only for notes.
- Review your journals periodically. You might find that you can now expand on some pieces because you have gained more understanding.
- Share some of your entries with other members of the class.
- Review your journal at the end of each marking period to see how your understanding of math is growing.

Some Suggested Math Journal Topics

Notes on skills.

Notes on how to solve certain problems.

Reflections or impressions about math class.

Expression of "frustration" about a tough problem.

Expression of joy (or relief!) after solving that tough problem.

Questions (specific or general).

Comments about interesting problems.

Notes on practical applications of math.

Notes on how math relates to other fields.

Alternate problems.

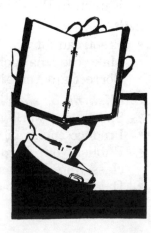

The Math Teacher's Book of Lists, © 1995 by Prentice Hall

section 2
MEASUREMENT

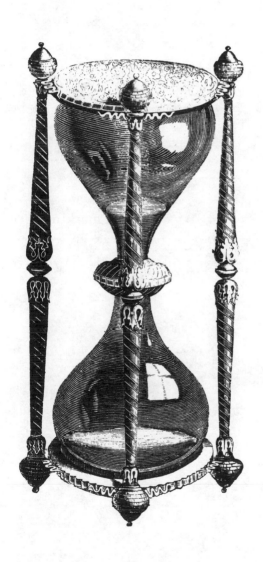

LIST 50 THINGS THAT MEASURE

Unless they really think about it, most people don't realize how many things we measure. The following list gives some samples.

Measuring Device	What It Measures
Accelerometer	increase of speed
Altimeter	altitude
Ammeter	amperage
Anemometer	velocity of wind
Atomic clock	time
Audiometer	hearing
Balance	weight
Barometer	atmospheric pressure
Beaker	capacity
Calendar	days, weeks, months
Caliper	dimensions of a place
Chronometer	time (used on ships)
Clock	time
Eggtimer	timer for cooking eggs
Electric meter	kilowatts used
Eyedropper	small liquid quantities
Fathometer	depth of water
Flask	capacity
Galvanometer	electric current
Gas gauge	amount of gas in tank
Gas meter	quantity of gas
Gasometer	gasses
Geiger counter	atomic radiation
Hourglass	time (by grains of sand)
Hydrometer	density of a liquid
Hygrometer	relative humidity
IQ tests	intelligence
Jeweler's stick	ring size
Light meter	light (in photography)
Manometer	pressure (gases, liquids)
Measuring cup	capacity
Measuring spoons	capacity
Meterstick	length
Metronome	tempo (in music)
Micrometer	very small distances
Odometer	distance traveled
Oil gauge	oil pressure
Pedometer	number of steps taken
Platform scale	weight (heavy objects)
Potentiometer	voltage

LIST 50   (Continued)

Measuring Device	What It Measures
Protractor	angles
Radiometer	radiation
Rain gauge	amount of rainfall
Ruler	length
Scale	weight
Seismograph	earthquakes
Sextant	angular distance
Snow gauge	amount of snowfall
Speedometer	speed of a vehicle
Sphygmomanometer	blood pressure
Spirometer	volume of air entering and leaving lungs
Stopwatch	short periods of time
Sundial	time of day
Tachometer	speed of rotation
Tape measure	length
Temperature gauge	temperature
Theodolite	angles (in surveying)
Thermometer	temperature
Timer	time
Tire gauge	air pressure in tires
Voltmeter	electrical force
Watch	time
Water meter	amount of water
Yardstick	length

LIST 51 THE ORIGIN OF MEASUREMENTS

When our ancestors first found the need to measure things, it was natural that they would use objects that they were most familiar with. Fingers, hands, arms, and feet were some of the earliest units for the measurement of length. Stones were often designated as units of weight, and baskets could easily be used for capacity. Of course, problems arose when someone's foot was bigger than another's, or one village relied on different sizes in baskets to measure corn. Clearly, our units of measurement today are improvements over what our ancestors used. Following is just a sampling of early units of measure.

Length

inch—the length of three barley grains placed end to end. (Sometimes corn kernels or other grains were used.)

digit—the breadth of a finger, about .75 inch.

palm—the breadth of a hand, about 4 inches.

hand—the length from the wrist to the end of the middle finger, about 8 inches.

cubit—the length of the forearm from the point of the elbow to the end of the middle finger, about 18 inches.

foot—in many ancient cultures the length of a man's foot, about 12 inches. In ancient Rome a foot equaled 4 palms.

fathom—the length of rope when pulled between a man's two outstretched arms. It was used by sailors to measure the depth of the water on which the ship sailed. The fathom, still used today, is 6 feet.

furlong—the length of a short race. Today the furlong is equal to one-eighth of a mile.

mile—the distance of a thousand paces, as marked off by a length of 5 feet between lifts of the same foot. Our modern mile is 5,280 feet.

league—the distance a person can see across a flat field, about 3 miles.

Capacity and Weight

Depending on the time and place, jars, bowls, and baskets were all used to measure capacity. The measuring of weight also varied. Simple balances compared the weight of one object with that of another. Sometimes, stones were designated as standards for comparing weight.

LIST 52   OBSOLETE UNITS OF MEASURE

Just as language changes over time, so do the types of units we use for measurement. It's likely you never heard of some of the following units of measurement.

Length	Dry Measure	Liquid Measure
3 barleycorns = 1 inch	2 quarts = 1 bottle	4 gills = 1 pint
2½ inches = 1 nail	2 bottles = 1 gallon	1 hogshead = 63 gallons
4 nails = 1 quarter	2 gallons = 1 peck	
4 quarters = 1 yard	3 bushels = 1 sack	
4 inches = 1 hand	4 bushels = 1 coomb	
3 inches = 1 palm	9 bushels = 1 vat	
4 digits = 1 palm	2 coombs = 1 quarter	
3 palms = 1 span	5 quarters = 1 wey	
7 palms = 1 cubit	2 weys = 1 last	
18 inches = 1 cubit		
5 feet = 1 pace		
5½ yards = 1 pole		
40 poles = 1 furlong		
8 furlongs = 1 mile		
3 miles = 1 league		

In time, assuming that the United States makes a total conversion to the Metric system, it is quite possible that most of the English units of measurement will join the above obsolete measuring units.

The Math Teacher's Book of Lists, © 1995 by Prentice Hall

LIST 53   MEASUREMENT ABBREVIATIONS

The following list includes abbreviations for both the English system and Metric system.

English System	*Metric System*
inch—in, "	nanometer—nm
foot—ft, '	millimeter—mm
yard—yd	centimeter—cm
rod—rd	decimeter—dm
furlong—fur	meter—m
mile—mi	dekameter or decameter—dkm or dam
fathom—fm	hectometer—hm
	kilometer—km
grain—gr	
pennyweight—dwt	milliliter—ml
ounce (troy)—oz t	centiliter—cl
pound (troy)—lb t	deciliter—dl
	liter—l
dram—dr	dekaliter or decaliter—dkl or dal
ounce—oz	hectoliter—hl
pound—lb, #	kiloliter—kl
hundredweight—cwt	
ton—T	milligram—mg
short ton—sh t	centigram—cg
long ton—l t	decigram—dg
	gram—g
gill—gi	dekagram or decagram—dkg or dag
pint—pt	hectogram—hg
quart—qt	kilogram—kg
gallon—gal	metric ton—t
barrel—bbl	
	square millimeter—mm^2
peck—pk	square centimeter—cm^2
bushel—bu	square decimeter—dm^2
	square meter—m^2
chain—ch	square dekameter or square decameter—dkm^2 or dam^2
cup—c	hectare or square hectometer—hm^2
teaspoon—t, tsp	square kilometer—km^2
tablespoon—T, tbsp	
fluid ounce—fl oz	cubic millimeter—mm^3
	cubic centimeter—cm^3, cc
square inches—sq in	cubic decimeter—dm^3
square feet—sq ft	cubic meter—m^3
square yard—sq yd	cubic dekameter or cubic decameter—dkm^3 or dam^3
square rod—sq rd	cubic hectometer—hm^3
acre—A	cubic kilometer—km^3
square mile—sq mi	
cubic inches—cu in	
cubic feet—cu ft	
cubic yard—cu yd	
cord—cd	

LIST 54   THE ENGLISH SYSTEM OF WEIGHTS AND MEASURES

The United States is one of the few countries to still use the English system of measurement. Much of the rest of the world relies on the Metric system. Although the United States is slowly changing over to the Metric system, the English system is not a relic yet and many Americans would have trouble measuring anything without it.

Linear Measure (Length)

1,000 mils = 1 inch
12 inches = 1 foot
3 feet = 1 yard
5.5 yards = 1 rod
4 rods = 1 chain
10 chains = 1 furlong
40 rods = 1 furlong
8 furlongs = 1 statute mile
5,280 feet = 1 mile
1,760 yards = 1 statute mile
3 miles = 1 league

Nautical Linear Measure

6 feet = 1 fathom
100 fathoms = 1 cable's length
120 fathoms = 1 cable's length (U.S. Navy)
10 cable's length = 1 nautical mile
1 nautical mile = 6,076.11549 feet
1 nautical mile = 1.508 statute miles
60 nautical miles = 1 degree of a great circle of the earth

Surveyor's Measure

7.92 inches = 1 link
100 links = 1 chain
66 feet = 1 chain
10 chains = 1 furlong
80 chains = 1 mile

Square Measure (Area)

144 square inches = 1 square foot
9 square feet = 1 square yard
30.25 square yards = 1 square rod
160 square rods = 1 acre
4,840 square yards = 1 acre
640 acres = 1 square mile

The Math Teacher's Book of Lists, © 1995 by Prentice Hall

LIST 54   (Continued)

Cubic Measure (Volume)

    1,728 cubic inches = 1 cubic foot
    27 cubic feet = 1 cubic yard
    231 cubic inches = 1 gallon (U.S.)
    277.27 cubic inches = 1 gallon (U.K.)
    2,150.42 cubic inches = 1 bushel (U.S.)
    2,219.36 cubic inches = 1 bushel (U.K.)

Liquid Measure (Capacity)

    3 teaspoons = 1 tablespoon
    2 tablespoons = 1 fluid ounce
    4 fluid ounces = 1 gill
    8 fluid ounces = 1 cup
    2 cups = 1 pint
    4 gills = 1 pint
    2 pints = 1 quart
    4 quarts = 1 gallon

Dry Measure (Capacity)

    2 pints = 1 quart
    8 quarts = 1 peck
    4 pecks = 1 bushel
    1 British dry quart = 1.032 U.S. dry quarts

Weight (Avoirdupois)

The Avoirdupois system is used for general weighing.

    27.3438 grains = 1 dram
    16 drams = 1 ounce
    16 ounces = 1 pound
    14 pounds = 1 stone
    2 stones = 1 quarter
    4 quarters = 1 long hundredweight (U.K.)
    100 pounds = 1 short hundredweight (U.S.)
    2,000 pounds = 1 short ton (U.S.)
    2,240 pounds = 1 long ton (U.K.)

Weight (Troy)

The Troy system is used for weighing precious metals or gems.

    1 carat = 3.086 grains
    24 grains = 1 pennyweight
    20 pennyweights = 1 ounce
    12 ounces = 1 pound

LIST 54   (Continued)

Weight (Apothecaries)

The Apothecaries' system formerly was used by pharmacists. Today, most pharmacists rely on metric units.

20 grains = 1 scruple
3 scruples = 1 dram
8 drams = 1 ounce
12 ounces = 1 pound

Wood Measure

144 cubic inches = 1 board foot = 1' × 1' × 1'
16 cubic feet = 1 cord foot = 4' × 4' × 1'
8 cord feet = 1 cord

Angular or Circular Measure

60 seconds = 1 minute
60 minutes = 1 degree
30 degrees = 1 zodiac sign
57.2958 degrees = 1 radian
90 degrees = 1 quadrant or right angle
360 degrees = 1 circle

Hardness of Some Popular Gems

Note: The scale for hardness runs from 10 to 1, with 10 being the hardest. These are some examples.

Diamond—10
Corundum—9
Topaz—8
Quartz—7
Labradorite—6
Smithsonite—5
Fluorite—4
Calcite—3
Alabaster—2

The Math Teacher's Book of Lists, © 1995 by Prentice Hall

LIST 55 RULES FOR CONVERTING UNITS IN THE ENGLISH SYSTEM

Because the values of units in the English system of measurement vary—unlike the Metric system in which units are multiples of 10—converting one unit to the other often requires using equivalencies. List 54, "The English System of Weights and Measures," is a good source for the units of the English system.

To Convert from a Larger Unit to a Smaller Unit

- Refer to an equivalency table to find a relationship using both quantities.
- Multiply.
- Add if necessary.

Convert 4 ft 8 in to inches.

1 ft = 12 in

4 ft = 4 × 12 = 48 in

4 ft 8 in = 48 in + 8 in = 56 in

To Convert from a Smaller Unit to a Larger Unit

- Refer to an equivalency table to find a relationship using both quantities.

- Divide.

- Express the remainder as the smaller unit of equivalency.

Convert 20 fl oz to cups and fluid ounces.

8 fl oz = 1 cup

$$\begin{array}{r} 2R4 \\ 8\overline{)20} \\ \underline{16} \\ 4 \end{array}$$

20 fl oz = 2c 4fl oz

LIST 56   U.S. AND BRITISH UNITS OF MEASUREMENT

Although the U.S. system of measurement is based largely on traditional British units, there are some differences. Both the U.S. and traditional British system are commonly referred to as the English system. Sometimes, this can cause confusion.

Weight (Avoirdupois)

Unit	U.S. Equivalent	British Equivalent
1 ounce	437.5 grains	437.5 grains
1 pound	16 ounces	16 ounces
1 stone	none	14 pounds
1 hundredweight*	100 pounds	8 stones or 112 pounds
1 ton**	2,000 pounds	20 hundredweight or 2,240 pounds

*Hundredweight in the U.S. is known as a *short* hundredweight. In England it is a *long* hundredweight.

**The ton in the U.S. is the *short* ton, while in England it is a *long* ton.

Liquid Measure

Unit	U.S. Equivalent	British Equivalent
1 fluid ounce	1.8047 cubic inches	1.734 cubic inches
1 pint	16 fluid ounces or 28.88 cubic inches	20 (British) fluid ounces or 34.68 cubic inches
1 quart	2 pints or 57.75 cubic inches	2 (British) pints or 69.36 cubic inches
1 gallon*	4 quarts or 231 cubic inches	1 Imperial gallon**or 4 (British) quarts or 277.42 cubic inches

*1 U.S. gallon = 0.833 British Imperial gallons.

**1 British Imperial gallon = 1.201 U.S. gallons.

LIST 57   UNITS OF THE METRIC SYSTEM

The official name of the Metric system is the International System of Units (known throughout the world as SI). While most people are familiar with the meter, gram, and liter, the Metric system contains several more units of measurement. They are divided into three categories: the Basic Units, Supplementary Units, and Derived Units. Of the Derived Units, only the most common are included in this list.

Basic Units

Unit	Symbol	Quantity
meter	m	length
kilogram	kg	mass
second	s	time
ampere	A	electric current
kelvin	K	temperature
candela	cd	luminous intensity
mole	mol	amount of substance

Supplementary Units

Unit	Symbol	Quantity
radian	rad	plane angle
steradian	sr	solid angle

Derived Units

Unit	Symbol	Quantity
square meter	m^2	area
cubic meter	m^3	volume
kilogram per cubic meter	kg/m^3	density
meter per second	m/s	velocity
meter per second squared	m/s^2	acceleration
newton	N	force
joule	J	energy
hertz	Hz	frequency (electromagnetism)
watt	W	power
volt	V	voltage
ohm	Ω	electrical resistance

LIST 58   METRIC STANDARDS

Standards in measurement refer to the physical representations of the value of a unit of measure. The standards themselves are not used for direct measurement; they are used only for reference and ensure that units of measure remain accurate. They are so important that they are kept in vaults where temperature, humidity, and security can be controlled.

Basic Units

Meter (length)—equal to 1,650,763.73 wavelengths of the reddish-orange light emitted by the isotope krypton 86.

Kilogram (mass)—the unit of mass equal to the mass of the platinum-iridium cylinder kept at Serres in France.

Second (time)—the duration of 9,192,631,770 periods of radiation corresponding to a specific transition of the cesium-133 atom.

Ampere (electric current)—the constant current that, flowing in two parallel conductors one meter apart in a vacuum, will produce a force of 2×10^{-7} newtons per meter of length.

Kelvin (temperature)—based on the triple point of water, which is the point at which water can exist in three states: liquid, vapor, and ice. It is defined as 1/273.16 of the temperature of the triple point of water.

Candela (luminous intensity)—intensity of the black-body radiation from a surface of 1/600,000 square meter at the temperature of freezing platinum and at a pressure of 101,325 pascals.

Mole (amount of substance)—an amount of a substance in a system that contains as many elementary entities as there are atoms in 0.012 kilogram of carbon 12.

Supplementary Units

Following are the standards for the two supplementary units in the Metric system.

Radian (plane angle)—the plane angle between two radii of a circle that cut off on the circumference an arc whose length equals the radius.

Steradian (solid angle)—a solid angle whose vertex is in the center of a sphere, which cuts off an area of the surface of the sphere equal to that of a square with sides of length equal to the radius of the sphere.

LIST 58 (Continued)

Derived Units

Derived units are defined in terms of the basic units. In some cases they have special names and symbols. The major derived units and their standards are listed below.

Newton—the unit of force equal to the force needed to accelerate one kilogram by one meter per second squared.

Joule—the unit of energy and work equal to the work done when the point of application of a force on one newton moves one meter in the direction of the force.

Hertz—the unit of frequency in the field of electromagnetism defined as one cycle per second.

Watt—the unit of power defined as the power of one joule per second.

Volt—the unit of voltage defined as the difference of electrical potential between two points of a conductor carrying a constant current of one ampere when the power used between them equals one watt.

Ohm—the unit of electrical resistance equal to a resistance that passes a current of one ampere when there is an electrical potential difference of one volt across it.

LIST 59   METRIC PREFIXES

Most people are familiar with some of the prefixes of the Metric system, most notably *kilo* (meaning a thousand), *centi* (one-hundredth), and *milli* (one-thousandth). There are metric prefixes that describe numbers vastly bigger and incredibly smaller. For example, a megameter equals 1 million meters; a nanometer equals 1 billionth of a meter. In the following list the prefixes range from biggest to smallest.

Metric Prefix	Symbol	Value
exa	E	one quintillion or 10^{18}
peta	P	one quadrillion or 10^{15}
tera	T	one trillion or 10^{12}
giga	G	one billion or 10^{9}
mega	M	one million or 10^{6}
kilo	k	one thousand or 10^{3}
hecto	h	one hundred or 10^{2}
deca/deka	da or dk	ten or 10^{1}

The basic unit has no prefix.

deci	d	one-tenth or 10^{-1}
centi	c	one-hundredth or 10^{-2}
milli	m	one-thousandth or 10^{-3}
micro	μ	one-millionth or 10^{-6}
nano	n	one-billionth or 10^{-9}
pico	p	one-trillionth or 10^{-12}
femto	f	one-quadrillionth or 10^{-15}
atto	a	one-quintillionth or 10^{-18}

The Math Teacher's Book of Lists, © 1995 by Prentice Hall

LIST 60   WEIGHTS AND MEASURES IN THE METRIC SYSTEM

In the Metric system, the basic unit of length is the meter, the basic unit of weight is the gram, and the basic unit of capacity is the liter. To change a unit to a larger one, simply multiply by powers of 10. To change to a smaller unit, divide by powers of 10. There are few equivalences to remember; the most important items are the prefixes. The Metric system is now the standard for measurement in most countries.

Linear Measure

10 millimeters = 1 centimeter
10 centimeters = 1 decimeter
10 decimeters = 1 meter
10 meters = 1 dekameter or decameter
10 dekameters = 1 hectometer
10 hectometers = 1 kilometer

Square Measure

100 square millimeters
    = 1 square centimeter
100 square centimeters
    = 1 square decimeter
100 square decimeters
    = 1 square meter
100 square meters
    = 1 square dekameter or
    square decameter
100 square dekameters
    = 1 square hectometer or
    hectare
100 square hectometers
    = 1 square kilometer

Liquid Measure (Capacity)

10 milliliters = 1 centiliter
10 centiliters = 1 deciliter
10 deciliters = 1 liter
10 liters = 1 dekaliter or decaliter
10 dekaliters = 1 hectoliters
10 hectoliters = 1 kiloliter

Cubic Measure

1000 cubic millimeters
    = 1 cubic centimeter
    = 1 milliliter
1000 cubic centimeters
    = 1 cubic decimeter
    = 1 liter
1000 cubic decimeters
    = 1 cubic meter
1000 cubic meters
    = 1 cubic dekameter or
    cubic decameter
1000 cubic dekameters
    = 1 cubic hectometer
1000 cubic hectometers
    = 1 cubic kilometer

Mass Measure (Weight)

10 milligrams = 1 centigram
10 centigrams = 1 decigram
10 decigrams = 1 gram
10 grams = 1 dekagram or
    decagram
10 dekagrams = 1 hectogram
10 hectograms = 1 kilogram
100 kilograms = 1 quintal
10 quintals = 1 metric ton

LIST 61   CONVERTING ONE UNIT TO ANOTHER
IN THE METRIC SYSTEM

The values of Metric units are based on tens. This is why the Metric system—once a person learns it—is much easier to use than the English system. List 60, "Weights and Measures in the Metric System," shows the relationships between Metric units.

You can use the following steps to convert Metric units of length, liquid capacity, and mass.

To Convert from a Larger Unit to a Smaller Unit

- List the pertinent portions of the equivalency in order from greatest to least.

- Move the decimal point to the right every time you move from one unit to the other. Insert zeros as placeholders if necessary. (Moving the decimal point to the right is the same as multiplying by 10.)

Convert 2.8 kg to dg.

kg hg dkg g dg

   1 2 3 4

2.8000

2.8 kg = 28000dg

To Convert from a Smaller Unit to a Larger Unit

- List the pertinent portions of the equivalency in order from greatest to least.

- Move the decimal point to the left each time you move from one unit to the other. Insert zeros as placeholders if necessary. (Moving the decimal point to the left is the same as dividing by 10.)

Convert 35mm to dm.

dm cm mm

    2   1

  35

35mm = .35dm

The Math Teacher's Book of Lists, © 1995 by Prentice Hall

LIST 62   RULES FOR ADDING UNITS OF MEASUREMENT

When you are asked to add units in measurement, follow these steps.

- Line up the units in columns, just like an ordinary addition problem.
- Add each column (unit) separately.
- If necessary, convert the sum of each column.

Find the sum of 3 ft 7 in and 4 ft 8 in

$$\begin{array}{r} 3 \text{ ft } \ 7 \text{ in} \\ +4 \text{ ft } \ 8 \text{ in} \\ \hline 7 \text{ ft } 15 \text{ in} \end{array}$$

1 ft = 12 in

$$\begin{array}{r} 1 \text{ R}3 \\ 12\overline{)15} \\ \underline{12} \\ 3 \end{array}$$

15 in = 1 ft 3 in

7 ft 15 in = 7 ft + 1ft 3 in = 8 ft 3 in

LIST 63   RULES FOR SUBTRACTING UNITS OF MEASUREMENT

Use the following steps for subtracting units of measurements.

- Line up like units in columns. Remember to put the larger quantity on top.
- If necessary, regroup, using an equivalent. Working only with the top number, convert it to the smaller unit, and add the digits of the smaller unit.
- Subtract each unit separately.
- Make any final necessary conversions.

Find the difference of 3 hr 25 min and 1 hr 35 min.

$$\begin{array}{r} 3 \text{ hr } 25 \text{ min} \\ -1 \text{ hr } 35 \text{ min} \\ \hline \end{array}$$

Since 60 min = 1 hr

3 hr 25 min = 2 hr + 60 min + 25 min

$$\begin{array}{r} = 2 \text{ hr } 85 \text{ min} \\ -1\text{hr } 35 \text{ min} \qquad = \underline{1 \text{ hr } 35 \text{ min}} \\ 1\text{hr } 50 \text{ min} \end{array}$$

LIST 64   RULES FOR MULTIPLYING UNITS
OF MEASUREMENT

Multiplying units of measurement is similar to ordinary multiplication. The final step, however, is to simplify your answer as the list shows.

- Set up your problem like ordinary multiplication.
- Multiply from right to left, multiplying each column separately.
- If necessary, convert the units.

Find the product of 3 and 4 lb 9 oz.

$$\begin{array}{r} 4 \text{ lb} \quad 9 \text{ oz} \\ \times 3 \\ \hline 12 \text{ lb } 27 \text{ oz} \end{array}$$

Since 16 oz = 1 lb

$$16 \overline{)27} \quad {}^{1 \text{ R}11} \\ \underline{16} \\ 11$$

Therefore 27 oz = 1 lb 11 oz

12 lb 27 oz = 12 lb + 1 lb 11 oz = 13 lb 11 oz

LIST 65   RULES FOR DIVIDING UNITS
OF MEASUREMENT

The following steps are helpful for dividing units of measurement.

- Convert the quantity into the smallest unit.
- Add to combine the units.
- Divide.
- If possible, express your quotient in terms of the largest quantity.

Divide 9 ft 4 in by 2.

Since 1 ft = 12 in

9 ft = 9 × 12 in = 108 in

And   9 ft 4 in = 108 in + 4 in = 112 in

$$2 \overline{)112} \quad {}^{56 \text{ in}}$$

$$12 \overline{)56} \quad {}^{4 \text{ R}8} \\ \underline{48} \\ 8$$

56 in = 4 ft 8 in

The Math Teacher's Book of Lists, © 1995 by Prentice Hall

LIST 66 ENGLISH—METRIC EQUIVALENTS

Since the United States uses both the English and Metric systems of measurement, it is often helpful to know what a particular unit in the English system equals in Metrics. (Note that the values for fluid ounces, quarts, and gallons on this list are U.S. units, which vary slightly from British units.)

Length

    1 inch = 25.4 millimeters
    1 inch = 2.54 centimeters
    1 foot = 0.3048 meter
    1 yard = 0.9144 meter
    1 rod = 5.029 meters
    1 furlong = 201.17 meters
    1 mile = 1.6093 kilometers

Area

    1 square inch = 6.4516 square centimeters
    1 square foot = 929.03 square centimeters
    1 square foot = .092903 square meter
    1 square yard = 0.8361 square meter
    1 acre = 0.4047 hectare
    1 square mile = 258.999 hectares
    1 square mile = 2.5899 square kilometers

Volume

    1 cubic inch = 16.387 cubic centimeters
    1 cubic foot = 0.0283 cubic meter
    1 cubic yard = 0.765 cubic meter

Liquid Measure

    1 teaspoon = 5 milliliters
    1 fluid ounce = 29.573 milliliters
    1 pint = 0.4732 liter
    1 quart = 0.9463 liter
    1 gallon = 3.7853 liters

Weights (Avoirdupois)

    1 ounce = 28.350 grams
    1 pound = 453.59237 grams
    1 pound = 0.45359 kilogram

LIST 67   METRIC—ENGLISH EQUIVALENTS

The following list shows what Metric units equal in the English system.

Length

1 millimeter = 0.03937 inch
1 centimeter = .3937 inch
1 meter = 39.37 inches
1 meter = 3.28 feet
1 meter = 1.094 yards
1 kilometer = 0.621 mile

Area

1 square centimeter = 0.15499 square inch
1 square meter = 10.764 square feet
1 square meter = 1.196 square yards
1 hectare = 2.471 acres

Volume

1 cubic centimeter = 0.06102 cubic inch
1 cubic meter = 35.314 cubic feet
1 cubic meter = 1.308 cubic yards

Liquid Measure

1 centiliter = .338 fluid ounce
1 liter = 1.0567 quarts
1 kiloliter = 264.18 gallons

Weight

1 gram = 0.035 ounce (avoirdupois)
1 kilogram = 2.2046 pounds (avoirdupois)
1 metric ton = 2,204.623 pounds (avoirdupois)

LIST 68   CONVERSION FACTORS FOR LENGTH

Because we use both the English system and the Metric system for measuring length, it is helpful to be able to convert measurements from one system to the other.

Original Measurement	Converted to	Multiply by
inches	millimeters	25.4
inches	centimeters	2.54
inches	meters	0.0254
feet	meters	0.3048
yards	meters	0.9144
rods	meters	5.0292
furlongs	meters	201.168
miles	kilometers	1.60934
nautical miles	miles	1.15078
nautical miles	kilometers	1.852
millimeters	inches	0.03937
centimeters	inches	0.3937
meters	inches	39.3701
meters	feet	3.2808
meters	yards	1.09361
kilometers	miles	0.621371
kilometers	nautical miles	0.539957

The Math Teacher's Book of Lists, © 1995 by Prentice Hall

LIST 69 CONVERSION FACTORS FOR AREA

The following conversion factors are useful for comparing area in the English and Metric systems.

Original Measurement	Converted to	Multiply by
square inches	square centimeters	6.4516
square yards	square meters	0.836127
square rods	square meters	25.293
square miles	square kilometers	2.58999
acres	square meters	4,046.86
square centimeters	square inches	0.15499
square meters	square feet	10.7639
square meters	square yards	1.19599
square kilometers	square miles	0.386019

LIST 70 CONVERSION FACTORS FOR VOLUME

When converting units of volume in the English and Metric systems, use the following factors.

Original Measurement	Converted to	Multiply by
cubic inches	cubic centimeters	16.387
cubic feet	cubic meters	0.0283168
cubic feet	liters	28.3168
cubic yards	cubic meters	0.764555
cubic centimeter	cubic inches	0.06102
cubic meter	cubic feet	35.314
cubic meter	cubic yards	1.308

LIST 71 CONVERSION FACTORS FOR LIQUID CAPACITY

Use the following factors for converting the English and Metric systems for liquid capacity.

Original Measurement	Converted to	Multiply by
gills	milliliters	118.3
fluid ounces	milliliters	29.573
pints	liters	0.4732
quarts	liters	0.9463
gallons	liters	3.7853
milliliters	fluid ounces	0.0338
centiliters	fluid ounces	0.338
liters	quarts	1.0567
liters	gallons	0.26418
kiloliters	gallons	264.18

The Math Teacher's Book of Lists, © 1995 by Prentice Hall

LIST 72   CONVERSION FACTORS FOR DRY CAPACITY

The following factors are handy for converting English and Metric units of dry capacity.

Original Measurement	Converted to	Multiply by
pints	liters	0.5505
quarts	liters	1.1012
pecks	liters	8.8096
bushels	liters	35.2383
liters	quarts	0.9081
dekaliters	pecks	1.135
hectoliters	bushels	2.838
kiloliters	bushels	28.38

LIST 73   CONVERSION FACTORS FOR MASS (WEIGHT)

Use the following factors for converting the English and Metric systems for mass (weight).

Original Measurement	Converted to	Multiply by
carats	milligrams	200.0
grains	milligrams	64.799
ounces (avoirdupois)	grams	28.3495
pounds (avoirdupois)	grams	453.59237
pounds (avoirdupois)	kilograms	0.453592
tons (short, 2,000 lbs)	kilograms	907.18
tons (long, 2,240 lbs)	kilograms	1,016.047
milligrams	grains	0.015
grams	ounces (avoirdupois)	0.035
kilograms	pounds (avoirdupois)	2.204623
tons (long)	tons (short)	1.12

The Math Teacher's Book of Lists, © 1995 by Prentice Hall

LIST 74 MEASURES OF FORCE AND PRESSURE

Force and pressure are closely linked. *Force* is anything that changes the motion or state of rest in a body. *Pressure* is a force acting upon a surface per unit of area.

Dyne—the force needed to accelerate a 1-gram mass 1 centimeter per second squared.

    1 dyne = 0.0000072 poundal
    1 dyne = 10^{-5} newtons

Poundal—the force needed to accelerate a 1-pound mass 1 foot per second squared.

    1 poundal = 13,825.5 dynes
    1 poundal = 0.138255 newtons

Newton—the force needed to accelerate a 1-kilogram mass 1 meter per second squared.

    1 newton = 10^5 dynes
    1 newton = 7.23300 poundals

Pascal—used to measure pressure. Equals 1 newton per square meter or 0.020855 pound per square foot.

Atmosphere—used to measure pressure. At sea level equals 14.6952 pounds per square inch; 2,116.102 pounds per square foot; 1.0332 kilograms per square centimeter; 101,323 newtons per square meter.

LIST 75   MEASUREMENT OF TIME

Time—it's so important to us that we have created numerous ways to measure it.

nanosecond = 1 billionth of a second (sec)
microsecond = 1 millionth of a second
millisecond = 1 thousandth of a second
60 seconds = 1 minute (min)
60 minutes = 1 hour (hr)
24 hours = 1 day (d)
7 days = 1 week (wk)
4 weeks = approximately 1 month (mn)
52 weeks = 1 year (yr)
30 days = 1 calendar month (individual months vary)
12 months = 1 year
365 days = 1 common year*
366 days = 1 leap year
10 years = 1 decade
100 years = 1 century
1,000 years = a millennium

Here are some other "timely" terms:

Sidereal Time—Also known as astronomical time, this method of measurement uses the movement of the stars to calculate time. An average sidereal day is 23 hours, 56 minutes, and 4.09 seconds long.

Solar Time—An outmoded measurement of time in which noon occurs when the sun is at its highest point over a given location. Of course, noon (and therefore time) varies from place to place.

Atomic Time—Atomic clocks calculate time with extreme accuracy based on energy states of the cesium-133 atom.

Standard Time—Introduced in 1883 by international agreement, Standard Time divided the Earth into 24 time zones. Calculated on solar time, the base of the system is the zero meridian that passes through the Royal Greenwich Observatory at Greenwich, England. Time is measured east or west of this Prime Meridian according to the time zones.

Daylight Saving Time—In the United States, Standard Time plus one hour. Daylight Saving Time seems to make the day last longer by an hour.

The Math Teacher's Book of Lists, © 1995 by Prentice Hall

---

*More precisely, a year equals 365¼ days. To keep the calendar accurate, an extra day is added every four years, resulting in a leap year.

LIST 76 TEMPERATURE FORMULAS

Three scales are used for measuring temperature. The most common are the Celsius and Fahrenheit scales. The third, the Kelvin scale, is used to measure the temperature in scientific experiments.

It is often necessary to convert from one scale to the other. Below are four formulas that may be used. Note that for the conversions to Celsius and Fahrenheit, the formulas are written in both fraction and decimal forms.

To convert from degrees Celsius (°C) to degrees Fahrenheit (°F) use:

$$F = \frac{9C}{5} + 32$$

$$F = (C \times 1.8) + 32$$

To convert from degrees Fahrenheit (°F) to degrees Celsius (°C) use:

$$C = \frac{(F - 32)}{9} \times 5$$

$$C = (F - 32) \div 1.8$$

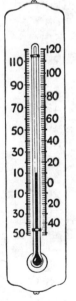

To convert from degrees Kelvin (°K) to degrees Celsius (°C) use:

$$C = K - 273.15$$

To convert from degrees Celsius (°C) to degrees Kelvin (°K) use:

$$K = C + 273.15$$

Following is a short list of important temperatures:

water boils	100°C =	212°F
normal body temperature	37°C =	98.6°F
water freezes	0°C =	32°F
Absolute zero	−273.15°C =	−459.67°F = 0°K

LIST 77   GETTING A FEEL FOR TEMPERATURE

The two most common scales used for measuring temperature are the Celsius and Fahrenheit scales. On the Celsius scale, named after Anders Celsius, the freezing point of water is 0°, and the boiling point of water is 100°. On the Fahrenheit scale, named after Gabriel Fahrenheit, the freezing point of water is 32°, and the boiling point is 212°.

Because the scales denote the freezing and boiling points of water at different degrees, people who are familiar with one scale usually have trouble understanding the other. Following are some degrees that you can use as reference points in comparing Celsius to Fahrenheit. Note that in some cases the conversions are approximations.

Degrees Celsius	Degrees Fahrenheit	Reference Point
327°C	621°F	lead melts
190°C	374°F	a hot oven
100°C	212°F	water boils
80°C	176°F	hot soup
66°C	151°F	hot faucet water
60°C	140°F	broiled steak
58°C	137°F	hottest air temperature recorded on earth
45°C	113°F	a hot bath
40°C	104°F	a high fever
38°C	101°F	a warm bath
37°C	98.6°F	normal body temperature
35°C	95°F	a hot day
20°C	68°F	room temperature on a winter day
10°C	50°F	cool fall day
7°C	45°F	cold water
1°C	33°F	ice water
0°C	32°F	water freezes
−5°C	23°F	snowy day
−11°C	12°F	frozen yogurt

The Math Teacher's Book of Lists, © 1995 by Prentice Hall

LIST 78   THE RICHTER SCALE

The Richter Scale, developed by seismologist Charles Richter, is used to express the amount of energy released at the focus of an earthquake. The scale is logarithmic, and based on a numerical system of exponents. For example, the difference between 6.0 and 7.0 on the Richter Scale is not one, but a factor of ten. Thus, an earthquake that measures 6.0 on the Richter Scale is a hundred times more powerful than an earthquake that measures 4.0. A quake of 8.0 is ten million times greater than a 1.0 quake.

Richter Number	Magnitude Increase	Comment
8	10,000,000	a disaster; few buildings left standing.
7	1,000,000	many buildings destroyed.
6	100,000	buildings shake; roads, walls crack.
5	10,000	strong rumbling; china, dishes break.
4	1,000	weak; much like a passing truck.
3	100	very weak; less than 3.5 detectable
2	10	only by seismographs.
1	1	

The great San Francisco earthquake of 1906 had a magnitude of 8.3. It leveled the city. This was hardly a burp compared to the earthquake that accompanied the volcanic explosion and sinking of the island of Krakatoa in 1883, which some experts estimate would have measured a 9.9 on the Richter Scale.

LIST 79   WIND SPEED

Description of the wind can be rather inaccurate, depending on an individual's point of view. To give some order to describing the wind, Admiral Sir Francis Beaufort devised the following wind speed scale in 1805. It is still used today.

Description of Air	Wind Speed		
	MPH	Knots	Km/hr
0. Calm	below 1	below 1	below 1
1. Light Air	1–3	1–3	1–5
2. Slight Breeze	4–7	4–6	6–11
3. Gentle Breeze	8–12	7–10	12–19
4. Moderate Breeze	13–18	11–16	20–28
5. Fresh Breeze	19–24	17–21	29–38
6. Strong Breeze	25–31	22–27	39–49
7. High Wind	32–38	28–33	50–61
8. Gale	39–46	34–40	62–74
9. Strong Gale	47–54	41–47	75–88
10. Whole Gale	55–63	48–55	89–102
11. Storm	64–75	56–65	103–117
12. Hurricane	over 75	over 65	over 117

The Math Teacher's Book of Lists, © 1995 by Prentice Hall

LIST 80   COMPUTER MEMORY

Cutting edge computers offer astounding memory capacity. The basic memory units, however, come down to bits and bytes.

8 bits = 1 character = 1 byte
1000 bytes = 1 kilobyte
1,000,000 bytes = 1,000 kilobytes = 1 megabyte

Since one character might correspond to the letter "a," 1 megabyte of memory has the capacity of storing a million single letters. These of course can be combined to form words, numbers, formulas, and pictures.

LIST 81 PAPER MEASURES OR PAPER WEIGHTS

Upon hearing the phrase "paper weights," many people think of the decorative objects that are used to keep papers from flying off desks when a breeze gusts in through a window, or someone shuts a door too fast. But paper weight also refers to the thickness of paper. Sheets might be 20-pound paper, 60-pound paper, or more. What do these numbers mean?

As if understanding the weight of paper isn't enough, the way paper is packaged can be just as confusing. Most people have heard that a ream of paper contains 500 sheets. It can; but it can also contain 480.

The following list (which is printed on 50-pound paper, which measures 8½ by 11 inches) clarifies the confusion.

Some Standard Amounts

24 sheets = 1 quire
25 sheets = 1 printer's quire
20 quires = 1 ream
21.5 quires = 1 printer's ream
2 reams = 1 bundle
4 bundles = 1 case
4 reams = 1 printer's bundle
10 reams = 1 bale
480 sheets = 1 short ream
500 sheets = 1 long ream

Guidelines for Commercial Paper Weights

9 pounds—onionskin paper
16 pounds—mimeograph paper
20 pounds—standard typing paper
24 pounds—standard letterhead paper
60 pounds—thick enough for printing on both sides because the ink won't bleed through
65 pounds—typical business cards
120 pounds—poster paper

LIST 82   U.S. MONEY—COINS AND BILLS

The following coins and bills are in current circulation in the United States.

$	.01	1¢	penny	$\frac{1}{100}$ of a dollar
	.05	5¢	nickel	$\frac{1}{20}$ of a dollar
	.10	10¢	dime	$\frac{1}{10}$ of a dollar
	.25	25¢	quarter	$\frac{1}{4}$ of a dollar
	.50	50¢	half dollar	$\frac{1}{2}$ of a dollar
	1.00		dollar (coin)	
	1.00		dollar (bill)	
	2.00		two dollars	
	5.00		five dollars	
	10.00		ten dollars	
	20.00		twenty dollars	
	50.00		fifty dollars	
	100.00		one hundred dollars*	

* Bills bigger than $100.00 are not issued any more.

Note that the one dollar coin and two dollar bill are seldom used.

The Math Teacher's Book of Lists, © 1995 by Prentice Hall

LIST 83 CURRENCIES AROUND THE WORLD

When is a dollar not a dollar? A peso not a peso? Or a franc not a franc?

Dollars, pesos, and francs are examples of currencies used by many countries around the world. Although Canada and the United States both use the dollar as their basic unit of money, the value of the Canadian dollar does not precisely equal that of the American dollar. Furthermore, due to the constant changes in the world's economy, the values of currencies are always fluctuating.

If you plan a trip to another country, you can easily find out the exchange rate of American dollars to the currency of your destination by calling your bank. Most banks maintain updated listings of exchange rates. The bank's representative can tell you how many pesos, francs, or deutsche marks you can "exchange" your American dollars for. Following is a list of some of the countries (and their currencies) you might one day be planning to visit.

Country	Currency	Country	Currency
Argentina	peso	Hungary	forint
Australia	dollar	Iceland	krona
Austria	schilling	India	rupee
Bahamas	dollar	Iran	rial
Belgium	franc	Iraq	dinar
Bolivia	peso	Israel	shekel
Brazil	cruzeiro	Italy	lira
Cambodia	riel	Japan	yen
Canada	dollar	Kenya	shilling
Chad	franc	Laos	kip
Chile	peso	Liberia	dollar
China		Macao	pataca
(People's		Mexico	peso
Republic of)	renminbi	Morocco	dirham
Colombia	peso	Netherlands	guilder
Costa Rica	colon	New Zealand	dollar
Cuba	peso	Nicaragua	cordoba
Czechoslovakia	crown	Norway	krone
Denmark	kroner	Oman	riyal-omani
Ecuador	sucre	Paraguay	guarani
Egypt	pound	Peru	sol
El Salvador	colon	Poland	zloty
Ethiopia	birr	Portugal	escudo
Finland	markka	Rumania	leu
France	franc	Russia	rouble
Greece	drachma	Saudi Arabia	riyal
Guatemala	quetzal	Singapore	dollar
Haiti	gourde	South Africa	rand
Honduras	lempira	South Korea	won
Hong Kong	dollar	Spain	peseta

LIST 83   (Continued)

Country	Currency	Country	Currency
Sweden	krona	United Arab	
Switzerland	franc	Emirates	dirham
Syria	pound	United Kingdom	pound
Taiwan	yuan	United States	
Thailand	baht	of America	dollar
Trinidad and		Venezuela	bolivar
Tobago	dollar	Vietnam	dong
Turkey	pound	Zambia	kwacha

GEOMETRY

LIST 84   UNDEFINED TERMS OF GEOMETRY

Geometry is the mathematics of properties, measurement, and the relationships of points, lines, angles, surfaces, and solids in space. It is based on three undefined terms: point, line, and surface. An understanding of these terms is necessary to understanding other geometric terms and principles. Although point, line, and surface remain undefined, they are described.

Point   —is represented by a dot.

  —has no length, width, or thickness.

Point A

  —is designated by a capital letter next to the dot.

Line   —has only length.

  —has no width or thickness.

Line $\overleftrightarrow{AB}$

  —is unlimited and extends infinitely in either direction.

  —is designated by two capital letters which represent two points on the line.

  —may also be designated by a small letter.

Line l

  —can be classified as:

    straight

    curved

    broken

    combination

  —unless stated otherwise, is understood to be straight.

  —is the shortest distance between two points.

Surface—has length and width.

  —does not have thickness.

  —may be represented by the side of a box, outside of a sphere, a wall with no windows or other openings.

  —a plane surface is a type of surface containing a straight line that connects any two points on the plane.

Plane K

  —a plane surface is sometimes denoted by a closed, four-sided figure with a capital letter at its vertex.

LIST 85   EUCLID'S AXIOMS AND POSTULATES

In his most famous work, *Elements,* Euclid (a Greek mathematician who lived around 300 B.C.) described geometry as a formal system of reasoning. Formal geometry is based on axioms, a set of "common notions," which are accepted to be true without proof. They apply to mathematics in general.

Postulates are assumptions that apply to a specific branch of mathematics—in this case geometry. Using the axioms and postulates, a person can define new terms and, using deductive reasoning, prove statements about them. These new statements are called theorems.

Euclid's Axioms

1. Things equal to the same thing are equal to each other.
2. If equals are added to equals, the sums are equal.
3. If equals are subtracted from equals, the differences are equal.
4. Things which coincide with one another are equal.
5. The whole is greater than any of its parts.

Euclid's Postulates

1. A straight line can be drawn between any two points.
2. Any straight line segment can be extended infinitely.
3. A circle with any radius may be described around a point as a center.
4. All right angles are equal to each other.
5. If a straight line falling on two straight lines makes the interior angles on the same side together less than two right angles, the two straight lines, if produced indefinitely, meet on that side on which the angles are together less than two right angles. (Because this fifth postulate is not felt to be a common notion and fit the definition of a postulate, John Playfair, a Scottish mathematician and physicist in the early 19th century, offered a revision of it: Given a line and a point not on the line, there is one and only one line parallel to the given line. Playfair's postulate is often substituted for the fifth postulate of Euclid.)

LIST 86   LINES AND PLANES

A line is one of the undefined terms in geometry. A description of a line is that it has length but no thickness or depth. In theory, a line may be extended infinitely in each direction.

A plane is a flat surface that extends infinitely in all directions. Imagine extending the length and width of a table top forever.

Lines that lie in the same plane are called coplanar lines. Any two coplanar lines must have one and only one of the characteristics listed below.

- The lines may intersect. If they intersect and form right angles, they are perpendicular lines.

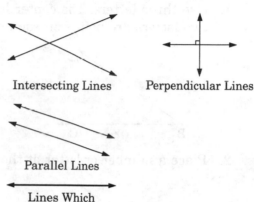

Intersecting Lines   Perpendicular Lines

- The lines may be parallel. Parallel lines will never meet.

Parallel Lines

- The lines may coincide. Lines that coincide are actually the same line.

Lines Which
Coincide

Lines that lie in different planes and do not intersect are called noncoplanar lines or skew lines.

- If two planes do not intersect, the planes are parallel.

- If two planes intersect, their intersection is a line.

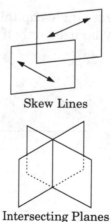

Skew Lines

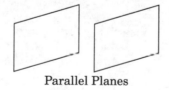

Parallel Planes

Intersecting Planes

LIST 87   STEPS FOR NAMING AN ANGLE

An angle is formed by two rays that have the same endpoint, which is called the vertex of the angle. The rays are called the sides of the angle. (A ray is a part of a line consisting of a given point called the endpoint. The ray continues forever in the other direction.) A point between the sides of the angle is in the interior of the angle. "∠" is the symbol for angle.

There are three ways to name an angle.

1. Use three letters. The center letter corresponds to the vertex. The other two letters are points on each ray.

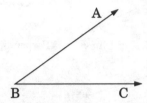

    The angle to the left can be named ∠ABC or ∠CBA. It can be read as "angle ABC or angle CBA."

2. Place a number or letter at the vertex in the interior of the angle.

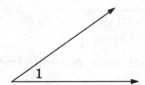

    The angle to the left can be named ∠1. It is read as "angle 1."

3. Use a single capital letter at the vertex in the interior of the angle. This may be used only if there is one angle at the vertex.

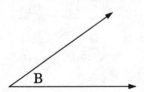

    The angle to the left can be named ∠B and read as "angle B."

The Math Teacher's Book of Lists, © 1995 by Prentice Hall

LIST 88 MEASURING ANGLES

We often describe the size of an object by comparing it to the size of something we know. The same is true of angles. The size of an angle has nothing to do with the lengths of its sides, which technically extend forever. The size of an angle depends upon the "opening" of the angle.

An angle is measured in *degrees* with an instrument called a *protractor*.

To measure an angle—

1. Compare its side to the corner of this page. The corner represents a *right angle,* whose measurement is 90°.

   —If the opening of the angle is smaller than the corner, the angle is an acute angle. Its measure is less than 90°.

   —If the opening is larger than the corner of the page, the angle is obtuse. Its measure is more than 90°.

2. Locate the point of your protractor which represents the vertex and align the vertex with the point.

3. Rotate the protractor, keeping the vertex aligned until one side of the angle is on the 0°-180° line of the protractor.

4. Read the angle measure that is determined by the side of the angle that is not on the 0°-180° line of the protractor. You may have to extend one side of the angle so that it crosses the scale.

   —If the angle is acute, read the smaller scale.

   —If the angle is obtuse, read the larger scale.

   —If the angle is a right angle, the measure is 90°.

5. Use the proper notation.

   —m is the symbol for "measure of."

   —Example: m∠ABC = 42° is read "the measure of angle ABC is 42°."

LIST 89   DRAWING ANGLES

Sometimes you may be asked to draw an angle that has a specific measure. You will need a protractor and a ruler.

To draw an angle, follow these steps—

1. Use your ruler (or the straight edge of your protractor) to draw a ray on your paper.

   Draw a 140° angle.

2. Align the point on the protractor, which represents the vertex of the angle, with the endpoint of the ray.

3. Using the right side of the protractor, align the ray with the 0°–180° line on the protractor.

4. Use the inner scale to find the measure of the angle you wish to draw. If the endpoint of the ray was located to the right of the ray (←), use the outer scale.

5. Mark that point on your paper.

6. Using your ruler, draw a ray from the vertex to the point you marked.

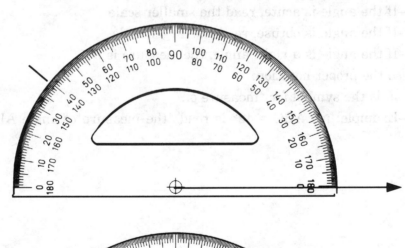

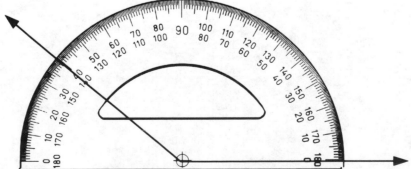

The Math Teacher's Book of Lists, © 1995 by Prentice Hall

LIST 90   TYPES OF ANGLES AND THE FACTS

There are five types of angles that are essential to the study of geometry. After you have a basic understanding of these, you can build upon your knowledge and skills.

Kinds of Angles

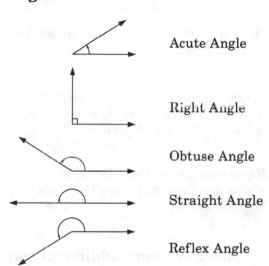

Acute angle—an angle whose measure is less than 90°.

Acute Angle

Right angle—an angle whose measure equals 90°. A box in the vertex denotes a right angle.

Right Angle

Obtuse angle—an angle whose measure is greater than 90° and less than 180°.

Obtuse Angle

Straight angle—an angle whose measure equals 180°.

Straight Angle

Reflex angle—an angle whose measure is greater than 180° and less than 360°.

Reflex Angle

Angle Facts

- Equal angles are angles that have the same number of degrees.
- A ray that bisects an angle divides it into 2 equal parts. The line is called the *angle bisector*.
- Congruent angles have the same measure.
- Perpendiculars are lines that form right angles.
- All right angles are congruent.
- The sides of a straight angle lie on a straight line.
- All straight angles are congruent.
- A perpendicular bisector of a line bisects the line and is perpendicular to the line.

LIST 91   FACTS ABOUT PAIRS OF ANGLES

A group of two angles is known as a pair of angles. Special angle pairs have their own names and distinguishing features.

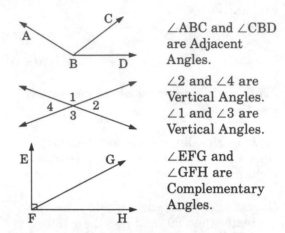

Adjacent angles—two angles that have the same vertex and a common side.

∠ABC and ∠CBD are Adjacent Angles.

Vertical angles—two nonadjacent angles formed by two intersecting lines.

∠2 and ∠4 are Vertical Angles.
∠1 and ∠3 are Vertical Angles.

Complementary angles—two angles whose measures add up to 90°. One angle is the complement of the other.

∠EFG and ∠GFH are Complementary Angles.

Supplementary angles—two angles whose measures add up to 180°. One angle is the supplement of the other.

There are 4 pairs of Supplementary Angles in the second diagram:

∠1 and ∠2	∠1 and ∠4
∠2 and ∠3	∠4 and ∠3

Here are some additional pairs of angles facts:

- If an angle is cut into two adjacent angles, then the sum of the measures of the adjacent angles equals the measure of the original angle.
- If the exterior sides of a pair of adjacent angles are perpendicular, then the angles are complementary.
- If the exterior sides of a pair of adjacent angles form a straight line, then the angles are supplementary.
- If two angles are congruent and supplementary, then each angle is a right angle.
- Complements of the same or congruent angles are congruent.
- Supplements of the same or congruent angles are congruent.
- Vertical angles are congruent.

LIST 92 ANGLES FORMED BY A TRANSVERSAL

A transversal is a line that cuts across two or more lines in the same plane. As it does, it forms five types of angles.

1. Interior angles—angles inside the region bounded by the two lines.
   - ∠1, ∠2, ∠3 and ∠4 are interior angles.

2. Exterior angles—angles outside the region bounded by the two lines.
   - ∠5, ∠6, ∠7 and ∠8 are exterior angles.

3. Same side interior angles—two nonadjacent interior angles that are on the same side as the transversal.
   - ∠2 and ∠4 are same side interior angles.
   - ∠1 and ∠3 are same side interior angles.

4. Alternate interior angles—two nonadjacent interior angles that are on opposite sides of the transversal.
   - ∠1 and ∠4 are alternate interior angles.
   - ∠2 and ∠3 are alternate interior angles.

5. Alternate exterior angles—two nonadjacent exterior angles that are on opposite sides of the transversal.
   - ∠5 and ∠8 are alternate exterior angles.
   - ∠6 and ∠7 are alternate exterior angles.

6. Corresponding angles—two nonadjacent angles (one is an interior angle and the other is an exterior angle) on the same side of the transversal.
   - Corresponding angles are listed below:
     ∠3 and ∠5
     ∠1 and ∠7
     ∠6 and ∠4
     ∠2 and ∠8

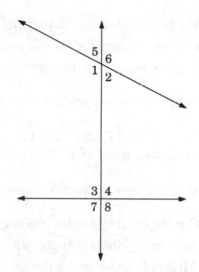

LIST 93   PRINCIPLES OF PARALLEL LINES

Parallel lines are lines which are in the same plane and never intersect. Imagine the lines made by the rails of a straight train track that extend forever. The distance between the lines remains constant.

∥ is the symbol for "is parallel to."

∦ is the symbol for "is not parallel to."

$l_1 \parallel l_2$ is read "line l_1 is parallel to line l_2."

Below are some properties of parallel lines.

The Parallel Postulate—Through a given point not on a line, exactly one line may be drawn parallel to the line.

If two lines are parallel, then:

Corresponding angles are congruent.

Alternate interior angles are congruent.

Alternate exterior angles are congruent.

Each pair of same side interior angles is supplementary.

A line perpendicular to one of the parallel lines is perpendicular to the other.

A line parallel to one of the parallel lines is parallel to the other.

To prove lines are parallel show that one of the following is true:

A pair of corresponding angles is congruent.

A pair of alternate interior angles is congruent.

A pair of alternate exterior angles is congruent.

A pair of same side interior angles is supplementary.

The lines are perpendicular to the same line.

The lines are parallel to the same line.

LIST 94 PRINCIPLES OF PERPENDICULAR LINES

Perpendicular lines intersect to form right angles. A line that is perpendicular to a segment and intersects the segment at its midpoint is called the *perpendicular bisector* of the segment.

$\perp$ is the symbol for perpendicular.

The following are principles of perpendicular lines:

- The lines intersect to form four right angles.
- There is only one perpendicular to a given line through a given point on the line.
- There is only one perpendicular to a given line through a given point not on the line.
- The distance between a line and a point not on the line is the length of the perpendicular segment drawn from the point to the line.

To prove that two lines are perpendicular show at least one of the following:

- The lines intersect to form a right angle.
- The lines intersect to form a pair of congruent adjacent angles.

LIST 95   TYPES OF POLYGONS

Polygons are closed, plane figures bounded by line segments. The following list contains useful information about these figures. n stands for the number of sides.

Polygon	Number of Sides	Number of Diagonals	Sum of Interior Angles*
Triangle	3	0	180°
Quadrilateral	4	2	360°
Pentagon	5	5	540°
Hexagon	6	9	720°
Heptagon	7	14	900°
Octagon	8	20	1,080°
Nonagon	9	27	1,260°
Decagon	10	35	1,440°
Undecagon	11	44	1,620°
Dodecagon	12	54	1,800°
N-gon	n	$(n^2 - 3n)/2$	$(n - 2)(180°)$

*The sum of the exterior angles for each polygon is 360°.

The Math Teacher's Book of Lists, © 1995 by Prentice Hall

LIST 96   REGULAR POLYGONS: TERMS AND FORMULAS

A regular polygon is equilateral (all sides are congruent) and equiangular (all angles are congruent). While some terms and formulas apply to all polygons, others apply only to regular polygons.

Terms

Center of a regular polygon—the common center of the inscribed and circumscribed circles. O is the center.

Radius of a regular polygon—the line segment which forms the center of the polygon to any vertex. $\overline{OA}$ is a radius.

Central angle of a regular polygon—an angle included between two radii drawn to successive vertices. $\angle AOB$ is a central angle.

Apothem of a regular polygon—a line segment from the center of the polygon that is perpendicular to one of its sides. $\overline{OC}$ is an apothem.

Diagonal of any polygon—a line segment drawn from one vertex to an another nonadjacent vertex. $\overline{DE}$ is a diagonal.

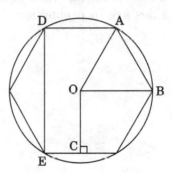

Formulas

1. The measure of each interior angle of a regular polygon is $\frac{180° (n-2)}{n}$ where n is the number of sides.

2. The measure of each exterior angle of a regular polygon is $\frac{360°}{n}$ where n is the number of sides.

3. The measure of each central angle of a regular polygon is $\frac{360°}{n}$ where n is the number of sides.

4. The sum of the interior angles of any polygon equals $(n-2)(180°)$ where n is the number of sides.

5. The sum of the exterior angles of any polygon is 360°.

6. The number of diagonals of any polygon is $\frac{n^2 - 3n}{2}$ where n is the number of sides.

LIST 97   PRINCIPLES OF REGULAR POLYGONS

Regular polygons share some unique characteristics, as the list below shows.

- A circle may be circumscribed about any regular polygon.
- A circle may be inscribed in any regular polygon.
- An equilateral polygon inscribed in a circle is a regular polygon.
- The radius of a regular polygon is a radius of the circumscribed circle.
- The radius of a regular polygon bisects the angle to which it is drawn.
- Apothems of regular polygons are equal.
- An apothem of a regular polygon bisects the side to which it is drawn.
- Regular polygons that have the same number of sides are similar.
- Corresponding lines of regular polygons that have the same number of sides are in proportion.

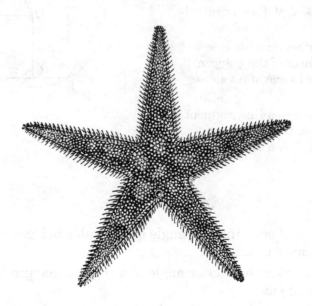

The Math Teacher's Book of Lists, © 1995 by Prentice Hall

LIST 98 SHAPES OF NUMBERS

The ancient Greeks, in the spirit of amusement and exploration, sometimes represented numbers by geometric figures. Whole numbers that can be depicted by geometric figures are called figurative numbers. Some figurative numbers are listed below:

Triangular numbers—numbers that can be presented by a triangular array of dots. (Triangles have 3 sides.)

1   3   6

Square numbers—numbers that can be represented by a square array of dots. (Squares have 4 congruent sides.)

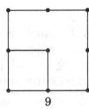

1   4   9

Pentagonal numbers—numbers that can be represented by a pentagonal array of dots. (Pentagons have 5 sides.)

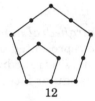

1   5   12

Hexagonal numbers—numbers that can be represented by a hexagonal array of dots. (Hexagons have 6 sides.)

1   6   15

Heptagonal numbers—numbers that can be represented by a heptagonal array of dots. (Heptagons have 7 sides.)

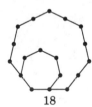

1   7   18

Octagonal numbers—numbers that can be represented by an octagonal array of dots. (Octagons have 8 sides.)

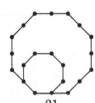

1   8   21

LIST 98   (Continued)

Nonagonal numbers—numbers that can be represented by a nonagonal array of dots. (Nonagons have 9 sides.)

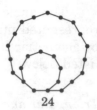

1   9   24

Some figurative numbers can be represented by arrays that show solid figures. Two of those:

Cubic numbers—numbers that can be represented by a cubic array of dots. (Cubes are solid figures that have six congruent squares as faces.)

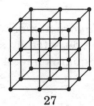

1   8   27

Tetrahedral numbers—numbers that can be represented by a tetrahedral array of dots. (Tetrahedra have four congruent triangular faces.)

1   4   10

LIST 99 FIGURATE NUMBER FORMULAS

Figurate numbers can be predicted by looking at the array of dots used to represent them. While some patterns are obvious, others require more study and numerical manipulations. Below is a list of the first five figurate numbers of each type and the generalization.

Shape	1st	2nd	3rd	4th	5th	n^{th}
Triangular	1	3	6	10	15	$\dfrac{n^2 + n}{2}$
Square	1	4	9	16	25	n^2
Pentagonal	1	5	12	22	35	$\dfrac{3n^2 - n}{2}$
Hexagonal	1	6	15	28	45	$2n^2 - n$
Heptagonal	1	7	18	34	55	$\dfrac{5n^2 - 3n}{2}$
Octagonal	1	8	21	40	65	$3n^2 - 2n$
Nonagonal	1	9	24	46	75	$\dfrac{7n^2 - 5n}{2}$
Cubic	1	8	27	64	125	n^3
Tetrahedral	1	4	10	20	35	$\dfrac{n^3 + 3n^2 + 2n}{6}$

LIST 100 POLYOMINOES

A polyomino is a plane figure made up of congruent squares that are connected to each other so that each square shares at least one side with one other square. Polyominoes are classified by a name whose prefix denotes the number of squares that are joined together. The first five polyominoes are listed.

	# of Squares	# of Arrangements	Arrangements
monomino	1	1	
domino	2	1	
tromino	3	2	
tetromino	4	5	
pentomino	5	12	

LIST 101 PENTOMINOES AND HEXOMINOES

Polyominoes are figures formed by joining congruent squares along the sides so that the sides are adjacent. *Pentominoes* are a special type of polyomino that consists of joining five congruent squares. *Hexominoes* are another special polyomino that consists of joining six congruent squares.

Pentominoes and hexominoes can be arranged in a variety of patterns. Some of the most interesting are those that may form boxes. Pentominoes form open boxes; hexominoes form closed boxes or cubes.

Of the 12 pentominoes, eight can be arranged so that they form an open box when cut out and folded along the dots. These are shown below.

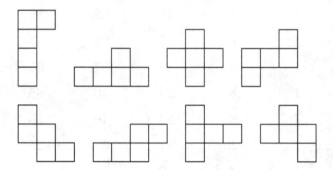

Of the 35 hexominoes, 11 can be arranged to form a closed box or cube when they are cut and folded along the dotted lines. These are shown below.

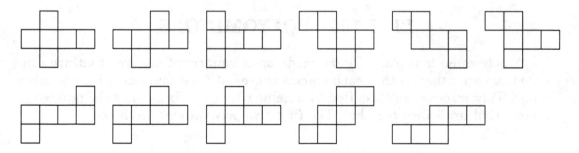

The Math Teacher's Book of Lists, © 1995 by Prentice Hall

LIST 102   BASIC FIGURES IN GEOMETRY

Geometry is all around us. You can find many examples of the following geometric figures every day.

Triangles

Triangles are three-sided figures. There are different kinds of triangles:

Equilateral triangle—all three sides have the same length and all three angles have the same measure.

Equilateral Triangle

Isosceles triangle—at least two sides have the same length.

Isosceles Triangle

Scalene triangle—all three sides have different lengths.

Scalene Triangle

Acute triangle—all angles measure less than 90°.

Acute Triangle

Right triangle—one angle measures 90°.

Right Triangle

Obtuse triangle—one angle measures greater than 90°.

Obtuse Triangle

Quadrilaterals

Quadrilaterals are closed figures with four sides. There are several common quadrilaterals.

Square—all sides are the same length; all angles are right angles.

Square

Rhombus—all sides are the same length; two pairs of sides are parallel.

Rhombus

The Math Teacher's Book of Lists, © 1995 by Prentice Hall

LIST 102   (Continued)

Rectangle—two pairs of sides are the
same length; all angles are right angles.   Rectangle

Parallelogram—two pairs of sides have
the same length, and two pairs of sides   Parallelogram
are parallel.

Trapezoid—one pair of sides is parallel.   Trapezoid

Circles

A *circle* is a plane figure bounded by a
curved line. Every point of the curved   Circle
line is equidistant from the center.

The Math Teacher's Book of Lists, © 1995 by Prentice Hall

LIST 103   TRIANGLE TERMS

The following words are used to describe triangles and their parts.

Triangle—a closed plane figure formed by three line segments, provided each line segment intersects another line segment at its endpoints.

Side—a line segment joining two endpoints.

Vertex—the point where two sides meet.

Vertices—the plural of vertex.

Angle of a triangle—the angle formed inside the triangle by two sides meeting at a vertex. It is also called the interior angle.

Angle bisector of a triangle—a line segment that bisects an angle and extends to the opposite side. $\overline{DE}$ is an angle bisector.

Exterior angle—an angle adjacent to an interior angle such that their exterior sides form a straight line. ∠a is an exterior angle.

Perpendicular bisector of a side of a triangle—a line segment that bisects the side and is perpendicular to it. $\overline{AB}$ is the perpendicular bisector.

Altitude of a triangle—a segment drawn from any vertex, perpendicular to the opposite side. It may be extended if necessary. $\overline{CF}$ is an altitude.

Height—the length of an altitude.

Median of a triangle—the line segment drawn from any vertex of a triangle to the midpoint of the opposite side. $\overline{CB}$ is a median.

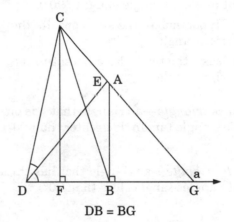

DB = BG

LIST 104   CLASSIFYING TRIANGLES

Triangles may be grouped according to the measure of their angles and the lengths of their sides.

Triangles Classified According to Angles

Right triangle—a triangle that has one right angle (an angle equal to 90°).

- Hypotenuse—the side opposite the right angle.
- legs—the two sides adjacent to the right angle.

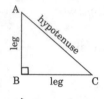

Right Triangle

Obtuse triangle—a triangle that has one obtuse angle (an angle greater than 90°).

Obtuse Triangle

Acute triangle—a triangle that has three acute angles (angles less than 90°).

Acute Triangle

Equiangular triangle—a triangle with three angles whose measures are each 60°.

Equiangular Triangle

Triangles Classified According to Sides

Scalene triangle—a triangle that has no congruent sides.

Scalene Triangle

Isosceles triangle—a triangle with at least two congruent sides.

- Legs—the congruent sides.
- Base—the side remaining.
- Base angles—angles on either side of the base and opposite the legs.
- Vertex—the angle opposite the base.

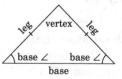

Isosceles Triangle

Equilateral triangle—a triangle that has three congruent sides.

Equilateral Triangle

The Math Teacher's Book of Lists, © 1995 by Prentice Hall

LIST 105   PRINCIPLES OF TRIANGLES

The following principles apply to all triangles.

- The sum of the measures of the angles of a triangle is 180°.
- The measure of each angle in an equiangular triangle is 60°.
- An equilateral triangle is isosceles and equiangular.
- A triangle may have at most one right or one obtuse angle.
- The acute angles of a right triangle are complementary.
- If two angles of one triangle are congruent to two angles of another triangle, then the remaining pair of angles are congruent.
- The measure of an exterior angle of a triangle is equal to the sum of the measures of the two nonadjacent interior angles.
- The measure of an exterior angle of a triangle is greater than the measure of either nonadjacent interior angles.
- An altitude of a triangle is perpendicular to the side to which it is drawn.
- Every triangle has three altitudes which intersect at a point called the *orthocenter*. This could happen in one of three ways:

  1) In the interior of an acute triangle.

  2) On the right triangle.

  3) In the exterior of an obtuse triangle.

- The median of a triangle bisects the side to which it is drawn.
- Every triangle has three medians which intersect at a point called the *centroid*.
- The length of each side of a triangle must be less than the sum of the lengths of the remaining sides.
- If two sides of a triangle are congruent, then the angles opposite those sides are congruent.
- If two angles of a triangle are congruent, then the opposite sides are congruent.

The Math Teacher's Book of Lists, © 1995 by Prentice Hall

LIST 106   CONCURRENT SEGMENTS
OF TRIANGLES

Three or more lines (or line segments) that intersect at a common point are said to be concurrent at that point. The following line segments are examples of concurrent segments of triangles.

- The perpendicular bisectors of the sides are concurrent at a point. This point of concurrency is equidistant from the vertices of the triangle and is called the "circumcenter of the triangle."

  O is the circumcenter of the triangle.
  OA = OB = OC

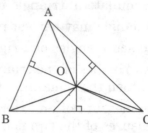

- Altitudes are concurrent at a point. This point of concurrency is called the "orthocenter of the triangle." The triangle formed by joining the feet of the vertices is known as the pedal triangle.

  H is the orthocenter of the triangle.

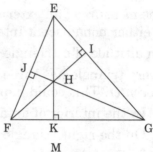

- The angle bisectors of the angles of a triangle are concurrent at a point that is equidistant from the sides of the triangle. This point of concurrency is the "center of the triangle."

  R is the center of the triangle.
  QR = RP = RO

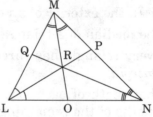

- The medians of a triangle are concurrent at a point called the "centroid of the triangle." This point is ⅔ of the distance from the vertex of the triangle to the midpoint of the side opposite the vertex.

  X is the centroid of the triangle.

  $VX = \frac{2}{3} VT$

  $YX = \frac{2}{3} YS$

  $UX = \frac{2}{3} UW$

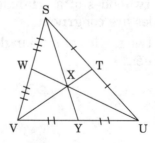

The Math Teacher's Book of Lists, © 1995 by Prentice Hall

LIST 107   SPECIAL RIGHT TRIANGLES

The 30°–60°–90° triangle is half of an equilateral triangle. The 45°–45°–90° triangle is half of a square. The legs and hypotenuse of these triangles enjoy a special relationship, as listed below.

Relationships in a 30°–60°–90° triangle:

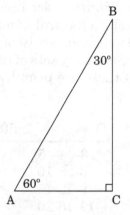

- The length of the leg opposite the 30° angle is ½ the length of the hypotenuse.

  AC = ½AB

- The length of the leg opposite the 60° angle equals ½ the length of the hypotenuse times √3.

  BC = ½AB √3

- The length of the leg opposite the 60° angle equals the length of the leg opposite the 30° angle times √3.

  BC = AC √3

Relationships in a 45°–45°–90° triangle:

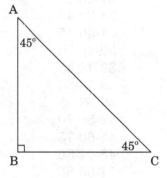

- The legs are congruent.

  AB = BC

- The length of the hypotenuse equals the length of either leg times √2.

  AC = AB √2

  AC = BC √2

- The length of either leg is equal to the product of the hypotenuse and ½ and √2.

  AB = ½AC √2

  BC = ½AC √2

LIST 108   PYTHAGOREAN TRIPLES

In the sixth century B.C. Pythagoras discovered a relationship between the hypotenuse of a right triangle and the two legs.

$a^2 + b^2 = c^2$ is called the Pythagorean Theorem. (a and b represent the legs and c stands for the hypotenuse.)

The most common right triangle is known as the 3,4,5 triangle. This set is called the *primitive set* because the numbers are relatively prime. Multiplying each value by a natural number, for example 2,3, or 4 results in another Pythagorean triple such as 6,8,10 or 9,12,15 or 12,16,20.

There are fifty sets of triples where each leg and hypotenuse is less than 100. Sixteen of these are primitive sets and denoted by * in the following list.

50 Pythagorean Triples

* 3- 4- 5	* 8-15-17	*33-56-65
6- 8-10	16-30-34	*36-77-85
9-12-15	24-45-51	*39-80-89
12-16-20	32-60-68	*48-55-73
15-20-25	40-75-85	*65-72-97
18-24-30	* 7-24-25	
21-28-35	14-48-50	
24-32-40	21-72-75	
27-36-45	* 9-40-41	
30-40-50	18-80-82	
33-44-55	*11-60-61	
36-48-60	*12-35-37	
39-52-65	24-70-74	
42-56-70	*13-84-85	
45-60-75	*16-63-65	
48-64-80	*20-21-29	
51-68-85	40-42-58	
54-72-90	60-63-87	
57-76-95	*28-45-53	
* 5-12-13		
10-24-26		
15-36-39		
20-48-52		
25-60-65		
30-72-78		
35-84-91		

The Math Teacher's Book of Lists, © 1995 by Prentice Hall

LIST 109   PROVING TRIANGLES CONGRUENT

Congruent triangles have the same size and shape. Two triangles can be proven to be congruent if they agree with any of the statements below. (Note that ≅ is the symbol for "is congruent to.")

Side-Side-Side (S-S-S)—If three sides of one triangle are congruent to corresponding sides of the other triangle, the two triangles are congruent.

Side-Angle-Side (S-A-S)—If two sides and the included angle of one triangle are congruent to the corresponding parts of the other triangle, the two triangles are congruent.

Angle-Side-Angle (A-S-A)—If two angles and the included side of one triangle are congruent to the corresponding parts of the other triangle, the two triangles are congruent.

Angle-Angle-Side (A-A-S)—If two angles and the side opposite one of the angles in a triangle are congruent to corresponding parts of the second triangle, the triangles are congruent.

To prove that right triangles are congruent, use any method above, or use—

- *Hypotenuse-Leg*—If the hypotenuse and either leg of one triangle is congruent to corresponding parts of the second triangle, the triangles are congruent.

LIST 110   PROPERTIES OF SIMILAR TRIANGLES

Similar triangles have the same shape but not the same size. Three pairs of corresponding angles are congruent and the lengths of corresponding sides are proportional. The symbol ~ means "is similar to."

Similar triangles have the following properties:

- Corresponding angles are congruent.
- Corresponding sides are in proportion.
- Two angles of one triangle are respectively congruent to two angles of the other triangle.
- An angle of one triangle is congruent to an angle of the other and the sides including these angles are in proportion.
- An acute angle of a right triangle is congruent to an acute angle of another triangle.

LIST 111   PROVING TRIANGLES SIMILAR

Similar triangles have the same shape but not the same size. You can prove that two triangles are similar by using any of the methods below.

Angle-Angle (A-A)—If two angles of one triangle are congruent to corresponding angles of the other triangle, then the triangles are similar.

Side-Side-Side (S-S-S)—If the corresponding sides of one triangle are in proportion to the corresponding sides of the other triangle, then the triangles are similar.

Side-Angle-Side (S-A-S)—If a pair of corresponding angles are congruent and the sides which include this angle are in proportion, then the triangles are similar.

To prove that right triangles are similar, use any method listed above, or—

- Prove that an acute angle in one right triangle is congruent to an acute angle in the other triangle.

Other Facts about Similar Triangles

The following have the same ratios as the lengths of any pair of corresponding sides.

- Corresponding altitudes.
- Corresponding medians.
- Corresponding perimeters.

LIST 112 RATIO AND PROPORTIONS

A ratio is a comparison of two values. For example, since a yard is equal to 3 feet, the ratio of 1 foot to 1 yard can be expressed as 1 to 3. When writing ratios, the units used for comparison must be the same. The first unit of comparison becomes the first number of the ratio.

Ratios can be expressed in three ways. A ratio of 1 to 3 may be written:

As a fraction $\frac{1}{3}$

In colon form $1:3$

With the word "to" 1 to 3

Sometimes a ratio can be simplified. The ratio can $\frac{8}{10}$ be written as $\frac{4}{5}$.

An equation that states two ratios are equal is a proportion and can be written in three ways:

$$\frac{8}{10} = \frac{4}{5}$$

$$8:10 = 4:5$$

8 to 10 = 4 to 5

Each term of a proportion has a name determined by its position in the proportion.

First Proportional Third Proportional
$\frac{a}{b} = \frac{c}{d}$
Second Proportional Fourth Proportional

The first and fourth terms are called the *extremes* of the proportion.

The second and third terms are called the *means* of the proportion.

Means
$\frac{a}{b} = \frac{c}{d}$ a:b = c:d   a to b = c to d
Extremes   Extremes   Extremes

In any proportion the product of the means equals the product of the extremes. Multiplying in this way is also called cross multiplying. If $\frac{a}{b} = \frac{c}{d}$ then bc = ad.

If the means of a proportion are the same, then either the second term or the third term of the proportion is called the *mean proportional* or *geometric mean* between the extremes.

Mean Proportional   Mean Proportional
$\frac{a}{b} = \frac{b}{c}$ or   a:b = b:c

LIST 113   DERIVING PROPORTIONS

From a given proportion, you may form other proportions by using some algebraic properties. The following proportions may be obtained from $\frac{a}{b} = \frac{c}{d}$, using the methods below.

- Switching numerators and denominators.

$$\text{If } \frac{a}{b} = \frac{c}{d} \quad \text{then} \quad \frac{b}{a} = \frac{d}{c} \quad \text{or} \quad \frac{d}{c} = \frac{b}{a}$$

- Switching the first proportion with the fourth proportion.

$$\text{If } \frac{a}{b} = \frac{c}{d} \quad \text{then} \quad \frac{d}{b} = \frac{c}{a} \quad \text{or} \quad \frac{c}{a} = \frac{d}{b}$$

- Adding the denominator to the numerator on each side of the equation.

$$\text{If } \frac{a}{b} = \frac{c}{d} \quad \text{then} \quad \frac{a+b}{b} = \frac{c+d}{d} \quad \text{or} \quad \frac{c+d}{d} = \frac{c+b}{b}$$

- Subtracting the denominator from the numerator on each side of the equation.

$$\text{If } \frac{a}{b} = \frac{c}{d} \quad \text{then} \quad \frac{a-b}{b} = \frac{c-d}{d} \quad \text{or} \quad \frac{c-d}{d} = \frac{a-b}{b}$$

LIST 114   PRINCIPLES RELATING TO PROPORTIONAL LINES

Parallel lines arc lines which are in the same plane and never intersect. The principles listed below relate parallel lines (and in one case the angle bisector) to proportional lines.

- If a line is parallel to one side of a triangle, then it divides the other two sides proportionally. $\frac{a}{b} = \frac{c}{d}$

- If a line is parallel to one side of a triangle, it divides the larger triangle into a smaller similar triangle. $\triangle ABC \sim \triangle ADE$

- If a line divides two sides of a triangle proportionally, it is parallel to the third side.

- Three or more parallel lines divide any two transversals proportionally. $\frac{m}{n} = \frac{r}{s}$

- The bisector of an angle of a triangle divides the opposite side into segments which are proportional to the adjacent sides. $\frac{f}{h} = \frac{g}{j}$

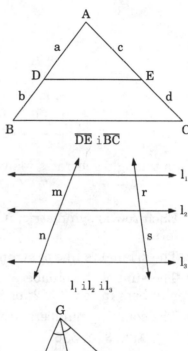

$\overline{DE} \parallel \overline{BC}$

$l_1 \parallel l_2 \parallel l_3$

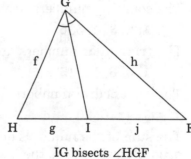

IG bisects ∠HGF

LIST 115   PASCAL'S TRIANGLE

The triangular array of numbers below is named for Blaise Pascal, a French mathematician who lived in the seventeenth century. Each number is the sum of the numbers to its immediate upper left and immediate upper right in the previous row.

```
                 1                          Row 0
              1     1                       Row 1
           1     2     1                    Row 2
        1     3     3     1                 Row 3
     1     4     6     4     1              Row 4
  1     5    10    10     5     1           Row 5
1     6    15    20    15     6     1       Row 6
  •     •     •     •     •     •     •
```

This triangle generates many interesting patterns, some of which are listed below.

- Each row is symmetric; it is read the same from left to right as right to left.
- The triangle's line of symmetry is the vertical center line.
- The sum of the numbers in row n equals 2^n. For example, the sum of the numbers in row 3 is 2^3 or 8.
- The counting numbers are listed along the second diagonal.

      1, 2, 3, 4, 5, 6 . . .

- The triangular numbers are listed along the third diagonal.

      1, 3, 6, 10, 15 . . .

- The tetrahedral numbers are listed along the fourth diagonal.

      1, 4, 10, 20 . . .

- The sum of the numbers on any diagonal is found by moving down the diagonal until you see the last number you wish to add and then moving diagonally right. For example, the sum of the first 5 counting numbers is obtained by moving down the second diagonal until you reach 5, then move diagonally right to 15. Thus, the sum of the first 5 counting numbers is 15.
- The sum of all the numbers above row n is $2^n - 1$. For instance, the sum of all the numbers above row 3 is $2^3 - 1$ or 7.
- Each row represents the coefficients in the expansion of $(x + y)^n$ where n represents the row of Pascal's triangle. For example, $(x + y)^2 = x^2 + 2xy + y^2$ has respective coefficients of 1, 2, 1, which are the numbers in row 2.

The Math Teacher's Book of Lists, © 1995 by Prentice Hall

LIST 116   THE HARMONIC TRIANGLE

The Harmonic Triangle is a triangular array of numbers associated with Gottfried Wilhelm Leibniz. Considered by many to be one of the brightest men of his times, Leibniz discovered the basic principles of infinitesimal calculus.

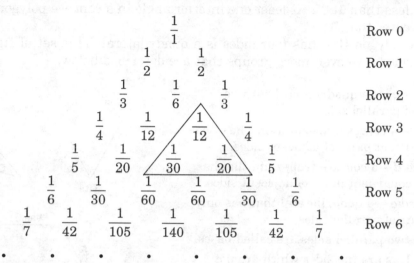

Row 0
Row 1
Row 2
Row 3
Row 4
Row 5
Row 6

Many patterns are generated by this triangle:

- Each row is symmetric. It reads the same from left to right as right to left.

- The vertical center line is the line of symmetry.

- The first number in each row is the reciprocal of the counting numbers.

- The second number in each row is the product of the first number in the row and the first number in the previous row. For example, $\frac{1}{6}$ the second number in row 2 equals $\frac{1}{2} \times \frac{1}{3}$.

- The denominators are multiples of the numbers in Pascal's Triangle.

- An equilateral triangle can be drawn to include three numbers anywhere on the triangle with the following result—the top fraction minus the bottom lefthand fraction equals the bottom righthand fraction. For example, in the small triangle drawn in row 3 and row 4, $\frac{1}{12} - \frac{1}{30} = \frac{1}{20}$.

- The numbers in each diagonal form an infinite sequence. For example, the terms of the sequence in the second diagonal are $\frac{1}{2}, \frac{1}{6}, \frac{1}{12}, \frac{1}{20}, \frac{1}{30}, \frac{1}{42} \cdots$

- The sum of the infinite series whose terms are the numbers in the second diagonal equals one.

- The sum of the infinite series whose terms are the numbers in the third diagonal equals one-half.

- The sum of the infinite series whose terms are the numbers in the fourth diagonal equals one-third.

- In general, the sum of the infinite series whose terms are the numbers in the nth diagonal equals the first number (or last) in the $n - 1$ row. For example, the sum of the numbers in the fifth diagonal equals the first (or last) number in row 4 which is $\frac{1}{5}$.

LIST 117   TYPES OF QUADRILATERALS

A polygon is a closed plane figure whose sides are line segments, which intersect only at their endpoints. Polygons may be concave or convex, depending upon the measure of their angles. Every interior angle in a convex polygon has a measure of less than 180°. At least one interior angle in a concave polygon has a measure greater than 180°.

A polygon that has four sides is a quadrilateral. This set of figures may be subdivided into even more groups that are described below.

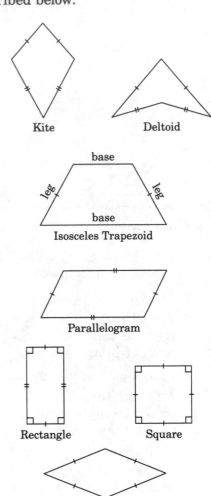

Trapezium—a quadrilateral with no pairs of parallel sides.

- *Kite*—a convex trapezium that has two congruent pairs of adjacent sides.

- *Deltoid*—a concave trapezium that has two congruent pairs of adjacent sides.

Trapezoid—a quadrilateral that has only one pair of parallel sides.

- The two parallel sides are called bases.

- The legs are the sides which are not parallel.

- The median joins the midpoints of the legs.

- An isosceles trapezoid is a special type of trapezoid whose legs are congruent. They are *not* parallel.

Parallelogram—a quadrilateral whose opposite sides are parallel. This is equivalent to saying it has two pairs of parallel sides. Some special types of parallelograms follow.

- *Rectangle*—a parallelogram that has four right angles.

- *Rhombus*—a parallelogram that has four congruent sides.

- *Square*—a parallelogram that has four congruent sides and four congruent angles.

LIST 118 PROPERTIES OF SPECIAL QUADRILATERALS

Quadrilaterals are four-sided polygons. The sum of the interior angles of a quadrilateral is 360°. In addition, some quadrilaterals possess special properties, which are listed below.

Properties of a Trapezoid

- Exactly one pair of parallel sides.
- The median is parallel to the bases.
- The length of the median equals one-half the sum of the length of the bases.

Properties of an Isosceles Trapezoid

- All the properties of a trapezoid.
- The lower base angles are congruent.
- The upper base angles are congruent.
- The diagonals are congruent.
- The legs are congruent.

Properties of a Parallelogram

- Opposite sides are parallel.
- Consecutive pairs of angles are supplementary.
- Opposite angles are congruent.
- Opposite sides are congruent.
- Diagonals bisect each other.

Properties of a Rectangle

- All the properties of a parallelogram.
- Diagonals are congruent.
- All angles are right angles.

Properties of a Rhombus

- All the properties of a parallelogram.
- All sides are congruent.
- The diagonals are perpendicular to each other.
- The diagonals bisect opposite angles.

Properties of a Square

- All the properties of a parallelogram.
- All the properties of a rectangle.
- All the properties of a rhombus.

LIST 119   CLASSIFICATION
OF QUADRILATERALS

Quadrilaterals—closed figures with four sides—may be classified according to their number of parallel sides, congruent segments, and right angles. Below is a summary of the types of quadrilaterals mentioned in List 117, "Types of Quadrilaterals."

You might think of it like this: every square is a rectangle, but not every rectangle is a square. A rectangle, however, is also a parallelogram, but a parallelogram may not be a rectangle (unless its angles are all right angles). The next time you find yourself engaged in a conversation that is lagging, you might bring up these fine points of geometry.

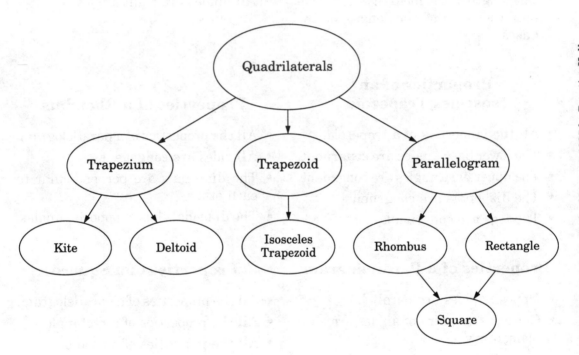

The Math Teacher's Book of Lists, © 1995 by Prentice Hall

LIST 120   PROOFS FOR QUADRILATERALS

List 118, "Properties of Special Quadrilaterals," contains the properties of special quadrilaterals. To prove a trapezoid is isosceles, a quadrilateral is a parallelogram, and a parallelogram is a rectangle, rhombus, or square, the other side of the issue must be examined.

Below is a list of the minimum information required for each proof.

To prove a trapezoid is isosceles show that any one of the following is true:

- Base angles (upper or lower) are congruent.
- Diagonals are congruent.
- Legs are congruent.

To prove a quadrilaterial is a parallelogram show that at least one of the following is true:

- Opposite angles are congruent.
- Opposite sides are parallel.
- Opposite sides are congruent.
- Diagonals bisect each other.
- A pair of sides is both parallel and congruent.
- Consecutive pairs of angles are supplementary.

To prove a parallelogram is a rectangle show that:

- It contains at least one right angle.
- Diagonals are congruent.

To prove a parallelogram is a rhombus show that at least one of the following is true:

- It contains at least one pair of congruent adjacent sides.
- Diagonals are perpendicular.
- Diagonals bisect the vertex angles.

To prove a parallelogram is a square show that at least one of the following is true:

- It is a rectangle and has one pair of congruent sides.
- It is a rhombus and has at least one right angle.

LIST 121   CIRCLES

Circles are everywhere. They are represented by coins, wheels, frisbees, and the red and black pieces used in checkers. Even a dart board has concentric circles. Following are words that have to do with circles.

Circle—the set of points in a plane, all of which are the same distance from a given point. ⊙ is the symbol for a circle.

Center of a circle—the fixed point from which all other points are equidistant. ⊙O is the symbol for a circle whose center is point 0.

Radius—the line segment from the center of a circle to a point on the circle.

Radii—the plural of radius.

Chord—a line segment which connects two points on the circle.

Diameter—a chord which connects the center to any two points on the circle. It is also called the diameteral chord.

Circumference—the distance around a circle. C = π d or C = 2 π r. C stands for the circumference, d for the diameter, r for the radius.

Pi—the ratio of the circumference to the length of the diameter. It is an irrational number approximately equal to 3.14 or $\frac{22}{7}$.

Secant—a straight line that intersects the circle at two points. D̄Ē is the secant line.

Secant segment—a line segment with an endpoint in the exterior of a circle, and the other endpoint on the circle, furthest from the external point. The secant segment is divided by the circle into two parts: the external secant segment and the internal secant segment. $\overline{DF}$ is the secant segment. $\overline{DE}$ is the internal secant segment. $\overline{EF}$ is the external secant segment.

Tangent—a line that intersects the circle at one and only one point. This point is called the point of tangency or point of contact. A̅B̅ is the tangent line.

Tangent segment—a line segment that has a point on the tangent line and the point of tangency as its endpoints. $\overline{AB}$ is the tangent segment.

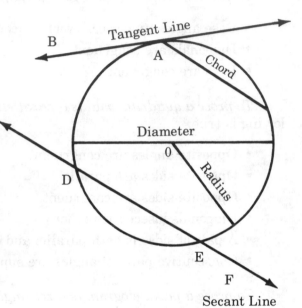

The Math Teacher's Book of Lists, © 1995 by Prentice Hall

LIST 122 SPECIAL CIRCLES

Based upon their relative positions, two circles in a plane or a circle and a polygon have special names. Following are some facts about these special circles.

Tangent circles—two circles that intersect only at one point.

There are two positions for tangent circles.

- Internally tangent circles—both circles are on the same side of the tangent line.

- Externally tangent circles—both circles are on opposite sides of the tangent line.

Concentric circles—two or more circles in a plane with the same center, but the lengths of their radii vary. The *annulus* is the region between concentric circles.

Eccentric circles—circles that have different centers.

Circumscribed circle—a circle passing through each vertex of a polygon.

Inscribed circle—a circle to which all the sides of a polygon are tangents.

Circumscribed polygon—a polygon that is outside the circle in such a way that all of its sides are tangent to the circle.

Inscribed polygon—a polygon that is inside a circle so that each of its vertices lie on the circle.

Externally Tangent Circles

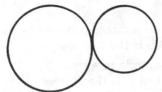

Internally Tangent Circles

Concentric Circles

Eccentric Circles

Circumscribed Circle
Inscribed Polygon

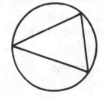

Inscribed Circle
Circumscribed Polygon

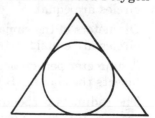

LIST 123   CIRCLES—LINE AND SEGMENT PRINCIPLES

The lines and segments that are parts of circles have certain relationships and properties that are useful in finding lengths of line segments and congruent segments.

The diameter divides a circle into two congruent parts. $\overline{AB}$ is the diameter.

If a chord divides a circle into two congruent parts, then it is the diameter.

The diameter is the longest chord.

The diameter equals twice the length of a radius. $\overline{OC}$ is the radius. AB = 2(OC)

The radius equals half the length of the diameter. OC = ½(AB)

Location of points and length of the radius:

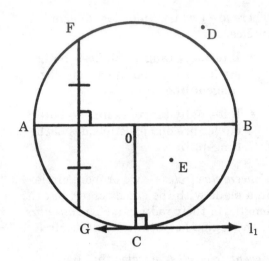

- A point is outside the circle if its distance from the center is greater than the length of the radius. D is outside the circle.

- A point is inside the circle if its distance from the center is less than the length of the radius. E is inside the circle.

- A point is on the circle if its distance from the center equals the length of the radius. F is on the circle.

The radii of the same or congruent circles are equal.

Diameters of the same or congruent circles are equal.

A diameter perpendicular to a chord bisects the chord. $\overline{AB}$ bisects $\overline{FG}$.

The radius is perpendicular to the tangent line at the point of tangency. $\overline{OC} \perp l_1$

If a radius is perpendicular to a line at the point at which the line intersects a circle, then the line is a tangent.

A perpendicular bisector of a chord passes through the center of the circle. $\overline{AB}$ is the perpendicular bisector of $\overline{FG}$.

The Math Teacher's Book of Lists, © 1995 by Prentice Hall

LIST 123   (Continued)

In the same or congruent circles, congruent chords are equidistant from the center.

In the same or congruent circles, chords that are equidistant from the center are congruent.

If two chords intersect in the interior of a circle, then the product of the lengths of the segments of one chord equals the product of the lengths of the segments of the other chord.

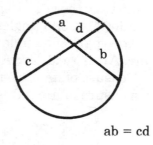

$$ab = cd$$

If two tangent segments are drawn to a circle from the same exterior point, then the tangent segments are congruent.

Secant-Secant Segment Theorem—If two secant segments are drawn to a circle from the same exterior point, then the product of the lengths of one secant segment and its external segment is equal to the product of the lengths of the other secant segment and its external segment.

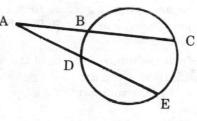

$$AC \cdot BA = AE \cdot AD$$

Tangent-Secant Segment Theorem—If a tangent segment and a secant segment are drawn to the circle from the same exterior point, then the square of the length of the tangent segment is equal to the product of the lengths of the secant segment and its external segment.

$$\frac{\text{Length of arc}}{\text{Circumference}} = \frac{\text{degree measure of arc}}{360°}$$

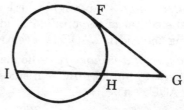

$$FG^2 = GI \cdot HG$$

LIST 124   CIRCLES—ARCS AND ANGLES

Just as there are special line segments that pertain to circles, there are names for arcs and angles.

Arc—part of a circle between any two points on the circle. ⌢ is the symbol for arc. $\overset{\frown}{AB}$ is read "arc AB."

Measure of an arc—$m\overset{\frown}{AB}$ is read "the measure of arc $\overset{\frown}{AB}$." mAB = 40 is read "the measure of arc AB is 40." Note that the symbol for degrees is omitted.

Types of Arcs and Angles

Semicircle—an arc equal to half of a circle.

Minor arc—an arc less than a semicircle. $\overset{\frown}{AC}$ is a minor arc.

Major arc—an arc greater than a semicircle but less than 360°. $\overset{\frown}{ABC}$ is a major arc.

Midpoint of an arc—point of the arc which divides the arc into two congruent arcs. B is the midpoint of $\overset{\frown}{ABC}$ since $\overset{\frown}{AB} \cong \overset{\frown}{AC}$.

Congruent arcs—arcs in the same or congruent circles that have the same degree measure. $\overset{\frown}{AB} \cong \overset{\frown}{AC}$.

Central angle—an angle whose vertex is at the center of the circle; its sides are along the radii. ∠AOC is a central angle.

Measure of a minor arc—the measure of its central angle. $m\overset{\frown}{AC} = n$ since m∠AOC = n°.

Measure of a major arc—360° minus the measure of the minor arc. $m\overset{\frown}{ABC} = 360° - m\overset{\frown}{AC}$.

Inscribed angle—an angle whose vertex is on the circle and whose sides are along two chords. ∠ABC is an inscribed angle.

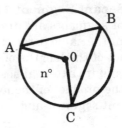

0 is the center of the circle

LIST 125   ARC AND ANGLE PRINCIPLES

Below are some facts relating to the arcs and angles of a circle.

A circle contains 360°.

In the same or equal circles, equal arcs have equal central angles.

In the same or equal circles, equal central angles have equal arcs.

In the same or equal circles, equal chords have equal arcs.

In the same or equal circles, equal arcs have equal chords.

In the same or equal circles, parallel chords cut off equal arcs. $\overset{\frown}{CF} \cong \overset{\frown}{BG}$

A diameter perpendicular to a chord bisects the arcs. $\overline{ED}$ bisects $\overset{\frown}{CB}$. $\overset{\frown}{DC} \cong \overset{\frown}{DB}$ and $\overset{\frown}{CFE} \cong \overset{\frown}{BGE}$

Arc Addition Postulate—If point D is on $\overset{\frown}{AB}$, then $m\overset{\frown}{AD} + m\overset{\frown}{DB} = m\overset{\frown}{AB}$.

Arc Sum Postulate—If points C and D are on $\overset{\frown}{AB}$ and $m\overset{\frown}{AC} = m\overset{\frown}{BD}$, then $m\overset{\frown}{AD} = m\overset{\frown}{BC}$.

Arc Difference Postulate—If points C and D are on $\overset{\frown}{AB}$ and $m\overset{\frown}{AD} = m\overset{\frown}{BC}$, then $m\overset{\frown}{AC} = m\overset{\frown}{BD}$.

Congruent central angles intercept congruent arcs.

Congruent arcs have congruent central angles.

Inscribed angle theorem—the measure of an inscribed angle is equal to one-half the measure of its intercepted arc. $m\angle IJK = \frac{1}{2}m\overset{\frown}{IK}$.

An angle inscribed in a semicircle is a right angle. $\overline{FG}$ divides $\odot O$ into 2 semicircles so $\angle FHG$ is a right angle.

If inscribed angles intercept the same or congruent arcs, then they are congruent.

If inscribed angles are congruent, then their intercepted arcs are congruent.

Chord-tangent angle theorem—the measure of an angle formed by a tangent and a chord drawn from a point of tangency is equal to one-half the measure of the intercepted arc. $\overline{IL}$ is

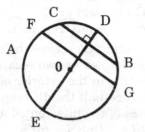

0 is the center of the circle

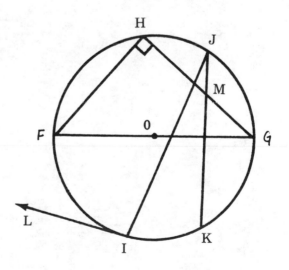

The Math Teacher's Book of Lists, © 1995 by Prentice Hall

LIST 125   (Continued)

tangent to $\overline{IJ}$. The measure of
$\angle JIL = \frac{1}{2}m\overset{\frown}{IFJ}$.

Chord-chord angle theorem—the
measure of an angle formed by two
chords intersecting in the interior of a
circle is equal to one-half the sum of the
measures of the two intercepted arcs. $\overline{JK}$
and $\overline{HG}$ intersect at M.
$m\angle HMK = \frac{1}{2}(m\overset{\frown}{KIH} + m\overset{\frown}{JG})$

Secant-secant theorem—the measure of
an angle formed by two secants
intersecting in the exterior of a circle is
equal to one-half the difference of the
measures of the intercepted arcs.
$m\angle PQR = \frac{1}{2}(m\overset{\frown}{SN} - m\overset{\frown}{PR})$

Secant-tangent theorem—the measure of
an angle formed by a secant and a
tangent intersecting in the exterior of a
circle is equal to one-half the difference
of the measures of the intercepted arcs.
$m\angle RQT = \frac{1}{2}(m\overset{\frown}{ST} - m\overset{\frown}{RT})$

Tangent-tangent theorem—the measure
of an angle formed by two tangents
intersecting in the exterior of a circle is
equal to one-half the difference of the
measures of the intercepted arcs.
$m\angle UQT = \frac{1}{2}(m\overset{\frown}{TSU} - m\overset{\frown}{TU})$

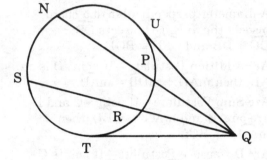

The Math Teacher's Book of Lists, © 1995 by Prentice Hall

LIST 126   SOLIDS

Solid figures, which are also called space figures, are three-dimensional shapes. There are two types of solid figures:

1.   Polyhedron (plural is polyhedra)—a solid whose flat surfaces are polygons.
2.   Solid figures whose surfaces are curved.

The following vocabulary is necessary to discuss solid figures:

Face—the flat surface of a solid.

Edge—line segment of a solid where 2 faces intersect.

Vertex—the point where the edges of a solid meet.

Types of Polyhedra

Prism—a polyhedron with 2 faces that are polygons which are both parallel and congruent. These are called the bases. The other faces (called lateral faces) are parallelograms.

Types of Prisms

• Right prism—a prism whose lateral faces are rectangles. Its bases may be any type of polygon.

Right Prism
(In this example the bases are pentagons.)

• Triangular prism—a prism that has 2 triangular bases and 3 lateral faces.

Triangular Prism

• Parallelopiped—a prism with 6 faces that are parallelograms.

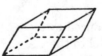

Parallelopiped

• Rectangular solid (also called a box)—a parallelopiped whose faces are rectangles.

Rectangular Solid

• Cube—a rectangular solid whose faces are squares.

Cube

LIST 126   (Continued)

Pyramid—a polyhedron that has 1 base.
The lateral faces are triangles.

Regular pyramid—a pyramid whose base
is a regular polygon and whose altitude
joins the vertex and the center of the base.

*Platonic solids (also called regular
polyhedra)*—polyhedra with congruent
faces. These are 5 solids. See List 127,
"Platonic Solids."

Pyramids

Triangular Base   Square Base

Solid Figures That Have Curved Surfaces

These 3-dimensional figures are not polyhedra because their faces are not
polygons. They include:

Cylinder—a solid figure with 2
congruent circular bases that are
parallel. The line segment joining the
center of the bases is an axis of the
cylinder. If the axis is perpendicular to
the base, then it is a right cylinder;
otherwise it is an oblique cylinder.

Cylinder

Cone—a solid figure that has 1 circular
base and a vertex. The line segment
joining the vertex to the center of the base
is an axis of the cone. If the axis is
perpendicular to the base, then it is a
right cone; otherwise it is an oblique cone.

Cone

Sphere—the set of points in space that
are equidistant from the center.

Sphere

A geometric solid may be produced by a
plane cutting the solid parallel to the
base or by 2 parallel planes cutting the
solid. This figure is called a *frustum*.

Frustum of a Pyramid

LIST 127   PLATONIC SOLIDS

Regular polyhedra are solid figures bounded by regular polygons in a manner that the same number of faces meet at each vertex. There are only five regular polyhedra, which are also called Platonic Solids.

Name	*Faces*	*Edges*	*Vertices*	*Types of Faces*
1. Regular Tetrahedron	4	6	4	equilateral triangles
2. Regular Hexahedron or Cube	6	12	8	squares
3. Regular Octahedron	8	12	6	equilateral triangles
4. Regular Dodecahedron	12	30	20	regular pentagons
5. Regular Icosahedron	20	30	12	equilateral triangles

Euler's Formula: $V - E + F = 2$, where V stands for the number of vertices, E stands for the number of edges, F stands for the number of faces, applies to the Platonic Solids as well as other polyhedra.

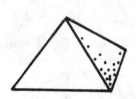

Regular Tetrahedron

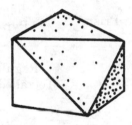

Regular Octahedron

Regular Icosahedron

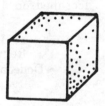

Regular Hexahedron

Regular Dodecahedron

LIST 128   CLASSIFICATION OF SOLIDS

Solids may be grouped according to the hierarchy below.

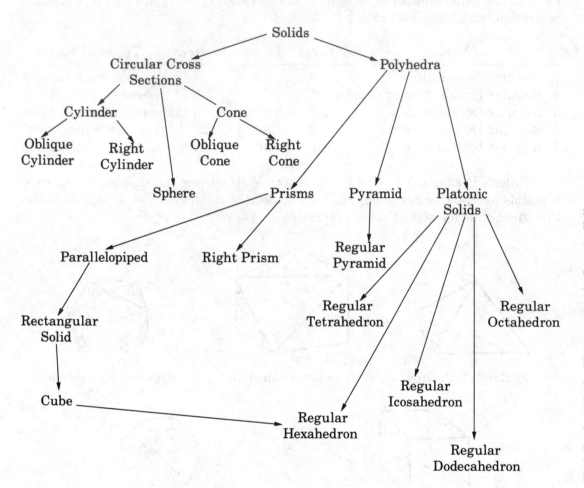

The Math Teacher's Book of Lists, © 1995 by Prentice Hall

LIST 129 PATTERNS OF A PAINTED CUBE

By exploring the characteristics of a cube, you can see some of the important relationships as well as some number patterns.

Suppose you dipped a cube in paint and cut it both horizontally and vertically so that the number of segments on each edge is listed in the first column. The resulting number of cubes and ratios is as follows:

Number of Segments on Each Edge	Total Number of Cubes	Ratio of the Volume of Each Cube to the Volume of the Original Cube	Number of Cubes with the Given Number of Painted Sides			
			0	1	2	3
2	$2^3 = 8$	$\frac{1}{2^3}$ or $\frac{1}{8}$	0	0	0	8
3	$3^3 = 27$	$\frac{1}{3^3}$ or $\frac{1}{27}$	1	6	12	8
4	$4^3 = 64$	$\frac{1}{4^3}$ or $\frac{1}{64}$	8	24	24	8
5	$5^3 = 125$	$\frac{1}{5^3}$ or $\frac{1}{125}$	27	54	36	8
6	$6^3 = 216$	$\frac{1}{6^3}$ or $\frac{1}{216}$	64	96	48	8
7	$7^3 = 343$	$\frac{1}{7^3}$ or $\frac{1}{343}$	125	150	60	8
n	n^3	$\frac{1}{n^3}$	$(n-2)^3$	$6(n-2)^2$	$12(n-2)$	8

LIST 130   SCALE FACTORS FOR SIMILAR PLANE FIGURES AND SOLIDS

A scale factor for similar figures is the ratio of lengths of two corresponding sides. (Similar polygons are plane figures that have the same shape but not necessarily the same size.) Corresponding angles are congruent and corresponding sides are in proportion. The following holds true for two similar polygons.

If the scale factor is a : b, then

- The ratio of the perimeters is a : b.
- The ratio of the areas is $a^2 : b^2$.

Similar solids are solids that have the same shape but not necessarily the same size. To determine if two solids are similar, determine if the bases are similar and corresponding heights are proportional. The following is true for two similar solids.

If the scale factor is a : b, then

- The ratio of the corresponding perimeters is a : b.
- The ratio of base areas is $a^2 : b^2$.
- The ratio of lateral areas is $a^2 : b^2$.
- The ratio of total areas is $a^2 : b^2$.
- The ratio of the volumes is $a^3 : b^3$.

The Math Teacher's Book of Lists, © 1995 by Prentice Hall

LIST 131   TYPES OF SYMMETRY

A geometric figure is said to have symmetry (or be symmetric) with respect to a point, line or plane if there is an exact balance in the figure. Below are more precise definitions.

Symmetry with Respect to a Line

Two points A and B are symmetric with respect to a line if and only if the line is the perpendicular bisector of $\overline{AB}$. The line is called the axis of symmetry or the line of symmetry.

A geometric figure is symmetric with respect to a line if and only if every point of the figure is balanced by a symmetrical point on the other side of the axis or line of symmetry.

Symmetry with Respect to a Plane

Two points A and B are symmetric with respect to a plane if and only if the plane perpendicularly bisects $\overline{AB}$. The plane is called the plane of symmetry.

A geometric figure is symmetric with respect to a plane if and only if every point on the figure is balanced by a symmetrical point on the other side of the plane.

Symmetry with Respect to a Point

Two points A and B are symmetric with respect to a point C if and only if C bisects $\overline{AB}$. The point is called the point of symmetry.

A geometric figure is symmetric with respect to a point if and only if every point on the figure is balanced by a symmetrical point on the other side of the point.

Some types of symmetry, which are also known as the three basic rigid motions of geometry, are listed below:

- Symmetry by reflection—the property of being divisible into two parts that are mirror images of each other. A reflection if also called a *flip*.

- Symmetry by rotation—the property that a figure coincides with its original position when rotated about a point of symmetry through an angle of 360°. A rotation is also called a *turn*.

- Symmetry by translation—the property that a figure coincides with its original position when translated or shifted a fixed distance. A translation is also called a *glide*.

Note that some symmetries may be combinations of those listed above such as a glide reflection.

LIST 132 TYPES OF TRANSFORMATIONS

A transformation, or mapping, usually changes one quantity into another. In geometry, a transformation is the changing of one shape into another by moving each point in it to a different position, usually through a special procedure. See List 133, "Transformation Matrices." Some transformations are listed below.

Isometry—a geometric transformation that preserves distance. The size and shape of the figure remain the same.

Reflection (or flip)—geometric transformation of a point or set of points from one side of a point, line or plane to a symmetrical position on the other side.

Rotation (or turn)—a geometric transformation in which a figure is moved about a fixed point.

Translation (or glide)—a geometric transformation in which only position relative to the axes is changed, not its orientation, size, or shape.

Projection—a geometric transformation which maps a geometric figure on to a plane, producing a two-dimensional figure.

Dilation—a geometric projection in which a figure is "stretched." The resulting figure is similar to the original.

Enlargement—a dilation that produces an image larger, but similar to the original shape.

Reduction—a dilation that produces an image that is smaller, but similar to the original shape.

Deformation (or continuous deformation)—a geometric transformation that stretches, shrinks, or twists a shape without breaking its lines or surfaces.

Shear—a transformation that represents a shearing motion for which each point of a coordinate plane is mapped into itself.

The Math Teacher's Book of Lists, © 1995 by Prentice Hall

LIST 133   TRANSFORMATION MATRICES

A transformation can be represented by a 2×2 matrix. Below are some important transformation matrices.

Reflection in the x-axis $\begin{bmatrix} 1 & 0 \\ 0 & \text{-}1 \end{bmatrix}$

Reflection in the y-axis $\begin{bmatrix} \text{-}1 & 0 \\ 0 & 1 \end{bmatrix}$

Enlargement
  K is the scale factor > 1 $\begin{bmatrix} K & 0 \\ 0 & K \end{bmatrix}$

Reduction
  K is the scale factor < 1 $\begin{bmatrix} K & 0 \\ 0 & K \end{bmatrix}$

Stretch in the x-direction $\begin{bmatrix} K & 0 \\ 0 & 1 \end{bmatrix}$

Stretch in the y-direction $\begin{bmatrix} 1 & 0 \\ 0 & K \end{bmatrix}$

Shear in the x-direction by K $\begin{bmatrix} 1 & K \\ 0 & 1 \end{bmatrix}$

LIST 134   TESSELLATIONS

A design that covers a plane with no gaps and no overlaps is called a tessellation. Covering the plane in this manner is called "tessellating the plane," or "tiling the plane." Some "tessellating" facts follow.

- A pure tessellation uses only one shape to tile the plane.
- A regular tessellation uses only one regular polygon to tile the plane.
- A semiregular tessellation uses two or more types of regular polygons to tile the plane.
- There are only three polygons that tile the plane to form a regular tessellation:
  —square
  —triangle
  —hexagon
- Some types of polygons that form semiregular tessellations include:
  —hexagon and triangle
  —octagon and square
  —hexagon, square, and triangle
- Some shapes may form a semiregular tessellation around a sphere such as hexagons and pentagons on a soccer ball.
- Maurice C. Escher, a Dutch artist, used tessellation in over 150 of his sketches. He used modified versions of regular tessellations by using transformations such as translation and rotation.

LIST 135   FORMULAS FOR PERIMETER
AND CIRCUMFERENCE

The perimeter is the distance around the edge of a polygon. If you are running the bases in a baseball game, you are running along the perimeter of a square. On a major league field, the bases are 90 feet apart, which means that a runner (assuming he runs directly on the lines between each base) would run a total of 360 feet. That is the perimeter.

Since a circle is not a polygon, the distance around it is called the circumference.

Below are some formulas for finding perimeters and circumference.

Perimeter of a Square: Multiply the length of a side by 4.

$P = 4s$

Perimeter of a Rectangle: Multiply the length by 2. Multiply the width by 2. Add the products.

$P = 2L + 2W$
$P = L + W + L + W$
$P = 2(L + W)$

or

Add the lengths of all the sides together.

$P = a + b + c$

Perimeter of a Triangle: Add the lengths of all the sides together.

Perimeter of a Regular Polygon: A regular polygon is a figure such that all sides are the same length. To find the perimeter, multiply the length of the sides by the number of sides.

$P = ns$
n is the number of congruent sides.

Circumference of a Circle: Multiply the length of the diameter by π. (π ≈ 3.14 or $\frac{22}{7}$.)

$c = \pi d$

or

Multiply the radius by 2, then multiply the product by π. (π ≈ 3.14 or $\frac{22}{7}$.)

$c = 2r\pi$

LIST 136   AREA FORMULAS FOR
BASIC FIGURES

Area describes the space inside a region. Following are the formulas for several figures.

Square: Multiply the length of one side by another.

$A = s^2$

Rectangle: Multiply length by width.

$A = lw$

Parallelogram: Multiply the length of the base by the height.

$A = bh$

Triangle: Multiply the length of the base by the height, then divide by 2.

$A = \dfrac{bh}{2}$

Trapezoid: Add the lengths of the parallel bases, multiply this sum by the height, and divide the product by 2.

$A = \dfrac{(b_1 + b_2)h}{2}$

or

Multiply the height by the length of the median. The median is parallel to its bases and equals one-half the sum of the bases.

$A = mh$

Rhombus: Multiply the lengths of the diagonals, then divide by 2.

$A = \dfrac{d_1 \cdot d_2}{2}$

Circle: Square the length of the radius and multiply by π. $\pi \approx 3.14$ or $\frac{22}{7}$.

$A = \pi r^2$

or

Divide the length of the diameter by 2, square the quotient, and multiply by π.

$A = \pi\left(\dfrac{d}{2}\right)^2$

LIST 137   MORE FORMULAS FOR AREA

Area is the space inside a given region. Following are several formulas for finding areas.

Area of a Kite:

- Find the product of lengths of the diagonals.
- Divide by 2.

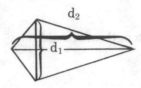

$$A = \frac{d_1 d_2}{2}$$

Area of a Triangle Using Heron's Formula:

- Let $s = \dfrac{a + b + c}{2}$
- $A = \sqrt{s(s - a)(s - b)(s - c)}$

Area of an Equilateral Triangle:

- Square the length of a side.

- Multiply by $\sqrt{3}$.

- Divide by 4.

$$A = \frac{s^2 \sqrt{3}}{4}$$

or

- Square the height.

- Multiply by $\sqrt{3}$.

- Divide by 3.

$$A = \frac{h^2 \sqrt{3}}{3}$$

Area of a Square:

- Square the length of a diagonal.

- Divide by 2.

$$A = \frac{d^2}{2}$$

or

- Square the length of a side.

$$A = s^2$$

Area of the Annulus—the area between concentric circles:

- Square the larger radius.
- Square the smaller radius.
- Subtract.
- Multiply by π.

$$A = (R^2 - r^2)\pi$$

The Math Teacher's Book of Lists, © 1995 by Prentice Hall

LIST 137   (Continued)

Area of a Sector—the part of the circle bounded by 2 radii and the intercepted arc:

- Find the area of the circle.
- Find the ratio of the degrees in the central angle to 360°.
- Multiply the area by the ratio.

$$A = \frac{n}{360}(\pi r^2)$$

Area of a Minor Segment—the part of the circle between a chord and its arc:

- Find the area of the sector.
- Find the area of the triangle formed by the radii and chord.
- Subtract.

A = area of
sector − area of
triangle

Area of a Regular Polygon:

- Find the product of the number of sides of the polygon and the length of each side.
- Multiply the product by the apothem.
- Divide the product by 2.

or

- Find the perimeter of the polygon.
- Multiply the perimeter by the apothem.
- Divide by 2.

$$A = \frac{nsa}{2}$$

n stands for the
number of sides

$$A = \frac{pa}{2}$$

p stands for
the perimeter

Area of an Ellipse:

- Find the product of the lengths of the minor and major axes.
- Divide by 4.
- Multiply by π.

$$A = \frac{mn}{4}\pi$$

LIST 138   FORMULAS FOR SURFACE AREA

The surface area of a space figure is the sum of all the faces of the figure. Following are the formulas for finding the surface area of several figures. Note that in all of the formulas, S stands for surface area.

Cube: $S = 6e^2$

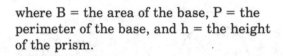

where e = the length of an edge.

Prism: $S = 2B + Ph$

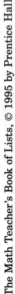

where B = the area of the base, P = the perimeter of the base, and h = the height of the prism.

Cylinder: $S = 2\pi r(r + h)$

where r = the radius of the circle and h = the height of the cylinder.

Cone: $S = \pi r^2 + \pi rs$

where r = the radius of the circle and s = the slant height.

Pyramid: $S = B + \dfrac{1}{2}Ps$

where B = the area of the base, P = the perimeter of the base, and s = the slant height of the lateral faces.

Sphere: $S = 4\pi r^2$

where r = the radius of the sphere.

LIST 139   FORMULAS FOR FINDING VOLUME

Volume refers to the amount of space a figure holds. Imagine a cardboard box, which is an example of a rectangular prism. The space inside the box is its volume. In all of the formulas below, V stands for volume.

Cube: $V = e^3$

where e = the length of an edge.

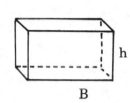

Prism: $V = Bh$

where B = the area of the base of the prism, and h = the height of the prism.

Cylinder: $V = \pi r^2 h$ or $V = Bh$

where r = the radius of the cylinder, h = the height of the cylinder, and B = the area of the base.

Cone: $V = \dfrac{\pi r^2 h}{3}$ or $V = \dfrac{Bh}{3}$

where r = the radius of the cone, h = the height of the cone, and B = the area of the base.

Pyramid: $V = \dfrac{Bh}{3}$

where B = the area of the base, and h = the height of the pyramid.

Sphere: $V = \dfrac{4\pi r^3}{3}$

where r = the radius of the sphere.

ALGEBRA

LIST 140   HOW TO EXPRESS OPERATIONS ALGEBRAICALLY

Changing verbal phrases into algebraic expressions is necessary to solve problems. The list below contains key words that will help you in your study of algebra.

Addition	Subtraction	Multiplication	Division
augment	decreased by	double (2×)	divided by
enlarge	depreciate	multiplied by	half (÷ by 2)
exceeds	difference	product	quotient
gain	diminish	quadruple (4×)	ratio
greater than	drop	times	
grow	less than	triple (3×)	
increased by	lose	twice (2×)	
larger than	loss		
more than	lower		
plus	minus		
rise	shorten		
sum	smaller than		
longer than			

LIST 141   ALGEBRAIC GROUPING SYMBOLS

The following symbols are important to grouping numbers, variables, and operations in algebra. Operations to be done first are included in grouping symbols.

Parentheses   (   )

Brackets   [   ]

Braces   {   }

Fraction Bar   ——

Absolute Value | |

LIST 142   PROPERTIES OF REAL NUMBERS

Real numbers include positive numbers, negative numbers, and zero. Since integers are a subset of the real numbers, all the properties of integers are also properties of real numbers. However, some properties of real numbers are not the properties of integers.

In the chart below, a, b, and c are real numbers.

	Addition	*Multiplication*
Closure Property	a + b is a unique real number	(a)(b) is a unique real number
Commutative Property	a + b = b + a	ab = ba
Associative Property	(a + b) + c = a + (b + c)	(ab)c = a(bc)
Identity Property	a + 0 = a	1(a) = a
Inverse Property	a + ⁻a = 0	$a \cdot \dfrac{1}{a} = 1 \qquad a \neq 0$
Property of Zero		a(0) = 0
Property of −1		−1 · a = −a
Properties of Opposites		−(−a) = a −(a+b) = −a + (−b) −(ab) = (−a)b = a(−b)
Zero Product Property		ab = 0 if and only if a = 0 or b = 0
Distributive Property	a(b + c) = ab + ac	
Completeness Property	Every real number can be paired with a point on the number line.	
Density Property	Between any two real numbers there is another real number.	

The Math Teacher's Book of Lists, © 1995 by Prentice Hall

LIST 143 SUMMARY OF PROPERTIES OF SETS OF NUMBERS

Each set of numbers—natural numbers, whole numbers, integers, rational numbers, irrational numbers, and real numbers—have specific properties. Below is a chart that summarizes the properties of each. A ✓ means the properties apply all the time. A blank means it is not always applicable.

	Natural	Whole	Integer	Rational	Irrational	Real
Closure (Add.)	✓	✓	✓	✓		✓
Closure (Subt.)			✓	✓		✓
Closure (Mult.)	✓	✓	✓	✓		✓
Closure (Div.)				✓		✓
Additive Identity	✓	✓	✓	✓	✓	✓
Multiplicative Identity	✓	✓	✓	✓	✓	✓
Additive Inverse			✓	✓	✓	✓
Multiplicative Inverse				✓	✓	✓

LIST 144   RELATING OPERATIONS ON THE REAL NUMBERS

From addition and multiplication of real numbers (see List 142, "Properties of Real Numbers"), we can define subtraction and division. Along with each definition, other equations relating the operations of addition, subtraction, multiplication, and division follow. In the equations, a, b, c, and d are real numbers.

- Definition of subtraction: $a - b = a + (-b)$.

- Definition of division: $a \div b = ab^{-1} = a\left(\dfrac{1}{b}\right)$. $b \neq 0$. Usually $\dfrac{a}{b}$ is written for $a \div b$.

- $\dfrac{ac}{bc} = \dfrac{a}{b}$ $b \neq 0, c \neq 0$

- $\dfrac{a}{c} + \dfrac{b}{c} = \dfrac{a+b}{c}$ $c \neq 0$

- $\dfrac{a}{c} - \dfrac{b}{c} = \dfrac{a-b}{c}$ $c \neq 0$

- $\dfrac{a}{c} + \dfrac{b}{d} = \dfrac{ad+bc}{cd}$ $c \neq 0, d \neq 0$

- $\dfrac{a}{c} - \dfrac{b}{d} = \dfrac{ad-bc}{cd}$ $c \neq 0, d \neq 0$

- $\dfrac{a}{c} \cdot \dfrac{b}{d} = \dfrac{ab}{cd}$ $c \neq 0, d \neq 0$

- $\dfrac{a}{c} \div \dfrac{b}{d} = \dfrac{a}{c} \cdot \dfrac{d}{b} = \dfrac{ad}{cb}$ $b \neq 0, c \neq 0, d \neq 0$

- If $\dfrac{a}{b} = \dfrac{c}{d}$ then $ad = bc$.

- $\dfrac{-a}{b} = \dfrac{a}{-b} = -\dfrac{a}{b}$ $b \neq 0$

- $\dfrac{-a}{-b} = \dfrac{a}{b}$ $b \neq 0$

LIST 145   AXIOMS OF EQUALITY

An axiom is a self-evident principle. In algebra (and also geometry), the four following statements about equality are true for all real numbers a, b, and c.

Reflexive Property   a = a   Any number is equal to itself
Symmetric Property   If a = b, then b = a
Transitive Property   If a = b and b = c, then a = c
Substitution Property   If a = b, then a may replace b or b may replace a

LIST 146   AXIOMS OF ORDER

Just as there are general statements about equality that apply to several areas of mathematics, there are Axioms of Order which are also known as Axioms of Inequality.

Trichotomy Property:

For all real numbers a and b, one and only one of the following statements is
    true:

$$a > b, a = b, \text{ or } a < b$$

Transitive Property:

For all real numbers a, b, and c

If a > b and b > c, then a > c
If a < b and b < c, then a < c

LIST 147   PROPERTIES OF EQUALITY

Pretend you are watching a basketball game and the score is tied. In the next two plays each team scores a basket. Do you agree that the score is tied once again? This is an example of the Addition Property of Equality. Try to find some examples of the other properties of equality listed below. The following hold true when a, b, and c are real numbers.

Addition Property:

If $a = b$, then $a + c = b + c$ and $c + a = c + b$

(If the same number is added to equal numbers, the sums are equal.)

Subtraction Property:

If $a = b$, then $a - c = b - c$

(If the same number is subtracted from equal numbers, the differences are
    equal.)

Multiplication Property:

If $a = b$, then $ac = bc$

(If equal numbers are multiplied by the same number, the products are
    equal.)

Division Property:

If $a = b$ and $c \neq 0$, then $a/c = b/c$

(If equal numbers are divided by the same nonzero number, the quotients are
    equal.)

The Math Teacher's Book of Lists, © 1995 by Prentice Hall

LIST 148   PROPERTIES OF INEQUALITIES

Inequalities are mathematical sentences in which the signs

less than, $<$,
less than or equal to, $\leq$,
greater than, $>$,
greater than or equal to, $\geq$, or
is not equal to, $\neq$, are used.

The following properties of inequalities hold true for all real numbers a, b, c, and d.

Addition:	if $a > b$, then $a + c > b + c$
	if $a < b$, then $a + c < b + c$
	if $a < b$ and $c < d$, then $a + c < b + d$
	if $a > b$ and $c > d$, then $a + c > b + d$
Subtraction:	if $a > b$, then $a - c > b - c$
	if $a < b$, then $a - c < b - c$
Multiplication*:	if $a > b$ and $c > 0$, then $ac > bc$
	if $a > b$ and $c < 0$, then $ac < bc$
	if $0 < a < b$ and $0 < c < d$, then $ac < bd$
Division*:	if $a > b$ and $c > 0$, then $a/c > b/c$
	if $a > b$ and $c < 0$, then $a/c < b/c$
	if $a < b$ and $ab > 0$, then $1/a > 1/b$

---

*For multiplication and division, the above properties are not valid if $c = 0$.

LIST 149   POWERS OF REAL NUMBERS

Some numbers may be written as the product of numbers which have identical factors. For example, $100 = 10 \times 10$ or 10^2. In this case, 10 is called the base and 2 is the exponent. The exponent shows the number of times the base is a factor.

Powers of a number can be written in factored form or in exponential form.

- Factored form indicates the products of the factors as in $b \cdot b \cdot b \cdot b \cdot b$.
- Exponential form indicates the base and exponents as in b^5.

Below are some powers of a real number b.

	Factored Form	Exponential Form	Read
Zero power of b	$1 \ (b \neq 0)$	b^0	1
First power of b	b	b^1 or b	b to the first power
Second power of b	$b \cdot b$	b^2	b to the second power, b squared, or the square of b
Third power of b	$b \cdot b \cdot b$	b^3	b to the third power, b cubed, or the cube of b
Fourth power of b	$b \cdot b \cdot b \cdot b$	b^4	b to the fourth power, or b to the fourth
nth power of b (n is a positive integer)	$\underbrace{b \cdot b \cdot b \cdot b \ldots b}_{n \text{ factors}}$	b^n	b to the nth power, or b to the nth
−nth power of b (n is a positive integer and $b \neq 0$)	$\dfrac{1}{\underbrace{b \cdot b \cdot b \cdot b \ldots b}_{n \text{ factors}}}$	b^{-n}	b to the −nth power, or b to the −nth

The Math Teacher's Book of Lists, © 1995 by Prentice Hall

LIST 150 RULES FOR EXPONENTS

The following rules for exponents hold for real numbers a and b. m and n are rational numbers. See also List 172, "Nth Roots."

For Multiplication: $a^m \cdot a^n = a^{m+n}$

For Division: $a^m/a^n = a^{m-n}$

   $a \neq 0$

For a Power of a Power: $(a^m)^n = a^{mn} = (a^n)^m$

For a Power of a Product: $(ab)^m = a^m b^m$

For a Power of a Quotient: $(a/b)^m = a^m/b^m$

   $b \neq 0$

For a Zero Exponent: $a^0 = 1$

   $a \neq 0$

For an Exponent of 1: $a^1 = a$

For a Negative Exponent: $a^{-n} = 1/a^n$

   $a \neq 0$

For a Base of 1: $1^n = 1$

LIST 151   ORDER OF OPERATIONS

In algebra, often finding the right answer to a problem depends on the way you go about solving it. There is a specific "order of operations" that you must follow.

1. Simplify expressions within grouping symbols. If several grouping symbols are used, simplify the innermost grouping first and continue simplifying to the outermost group. As you do so, be sure to follow steps 2, 3, and 4.

2. Simplify powers.

3. Perform all multiplicative operations (multiplication and division) from left to right.

4. Perform all additive operations (addition and subtraction) from left to right.

LIST 152   HOW TO CONSTRUCT A NUMBER LINE

Use the following steps to construct number lines accurately.

1. Use a ruler to draw a line segment.
2. Show continuity by drawing arrows on both ends.
3. Using a ruler, divide the line into equal segments.
4. Pair the endpoints or successive endpoints with integers listed in chronological order. Be sure to label numbers to the left of zero with a negative sign.

Steps

1) ——————————————

2) ⟨————————————————⟩

3) ⟨+—+—+—+—+—+—+—+—+—+—+⟩

4) ⟨+—+—+—+—+—+—+—+—+—+—+⟩
     -5 -4 -3 -2 -1 0 1 2 3 4 5

LIST 153   STEPS FOR GRAPHING ON A NUMBER LINE

Graphing is a required skill for most students. The following list provides simple procedures for graphing points and inequalities on number lines.

To Graph a Point

- Locate the coordinate (number) on the number line.
- Place a dot on the number line above the coordinate.

    Example: x = 5

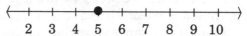

To Graph an Inequality

- Locate the coordinate (number) on the number line.
- If x is > a number, circle that number on the number line and shade the number line to the right.
- If x is ≥ a number, place a dot on the number line and shade the number line to the right.
- If x is < a number, circle that number on the number line and shade the number line to the left.
- If x is ≤ a number, place a dot on the number line and shade the number line to the left.
- If x is ≠ a number, circle that number on the number line and shade to left and right.

    Examples:

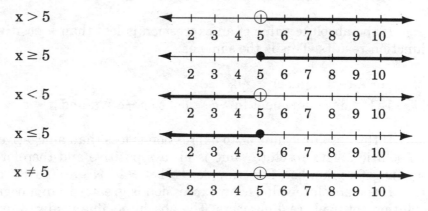

LIST 154   THE ABSOLUTE FACTS ON
ABSOLUTE VALUE

Absolute value is defined as the distance that a number is from zero on the number line.

$|a| = a$ if $a \geq 0$
$|a| = -a$ if $a < 0$

The distance between two real numbers a and b on the number line can be found by $|a - b|$ or $|b - a|$.

To evaluate an expression using absolute value, evaluate the expression within the absolute value first. They have the same priority as parentheses in the order of operations.

The absolute value of a sum is less than or equal to the sum of the absolute values.

$|a + b| \leq |a| + |b|$

The absolute value of a product is the product of the absolute values.

$|ab| = |a|\, |b|$

If the absolute value of an expression is greater than a positive number, a disjunction results. This is the same as:

For a real number $c > 0$,
$|a| > c$ is equivalent to $a < -c$ or $a > c$.

If the absolute value of an expression is less than a positive number, a conjunction results. This is the same as:

For a real number $c > 0$,
$|a| < c$ is equivalent to $-c < a < c$ or $-c < a$ and $a < c$

If the absolute value of an expression is less than a negative number, there is no solution. The absolute value is always positive and therefore is greater than any negative number. For example: $|N| < -4$ $N = \varnothing$ (no solution)

If the absolute value of an expression is greater than a negative number, the solution set is all real numbers. The absolute value is always positive and therefore is always greater than a negative number. For example $|N| > -4$ $N =$ all real numbers.

The Math Teacher's Book of Lists, © 1995 by Prentice Hall

LIST 155   STEPS TO SOLVE AN EQUATION
IN ONE VARIABLE

Equations which have the same solution are called equivalent equations. The following is a step-by-step list to rewrite and transform the original equation into an equivalent equation which has the same solution or root. If a step does not apply simply go on to the next one.

1. Substitute an equivalent expression for any expression in the equation.

2. Simplify each side of the equation. This may include:

   Combining similar terms within grouping symbols

   or

   Using the Distributive Property

   or

   Removing any unnecessary parentheses

   or

   Combining similar terms.

3. Add (or subtract) the same real number to (or from) each side of the equation. (If you add or subtract zero, an equivalent equation will result. It will be the same as the previous equations and will not be easier to solve. Although you can add or subtract zero, it is an unnecessary step and should be avoided.)

4. Multiply (or divide) each side of the equation by the same nonzero real number. (If you multiply each side of the equation by zero, the result will always be $0 = 0$ and the equation would not be solved. You can't divide each side of an equation by zero because division by zero is undefined.)

5. In most cases there is only one solution. The final transformation will result with the variable equaling a real number.

6. If the final transformation is equivalent to a false statement—such as $3 = 7$, $0 = 8$, etc.—the equation has no solution or root. It is written as $\varnothing$.

7. If the final transformation is equivalent to a statement which is always true—such as $x = x$, $3 = 3$, etc.—the equation is called an *identity* and is true for all real numbers.

LIST 156   STEPS TO SOLVE AN INEQUALITY
IN ONE VARIABLE

Just as equivalent equations have the same solution set, equivalent inequalities have the same solutions. To solve an inequality, try to rewrite it and transform it into an equivalent inequality using many of the same steps you use to solve equations. Be careful, however, when you multiply both sides of the inequality by the same negative number because that reverses the direction of the inequality. To solve an inequality in one variable, follow the steps below. If a step does not apply, go on to the next one.

1.   Substitute an equivalent expression for any expression in the inequality.
2.   Simplify each side of the inequality. This may include:
     Combining similar terms within grouping symbols
     or
     Using the Distributive Property
     or
     Removing any unnecessary parentheses
     or
     Combining similar terms.
3.   Add (or subtract) the same real number to (or from) each side of the inequality. Adding or subtracting zero should be avoided.
4.   Multiply (or divide) each side of the inequality by the same positive real number.
5.   Multiply (or divide) each side of the inequality by the same negative real number and reverse the direction of the inequality.
6.   In most cases the final transformation will be a comparison of a variable and real number, such as $x > 7$.
7.   If the final transformation is equivalent to a false statement—such as $2 > 7$, $6 > 9$, $x < x$, etc.—the inequality has no solution or root.
8.   If the final transformation is equivalent to a statement which is always true—such as $x \geq x$, $4 < 5$, etc.—the inequality is true for all real numbers.

The Math Teacher's Book of Lists, © 1995 by Prentice Hall

LIST 157 POLYNOMIALS

A monomial is an expression that is either 1) a real number, 2) a variable, or 3) the product of a real number and one or more variables. Remember that a variable can't be in the denominator.

The degree of a monomial is the sum of the exponents of its variables.

A polynomial is the sum or difference of monomials. Monomials that make up a polynomial are called its terms. Polynomials of two or three terms have special names.

Binomial—a polynomial with two terms.

Trinomial—a polynomial with three terms.

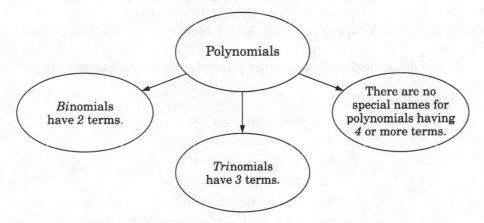

To simplify a polynomial combine similar terms. Similar terms contain the same variables and the same exponents.

Simplified polynomials can be arranged in

descending order in which the degree of each term decreases in successive terms, or

ascending order in which the degree of each term increases in successive terms.

The degree of a polynomial is the highest degree of any of its terms after it has been simplified.

LIST 158   MULTIPLICATION WITH MONOMIALS AND POLYNOMIALS

To multiply a polynomial by a monomial use the distributive property:

$$a(b + c + d) = ab + ac + ad$$

To multiply two binomials use the FOIL method.

$$(a + b)(c + d) = ac + ad + bc + bd$$

F—product of the FIRST terms   ac
O—product of the OUTERMOST terms   ad
I—product of the INNERMOST terms   bc
L—product of the LAST terms   bd

If the outermost and innermost products can be simplified, do so.

Special cases:

$$c(a + b) = ca + cb$$
$$c(a - c) = ca - cb$$
$$(a + b)^2 = a^2 + 2ab + b^2$$
$$(a - b)^2 = a^2 - 2ab + b^2$$
$$(a - b)(a + b) = a^2 - b^2$$
$$(a + c)(a + d) = a^2 + (c + d)a + cd$$

LIST 159   GUIDELINES FOR FACTORING POLYNOMIALS OF DEGREE 2

A polynomial is factored completely when it is written as the product of a prime polynomial and monomial, or it is the product of prime polynomials. A prime polynomial is a polynomial that cannot be factored. Use the following suggestions for factoring polynomials completely.

- Factor out the greatest monomial factor (GMF). The GMF is the largest monomial that is a factor of each term in the polynomial.
- If the polynomial has two terms, look for the difference of squares.
- If the polynomial has three terms, look for a perfect square trinomial or a pair of binomial factors.
- If the polynomial has four or more terms, group terms, if possible, in ways that can be factored. Factor out common polynomials.
- Be sure each polynomial is prime.
- Check by multiplying all factors.
- Remember that not all polynomials can be factored.
- See also List 160, "Common Factoring Formulas."

LIST 160   COMMON FACTORING FORMULAS

While there are many examples of ways to factor polynomials, some formulas are more common than others. The list below contains formulas for factoring polynomials of degree 2 and higher.

Factoring the Greatest Common Factor

$$ca + cb = c(a + b)$$
$$ca - cb = c(a - b)$$

Difference of Squares

$$a^2 - b^2 = (a - b)(a + b)$$

Sum of Squares

$$a^2 + b^2 \quad \text{prime polynomial (cannot be factored over the real numbers)}$$

Perfect Square Trinomials

$$a^2 + 2ab + b^2 = (a + b)(a + b) = (a + b)^2$$
$$a^2 - 2ab + b^2 = (a - b)(a - b) = (a - b)^2$$

Other Polynomials

$$a^2 + (c + d)a + cd = (a + c)(a + d)$$
$$a^3 + 3a^2b + 3ab^2 + b^3 = (a + b)^3$$
$$a^3 - 3a^2b + 3ab^2 - b^3 = (a - b)^3$$
$$a^4 - 4a^3b + 6a^2b^2 + 4ab^3 + b^4 = (a - b)^4$$
$$a^3 - b^3 = (a - b)(a^2 + ab + b^2)$$
$$a^3 + b^3 = (a + b)(a^2 - ab + b^2)$$
$$1 - a^n = (1 - a)(1 + a + a^2 + \ldots + a^{n-1})$$
$$a^n - b^n = (a - b)(a^{n-1} + ba^{n-2} + b^2a^{n-3} + \ldots + b^{n-2}a + b^{n-1}) \text{ for n positive}$$
$$a^n + b^n = (a + b)(a^{n-1} - ba^{n-2} + b^2a^{n-3} - \ldots - b^{n-2}a + b^{n-1}) \text{ for n positive and odd}$$

The Math Teacher's Book of Lists, © 1995 by Prentice Hall

LIST 161   CHARACTERISTICS OF THE COORDINATE PLANE

The Coordinate Plane may be thought of as a flat surface divided into four parts or quadrants by the intersection of a vertical number line (called the y-axis) and a horizontal number line (called the x-axis). It is used to graph ordered pairs of the form (x,y), straight lines, and other functions or relations. The x-coordinate of the ordered pair is called the *abscissa*. The y-coordinate of the ordered pair is called the *ordinate*. Below is a coordinate plane and some of its important characteristics.

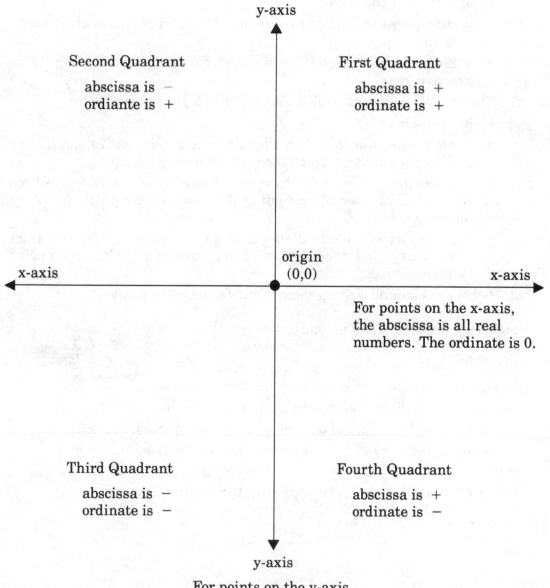

y-axis

Second Quadrant

abscissa is −
ordiante is +

First Quadrant

abscissa is +
ordinate is +

x-axis

origin
(0,0)

x-axis

For points on the x-axis,
the abscissa is all real
numbers. The ordinate is 0.

Third Quadrant

abscissa is −
ordinate is −

Fourth Quadrant

abscissa is +
ordinate is −

y-axis

For points on the y-axis,
the ordinate is all real numbers.
The abscissa is 0.

LIST 162   PLOTTING POINTS ON THE COORDINATE PLANE

Plotting, or graphing, points on the coordinate plane involves moving horizontally and vertically, depending on the values of x and y. The following "points" will help you to graph correctly.

1. In the ordered pair (x,y), the first coordinate (called the abscissa) is the value of x. Start from the origin.

    If the abscissa is

    - 0, remain at the origin.

    - positive, move to the right the required number of spaces along the x-axis and stop.

    - negative, move to the left the required number of spaces along the x-axis and stop.

2. The second coordinate (called the ordinate) is the value of y.

    If the ordinate is

    - 0, don't move up or down from the point where your pencil stopped after finding the abscissa. Graph the point by marking a dot.

    - positive, move directly up the required number of spaces from where your pencil stopped after finding the abscissa. Graph the point by marking a dot.

    - negative, move directly down the required number of spaces from where your pencil stopped after finding the abscissa. Graph this point by marking a dot.

3. Label the point by writing the coordinates near the point.

Following are some special points.

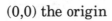

(0,0) the origin

(0,y) a point on the y-axis, provided y is a real number.

(x,0) a point on the x-axis, provided x is a real number.

When x > 0 and y > 0, (x,y) is a point in the first quadrant.

When x < 0 and y > 0, (x,y) is a point in the second quadrant.

When x < 0 and y < 0, (x,y) is a point in the third quadrant.

When x > 0 and y < 0, (x,y) is a point in the fourth quadrant.

The Math Teacher's Book of Lists, © 1995 by Prentice Hall

LIST 163 COMMON FORMS OF LINEAR EQUATIONS

A linear equation is an equation whose graph is a straight line. It is an equation of the first degree and is usually expressed in one of the following forms.

$ax + by = c$ Standard Form
a, b, and c are integers
Both a and b cannot equal zero

$x = k$ Vertical Line
k is any real number
Vertical lines have no slope

$y = k$ Horizontal Line
k is any real number
Horizontal lines have a slope of zero

$y = mx + b$ Slope-intercept Form
m stands for the slope
b stands for y-intercept

$y = mx$ Slope-intercept Form of a line passing through the origin
m stands for the slope

$y - y_1 = m(x - x_1)$ Point-slope Form
m stands for the slope
(x_1, y_1) is a point on the line

LIST 164 FORMULAS AND THE COORDINATE PLANE

Some equations are frequently used to graph lines or points on the coordinate plane. They are summarized below.

- Slope of a line given 2 points (x_1, y_1) and (x_2, y_2).

  $$m = \frac{y_2 - y_1}{x_2 - x_1}$$

  m stands for the slope.

  Horizontal lines have a slope of 0.

  Vertical lines have no slope.

- Slope-intercept Equation: $y = mx + b$.

  m stands for the slope. b stands for the y-intercept.

- Standard form of a linear equation: $ax + by + c = 0$.

  a,b,c are integers. Both a and b cannot equal 0.

- Point-slope Form: $y - y_1 = m(x - x_1)$.

  m stands for the slope. (x_1, y_1) is a point on the line.

- Distance Formula: $d = \sqrt{(x_2 - x_1)^2 + (y_2 - y_1)^2}$

  d is the distance between two points, (x_1, y_1) and (x_2, y_2).

- Midpoint Formula: $\left(\dfrac{x_1 + x_2}{2}, \dfrac{y_1 + y_2}{2} \right)$

  This gives the coordinate of the point halfway between (x_1, y_1) and (x_2, y_2).

- Parallel lines have the same slope.

  $m_1 = m_2$ if and only if l_1 and l_2 are two nonvertical, noncollinear straight lines with slopes m_1 and m_2.

- The slopes of perpendicular lines are negative reciprocals of each other.

  $m_1 \cdot m_2 = -1$, $m_1, m_2 \neq 0$ if and only if l_1 and l_2 are nonvertical, nonhorizontal straight lines with slopes m_1 and m_2.

The Math Teacher's Book of Lists, © 1995 by Prentice Hall

LIST 165   GRAPHING LINEAR EQUATIONS IN TWO VARIABLES ON THE COORDINATE PLANE

You can graph linear equations in two variables on the coordinate plane in three ways: by plotting points, using intercepts, or using the slope-intercept method.

Plotting Points

1. Find two ordered pairs that satisfy the equation. This can be done by looking at the equation, or by choosing an x value (choose a value that will simplify the arithmetic) and then finding a corresponding y value.
2. Plot these points on the coordinate plane.
3. Draw a straight line through the points. This line is the graph of the equation.
4. Check your graph by plotting a third point. This should be on the line. If it is not, go back and check your work and graph. All points should be collinear (lie on the same line).

Using Intercepts

1. Transform the equation into the form ax + by = c.
2. Substitute 0 for y to find the x-intercept.
3. Substitute 0 for x to find the y-intercept.
4. Plot the intercept points.
5. Draw a straight line through the points. This is the graph of the line.

Using the Slope-Intercept Method

1. Transform the equation into the form of y = mx + b. If there is no y term, then the graph is a vertical line. Solve for x. This is the x-intercept.
2. Using the equation y = mx + b, and (assuming there is a y term) graph the point (0,b). This is the y-intercept.
3. Write the slope m as a fraction. Remember that m = rise/run.
4. From the y-intercept, count out the rise and run. Then graph this point. If the rise is positive, count up. If the rise is negative, count down. If the run is positive, count to the right. If the run in negative, count to the left.
5. Draw a straight line through the y-intercept and the point plotted by using the slope. This is the graph of the line.

LIST 166   GRAPHING A LINEAR INEQUALITY IN TWO VARIABLES ON THE COORDINATE PLANE

The following steps and table will help you to graph linear equalities in two variables on coordinate planes.

1. Graph the inequality as if it were an equation. This will enable you to find the boundary, which is the line that divides the coordinate plane into two half-planes. You may want to refer to List 165, "Graphing Linear Equations in Two Variables on the Coordinate Plane."

2. Graph the line. If the inequality symbol is $\geq$ or $\leq$, draw a solid line since these solutions are included. If the inequality symbol is $>$ or $<$, draw a broken line since these solutions are not included.

3. Choose a point in the plane that is not on the line. Substitute this in the inequality.

4. If the point satisfies the inequality, shade the half-plane which includes the point. If the point does not satisfy the inequality, shade the other half-plane.

The table below offers some guidelines:*

Equation	Type of Line	Shaded
$x \geq k$	Solid Vertical	Right
$x > k$	Broken Vertical	Right
$x \leq k$	Solid Vertical	Left
$x < k$	Broken Vertical	Left
$y \geq k$	Solid Horizontal	Above
$y > k$	Broken Horizontal	Above
$y \leq k$	Solid Horizontal	Below
$y < k$	Broken Horizontal	Below
$y \geq mx + b$	Solid	Above
$y > mx + b$	Broken	Above
$y \leq mx + b$	Solid	Below
$y < mx + b$	Broken	Below

*k stands for any real number, m stands for the slope and b stands for the y-intercept.

LIST 167   STEPS TO SOLVE A SYSTEM OF LINEAR EQUATIONS IN TWO VARIABLES

There are four methods to solve a system (more than one) of linear equations. Although any method can be used, some may be more efficient and direct than others. Below is a list of the methods and when they can be used best.

Graphing Method

1. Draw the graph of each equation on the same coordinate plane. The lines will either intersect at one point, be parallel, or coincide.
2. If the lines intersect, the coordinates of the point of intersection are the solution to the two equations.
3. If the lines are parallel, there is no solution.
4. If the lines coincide (that is the lines are identical), then each point on the line is a solution. The number of solutions is infinite.

Use this method when you wish to approximate the solution. It is also most helpful when the solution is near the origin. This method is used the least for solving systems of linear equations.

The Substitution Method

1. Solve one equation for one of the variables whose coefficient is one.
2. Substitute this expression in the equation you have not used. You should now have an equation in one variable. Solve this equation.
3. Substitute this expression in the equation you used in Step 1 and solve it.
4. Check your answers in both original equations.

Use this method when the coefficient of one of the variables is 1 or -1.

The Addition-or-Subtraction Method

1. Add or subtract equations to eliminate one variable. Add the equations if the coefficients of one of the variables are opposites; subtract if the coefficients of one of the variables are the same.
2. Solve the equation resulting from Step 1.
3. Substitute this value in either of the original equations.
4. Check your answer in both of the original equations.

Use this method if the coefficients of one of the variables are the same or if the coefficients are opposites.

LIST 167   (Continued)

Multiplication with Addition-or-Subtraction Method

1. Multiply one or both equations so that the coefficients of one of the variables will be the same or opposite.
2. Follow Steps 1 through 4 in the Addition-or-Subtraction Method.

Use this method for the following conditions:

*   to clear the equations of fractions.
*   if the coefficients of a variable are relatively prime (have a greatest common factor of 1).
*   if one of the coefficients of a variable is a factor (other than 1) of the other.

The Math Teacher's Book of Lists, © 1995 by Prentice Hall

LIST 168   TYPES OF FUNCTIONS

A function is a special type of relation in which every element in the domain is paired with exactly one element of the range. This is loosely translated "for each value of x there is only one y." As a counter example, if there are two or more y values for any value of x, the relation is not a function.

If a vertical line can be drawn anywhere on a graph and the vertical line intersects the graph at more than one point, then the graph is not the graph of a function. This is called the Vertical Line Test.

Following is a list of functions and their descriptions.

Linear: $y = mx + b$ or $f(x) = mx + b$ where m and b are real numbers (m stands for the slope, b stands for the y-intercept)

Special names for Linear Functions

Constant Function: $y = b$ or $f(x) = b$
Slope is zero
Graph is a horizontal line

Identity Function: $y = x$ or $f(x) = x$
Slope is 1
Graph is a line passing through the origin

Direct Variation: $y = mx$ or $f(x) = mx$
Slope $\neq 0$
Graph is a line passing through the origin

Absolute Value Function: $y = |x|$ or $f(x) = |x|$
If $x \geq 0$, the graph is like the graph of $y = x$
If $x < 0$, the graph is like the graph of $y = -x$

Greatest Integer Function: $y = [x]$ or $f(x) = [x]$
Finds the greatest integer that is not greater than x
Graph is a series of line segments with one open endpoint

Inverse Variation Function: $xy = k$ or $f(x) = k/x$ $k \neq 0$
Graph is a hyperbola

Quadratic Function: $y = ax^2 + bx + c$ or $f(x) = ax^2 + bx + c$ $a \neq 0$
Graph is a parabola

Cubic Function: $y = ax^3 + bx^2 + cx + d$ or $f(x) = ax^3 + bx^2 + cx + d$ $a \neq 0$
Graph resembles a sideways "S"

Exponential Function: $y = b^x$ or $f(x) = b^x$ $b > 0, b \neq 1$ x is a real number
Graph resembles part of a hyperbola

LIST 168   (Continued)

Logarithmic Function: $y = \log_a x$ if and only if $a^y = x$ $a > 0, a \neq 0$

It is the inverse of the Exponential Function.

Graph is the inverse of the graph of the Exponential Function.

Trigonometric Functions: See Lists 5, 189, and 192 for definitions.

Some functions may be classified as odd or even. The properties of each are listed below:

Even Function: $y = f(-x) = f(x)$ for all x in the domain

Graph is symmetric with respect to the y-axis. (If (x,y) is on the graph, then so is (−x,y).)

Examples: $y = |x|$, $y = x^2$

Odd Function: $y = f(-x) = -f(x)$ for all x in the domain

Graph is symmetric with respect to the origin. (If (x,y) is on the graph, then so is (−x,−y).)

Examples: $y = x$, $y = x^3$

LIST 169 DIRECT FACTS ON VARIATIONS

Some functions are used so frequently in science and math that they have special names and general formulas. Types of "variations" fall into this category.

Common Types of Variations*

FORMULA	MEANING
$y = kx$ $y_1/x_1 = y_2/x_2$	y varies directly as x or y is directly proportional to x
$y = kx^2$ $y_1/x_1^2 = y_2/x_2^2$	y varies directly as the square of x or y is directly proportional to the square of x
$y = kx^3$ $y_1/x_1^3 = y_2/x_2^3$	y varies directly as the cube of x or y is directly proportional to the cube of x
$y = k/x$ $xy = k$ $x_1y_1 = x_2y_2$	y varies inversely as x or y is inversely proportional to x
$y = k/x^2$ $x^2y = k$ $x_1^2y_1 = x_2^2y_2$	y varies inversely as the square of x or y is inversely proportional to the square of x
$z = kxy$ $z_1/x_1y_1 = z_2/x_2y_2$	z varies jointly as x and y
$z = kx/y$ $zy = kx$ $z_1y_1/x_1 = z_2y_2/x_2$	z varies directly as x and inversely as y. This is a combined variation.

*k is a nonzero constant. It is called the constant of variation or the constant of proportionality.

LIST 170   FUNCTIONAL FACTS
ABOUT FUNCTIONS

Functions are sometimes combined to form other sums, differences, products, quotients, composites, and inverses. Following are some functional facts.

If f and g are any two functions with a common domain then:

1. The sum of f and g, written $f + g$ is defined by $(f + g)(x) = f(x) + g(x)$.

2. The difference of f and g, written $f - g$ is defined by $(f - g)(x) = f(x) - g(x)$.

3. The product of f and g, written fg is defined by $(fg)(x) = f(x)g(x)$.

4. The quotient of f and g, written f/g is defined by $(f/g)(x) = f(x)/g(x)$.

5. The composite of f and g, written $f \circ g$ is defined by $[f \circ g](x) = f[g(x)]$.

6. To find the inverse of a function, interchange the values for x and y. By doing this the order of each pair in f is reversed. (Note that the inverse of a function is not always a function.)

7. Assume f and f^{-1} are inverse functions, then $f(a) = b$ if and only if $f^{-1}(b) = a$.

8. f and f^{-1} are inverse functions if and only if their composites are the identity function, meaning $[f \circ f^{-1}](x) = [f^{-1} \circ f](x) = x$

*Recall that $y = x$ or $f(x) = x$ is the identity function. See List 168, "Types of Functions."

The Math Teacher's Book of Lists, © 1995 by Prentice Hall

LIST 171   SQUARE ROOTS

Finding the square root of a number is the inverse of squaring a number. Since $5^2 = 25$ and $(-5)^2 = 25$, the square root of 25 is both 5 and -5. Square root notation and properties follow.

- $\sqrt{}$ is called the radical sign.
- $\sqrt{a}$ The number written beneath the sign, in this case a, is called the radicand.
- $\sqrt{a}$ is used to denote the principal or non-negative square root of a positive real number a.
- $-\sqrt{a}$ is used to denote the negative square root of a positive real number a.
- $\pm\sqrt{a}$ is used to denote the positive or negative square root of a positive real number a.
- The index of a root is the small number written above and to the left of the radical sign. It represents which root is to be taken. The index for square roots is 2. It is understood and therefore not included.
- $(\sqrt{a})^2 = a$ where a is a positive real number.
- $\sqrt{a^2} = |a|$ where a is a real number.
- $\sqrt{a^{2m}} = |a|^m$ where a is any real number, and m is any positive integer.
- 0 has only one square root, $\sqrt{0} = 0$.
- Negative numbers do not have square roots in the set of real numbers. See List 176, "Imaginary Numbers and Their Powers."
- Product Property of Square Roots $\sqrt{ab} = \sqrt{a}\sqrt{b}$ where a and b are non-negative real numbers.
- Quotient Property of Square Roots $\sqrt{\frac{a}{b}} = \frac{\sqrt{a}}{\sqrt{b}}$ where a is any non-negative real number and b is a positive real number.
- Property of Square Roots of Equal Numbers $a^2 = b^2$ if and only if $a = b$ or $a = -b$ where a and b are real numbers.
- A radical is in simplest form when

  —no radicand has a square root factor (other than 1).

  —the radicand is not a fraction.

  —no radicals are in the denominator.
- Only radicals with like radicands may be added or subtracted.

LIST 172   NTH ROOTS

If the volume of a cube is 125 cubic units, then any side of the cube has a length of 5 cubic inches. You can write $\sqrt[3]{125} = 5$ because $5^3 = 125$. We can also say $\sqrt[3]{a} = b$, if $b^3 = a$.

The small number written in the upper lefthand corner of the radical is called the index. When finding the square root of a number, the index is generally not stated. It is understood to be 2.

For any integer $n \geq 2$, the nth root is defined as follows:

$$\sqrt[n]{a} = b$$

if and only if $b^n = a \begin{cases} \text{for } a \geq 0 \text{ and } b \geq 0 \text{ if } n \text{ is even.} \\ \text{for any real number } a \text{ if } n \text{ is odd.} \end{cases}$

Note that when n is an even integer, $\sqrt[n]{a}$ is defined for non-negative values of a.

Properties of Nth Roots

a and b are real numbers. m and n are positive integers. Each property is valid for all values of a and b for which the equation is defined.

- $(\sqrt[n]{a})^n = a$

- $\sqrt[n]{a^n} = \begin{cases} |a| \text{ if } n \text{ is even} \\ a \text{ if } n \text{ is odd} \end{cases}$

- $\sqrt[n]{ab} = \sqrt[n]{a} \ \sqrt[n]{b}$

- $\sqrt[n]{\dfrac{a}{b}} = \dfrac{\sqrt[n]{a}}{\sqrt[n]{b}}$

- $\sqrt[m]{\sqrt[n]{a}} = \sqrt[mn]{a} = \sqrt[n]{\sqrt[m]{a}}$

LIST 173   POWERS AND ROOTS

The following table shows the squares, square roots, cubes, and cube roots of the numbers from 1 to 100. Where necessary, they have been rounded to the nearest thousandth.

n	n^2	$\sqrt{n}$	n^3	$\sqrt[3]{n}$	n	n^2	$\sqrt{n}$	n^3	$\sqrt[3]{n}$
1	1	1.000	1	1.000	51	2,601	7.141	132,651	3.708
2	4	1.414	8	1.260	52	2,704	7.211	140,608	3.733
3	9	1.732	27	1.442	53	2,809	7.280	148,877	3.756
4	16	2.000	64	1.587	54	2,916	7.348	157,464	3.780
5	25	2.236	125	1.710	55	3,025	7.416	166,375	3.803
6	36	2.449	216	1.817	56	3,136	7.483	175,616	3.826
7	49	2.646	343	1.913	57	3,249	7.550	185,193	3.849
8	64	2.828	512	2.000	58	3,364	7.616	195,112	3.871
9	81	3.000	729	2.080	59	3,481	7.681	205,379	3.893
10	100	3.162	1,000	2.154	60	3,600	7.746	216,000	3.915
11	121	3.317	1,331	2.224	61	3,721	7.810	226,981	3.936
12	144	3.464	1.728	2.289	62	3,844	7.874	238,328	3.958
13	169	3.606	2,197	2.351	63	3,969	7.937	250,047	3.979
14	196	3.742	2,744	2.410	64	4,096	8.000	262,144	4.000
15	225	3.873	3,375	2.466	65	4,225	8.062	274,625	4.021
16	256	4.000	4,096	2.520	66	4,356	8.124	287,496	4.041
17	289	4.123	4,913	2.571	67	4,489	8.185	300,763	4.062
18	324	4.243	5,832	2.621	68	4,624	8.246	314,432	4.082
19	361	4.359	6,859	2.668	69	4,761	8.307	328,509	4.102
20	400	4.472	8,000	2.714	70	4,900	8.367	343,000	4.121
21	441	4.583	9,261	2.759	71	5,041	8.426	357,911	4.141
22	484	4.690	10,648	2.802	72	5,184	8.485	373,248	4.160
23	529	4.796	12,167	2.844	73	5,329	8.544	389,017	4.179
24	576	4.899	13,824	2.884	74	5,476	8.602	405,224	4.198
25	625	5.000	15,625	2.924	75	5,625	8.660	421,875	4.217
26	676	5.099	17,576	2.962	76	5,776	8.718	438,976	4.236
27	729	5.196	19,683	3.000	77	5,929	8.775	456,533	4.254
28	784	5.292	21,952	3.037	78	6,084	8.832	474,552	4.273
29	841	5.385	24,389	3.072	79	6,241	8.888	493,039	4.291
30	900	5.477	27,000	3.107	80	6,400	8.944	512,000	4.309
31	961	5.568	29,791	3.141	81	6,561	9.000	531,441	4.327
32	1,024	5.657	32,768	3.175	82	6,724	9.055	551,368	4.344
33	1,089	5.745	35,937	3.208	83	6,889	9.110	571,787	4.362
34	1,156	5.831	39,304	3.240	84	7,056	9.165	592,704	4.380
35	1,225	5.916	42,875	3.271	85	7,225	9.220	614,125	4.397
36	1,296	6.000	46,656	3.302	86	7,396	9.274	636,056	4.414
37	1,369	6.083	50,653	3.332	87	7,569	9.327	658,503	4.431
38	1,444	6.164	54,872	3.362	88	7,744	9.381	681,472	4.448
39	1,521	6.245	59,319	3.391	89	7,921	9.434	704,969	4.465
40	1,600	6.325	64,000	3.420	90	8,100	9.487	729,000	4.481
41	1,681	6.403	68,921	3.448	91	8,281	9.539	753,571	4.498
42	1,764	6.481	74,088	3.476	92	8,464	9.592	778,688	4.514
43	1,849	6.557	79,507	3.503	93	8,649	9.644	804,357	4.531
44	1,936	6.633	85,184	3.530	94	8,836	9.695	830,584	4.547
45	2,025	6.708	91,125	3.557	95	9,025	9.747	857,375	4.563
46	2,116	6.782	97,336	3.583	96	9,216	9.798	884,736	4.579
47	2,209	6.856	103,823	3.609	97	9,409	9.849	912,673	4.595
48	2,304	6.928	110,592	3.634	98	9,604	9.899	941,192	4.610
49	2,401	7.000	117,649	3.659	99	9,801	9.950	970,299	4.626
50	2,500	7.071	125,000	3.684	100	10,000	10.000	1,000,000	4.642

LIST 174   CONDITIONS FOR SIMPLIFYING RADICAL EXPRESSIONS

An expression having a square-root radical is in simplest form when:

✓ No radicand has a square factor other than 1.

✓ The radicand is not a fraction.

✓ No radicals are in the denominator.

This can be extended for all radical expressions (not only square root radicals) by adding an additional stipulation.

A radical expression is in simplest form when:

✓ None of the factors of the radicand can be written as powers greater than or equal to the index. (No perfect squares, except 1, can be factors of the quantity under the square root sign, no perfect cubes, except 1, can be factors of the quantity under the cube root sign, and so on.)

✓ The radicand is not a fraction.

✓ No radicals are in the denominator.

LIST 175 STEPS FOR SOLVING A QUADRATIC EQUATION

There are four methods to solving quadratic equations: 1) factoring, 2) using the square-root property, 3) completing the square, and 4) using the quadratic formula. Factoring and using the square-root property may only be used under certain conditions, while completing the square and using the quadratic formula can always be used. Below is a brief description of each method and when it may be used best.

Any quadratic equation has at most two solutions. Some may have the same solution twice. Others may have no real solutions. Some may only have one solution.

Factoring

Use this method if $ax^2 + bx + c$ can be factored.

1. Write the equation in the form $ax^2 + bx + c = 0$. a, b, and c are real numbers, $a \neq 0$.

2. Factor the polynomial.

3. Use the Zero-Product Property to set each factor equal to zero.

4. Solve each linear equation which results.

Solve $x^2 + 3x = 4$

$x^2 + 3x - 4 = 0$

$(x + 4)(x - 1) = 0$

$(x = 4) = 0 \qquad (x - 1) = 0$

$x = -4 \qquad\qquad x = 1$

Using the Square-Root Property

Use this method if $x^2 = k$ or $(ax + b)^2 = k$, $k \geq 0$.

1. Transform the equation so that a perfect square is on one side and a constant greater than or equal to zero is on the other.

2. Use the square-root property to find the square root of each member. Remember that finding the square root of a constant yields positive and negative values.

3. Solve each resulting equation. (If you are finding the square root of a negative number, there is no real solution.)

Solve $x^2 - 16 = 0$
$x^2 = 16$

$\sqrt{x^2} = \sqrt{16}$

$x = \pm 4$

LIST 175   (Continued)

Completing the Square

This method may always be used. It is best used, however, if the coefficient of the linear term is even.

1. Transform the equation so that the quadratic term plus the linear term equals a constant.

Solve $x^2 + 12x + 2 = 0$

$x^2 + 12x = -2$

2. Divide each term by the coefficient of the quadratic term if it does not equal 1.

$$12 \cdot \frac{1}{2} = 6$$

$$6^2 = 36$$

3. Complete the square:
   - Multiply the coefficient of x by ½.
   - Square this value.
   - Add the result to both members.
   - Express one side of the equation as the square of a binomial and the other as a constant.

$x^2 + 12x + 36 = -2 + 36$

$(x + 6)^2 = 34$

$\sqrt{(x + 6)^2} = \sqrt{34}$

$x + 6 = \pm\sqrt{34}$

$x = -6 + \sqrt{34}$

4. Follow steps 2 and 3 of "Using the Square-Root Property."

$x = -6 - \sqrt{34}$

Using the Quadratic Formula

This method may always be used for any equation of the form $ax^2 + bx + c = 0$.

1. Write the equation in the form $ax^2 + bx + c = 0$. a, b, and c are real numbers, a ≠ 0.

Solve $3x^2 = 8x - 2$

$3x^2 - 8x + 2 = 0$

2. The two roots (if they exist) are
$$x = \frac{-b \pm \sqrt{b^2 - 4ac}}{2a}$$

$$x = \frac{8 \pm \sqrt{64 - 24}}{6}$$

$$= \frac{8 \pm \sqrt{40}}{6}$$

$$= \frac{8 \pm 2\sqrt{10}}{6}$$

$$= \frac{4 \pm \sqrt{10}}{3}$$

LIST 176 IMAGINARY NUMBERS AND THEIR POWERS

Equations such as $x^2 = -25$ have no solution in the set of real numbers. Equations like this have solutions that fall in the realm of imaginary numbers. Imaginary numbers use the imaginary unit, i, which is defined to be the square root of -1.

$$i = \sqrt{-1} \qquad i^2 = -1$$

The solution to the equation $x^2 = -25$ in the set of imaginary numbers is $x = \pm 5i$.

Generally, if $r > 0$ then $\sqrt{-r} = i\sqrt{r}$

Some interesting patterns emerge for the powers of i as the exponent increases, as shown below.

$i = \sqrt{-1}$ by definition
$i^2 = -1$ by definition
$i^3 = i^2 \cdot i = -1 \cdot i = -i$
$i^4 = i^2 \cdot i^2 = -1 \cdot -1 = 1$
$i^5 = i^4 \cdot i = 1 \cdot i = i$
$i^6 = i^3 \cdot i^3 = -i \cdot -1 = -1$
$i^7 = i^3 \cdot i^4 = -i \cdot 1 = -i$
$\vdots$

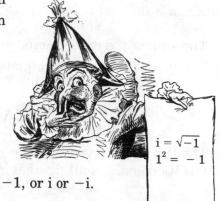

Any positive integer power of i equals 1, -1, or i or $-i$.

LIST 177   DISCRIMINANT AND COEFFICIENTS

A quadratic equation of the form $ax^2 + bx + c = 0$ where a, b, and c are real numbers, $a \neq 0$, has a discriminant equal to $b^2 - 4ac$ which determines the number and the kinds of solutions to the equation.

If $b^2 - 4ac$ is	then the equation will have
Negative	2 (conjugate) imaginary roots
Zero	1 real root (double real root)
Positive	2 different real roots

For any rational numbers a, b, and c, $a \neq 0$

If $b^2 - 4ac$ is	then the 2 roots are
Positive and the square of a rational number	rational
Positive and is not the square of a rational number	irrational

For any quadratic equation of the form $ax^2 + bx + c = 0$ a, b, and c are real numbers $a \neq 0$.

The sum of the roots equals $-b/a$ and

The product of the roots equals c/a.

LIST 178   QUADRATIC FUNCTIONS

The function f given by $f(x) = ax^2 + bx + c$ is a quadratic function, provided $a \neq 0$. If its domain is all the real numbers, then:

- Its graph is a parabola.
- Its vertex is the highest or lowest point on the graph, depending on the value of a.
- If $a > 0$ the vertex is the lowest point and the parabola opens upward.
- If $a < 0$ the vertex is the highest point and the parabola opens downward.
- The vertex is the point $\left(-\dfrac{b}{2a}, c - \dfrac{b^2}{4a} \right)$
- The axis of symmetry is the line $x = -\dfrac{b}{2a}$
- The x-intercepts (if any) can be found by solving $f(x) = 0$ for x by factoring or by using the Quadratic Formula.
- The y-intercept is c.

For reference, the Quadratic Formula is stated below—

If $ax^2 + bx + c = 0$, $a \neq 0$, and $b^2 - 4ac \geq 0$, then $x = \dfrac{-b \pm \sqrt{b^2 - 4ac}}{2a}$

The Math Teacher's Book of Lists, © 1995 by Prentice Hall

LIST 179   GRAPH OF A CIRCLE

A circle is one of the conic sections consisting of all points in a plane at a fixed distance (called the radius) from a fixed point (called the center). Below are some important principles of the graph of a circle centered at the origin.

- Standard form is $x^2 + y^2 = r^2$ $r \geq 0$. (If $r = 0$, then the circle is called a point-circle.)
- The center is $(0,0)$.
- Extreme points: $(-r,0)$
    $(r,0)$
    $(0,r)$
    $(0,-r)$
- Lines of symmetry are infinite in number and include $x = 0$ and $y = 0$.
- x-intercepts: r and $-r$
- y-intercepts: r and $-r$
- It is not a function.

The principles of a graph of a circle centered at (h,k) include:

- Standard form is $(x - h)^2 + (y - k)^2 = r^2$ $r \geq 0$. (If $r = 0$, then the circle is called a point-circle.)
- The center is (h,k).
- Extreme points: $(h - r, k)$
    $(h + r, k)$
    $(h, k + r)$
    $(h, k - r)$
- Lines of symmetry are infinite in number and include $x = h$ and $y = k$.
- x-intercepts: substitute $y = 0$ to find these.
- y-intercepts: substitute $x = 0$ to find these.
- It is not a function.

LIST 180   GRAPH OF AN ELLIPSE

One of the four conic sections is the ellipse. It is an elongated circle. Following are the principles of the graph of an ellipse centered at the origin.

- Standard form is $\dfrac{x^2}{a^2} + \dfrac{y^2}{b^2} = 1$ $a, b > 0$
- The center is (0,0).
- Extreme points: (a,0)
                   (−a,0)
                   (0,b)
                   (0,−b)
- Lines of symmetry: x = 0 and y = 0.
- x-intercepts: a and −a
- y-intercepts: b and −b
- It is not a function.
- If a = b, then the ellipse is a circle.
- If a > b, then the x axis is the major axis.
- If a < b, then the y axis is the major axis.

The principles of the graph of an ellipse centered at (h,k) include:

- Standard form: $\dfrac{(x − h)^2}{a^2} + \dfrac{(y − k)^2}{b^2} = 1$ $a, b > 0$
- The center is (h,k).
- Extreme points: (h + a,k)
                   (h − a,k)
                   (h,k + b)
                   (h,k − b)
- Lines of symmetry: x = h and y = k.
- x-intercepts (if they exist): Set y = 0 and solve for x.
- y-intercepts (if they exist): Set x = 0 and solve for y.
- It is not a function.
- If a = b, then the ellipse is a circle.
- If a > b, then the line y = k is the major axis.
- If a < b, then the line x = h is the major axis.

LIST 181 GRAPH OF A PARABOLA

A parabola is another conic section. It is shaped like a fountain. It can open up, down, to the left, or to the right. If it opens up or down, it is a quadratic function. Four general forms of the graphs are addressed below.

A parabola which opens up or down; its vertex is at the origin:

- Standard form: $y = ax^2$ $a \neq 0$
- Vertex: (0,0)
- Line of symmetry: $x = 0$
- y-intercept: 0
- Opens up if $a > 0$
- Opens down if $a < 0$
- It is a function.

A parabola which opens up or down. Its vertex is not the origin.

- Standard form: $y = ax^2 + bx + c$ $a \neq 0$
  This can be transformed to the form

$$y = a\left(x + \frac{b}{2a}\right)^2 + c - \frac{b^2}{4a}$$

  by completing the square.
- Vertex: $\left(-\dfrac{b}{2a}, \, c - \dfrac{b^2}{4a}\right)$
- Line of symmetry: $x = -\dfrac{b}{2a}$
- x-intercept if it exists: Use standard form and set $y = 0$
- y-intercept: c (from the standard form)
- Opens up if $a > 0$
- Opens down if $a < 0$
- It is a function.

A parabola which opens left or right. The vertex is the origin.

- Standard form: $x = ay^2$ $a \neq 0$
- Vertex: (0,0)
- Line of symmetry: $y = 0$
- x-intercept: 0
- It opens to the right if $a > 0$
- It opens to the left if $a < 0$
- It is not a function.

LIST 181   (Continued)

A parabola which opens left or right. The vertex is not the origin.

- Standard form: $x = ay^2 + by + c$ $a \neq 0$
  This can be transformed to the form

$$x = a\left(y + \frac{b}{2a}\right)^2 + c - \frac{b^2}{4a}$$

  by completeing the square.

- Vertex: $\left(c - \dfrac{b^2}{4a},\ -\dfrac{b}{2a}\right)$

- Line of symmetry: $y = -\dfrac{b}{2a}$

- x-intercept: c (from the standard form)
- y-intercept if it exists: Use standard form and set x = 0
- It opens to the right if a > 0
- It opens to the left if a < 0
- It is not a function.

LIST 182   GRAPH OF A HYPERBOLA

The fourth and final conic section is a hyperbola. A hyperbola is a curve with two branches each of which approaches other lines called asymptotes. The asymptotes are not part of the graph, but are helpful in drawing the graph. A hyperbola may open to the right and left or up and down.

Properties of the graph of a hyperbola which opens right and left. The center is the origin.

- Standard form: $\dfrac{x^2}{a^2} - \dfrac{y^2}{b^2} = 1$ $\qquad\qquad$ $a \neq 0, b \neq 0$
- Center: $(0,0)$
- Vertices: $(-a,0)$
  $\qquad\quad (a,0)$
- Lines of symmetry: $x = 0$ and $y = 0$
- Asymptotes: $y = -\dfrac{b}{a}x$ and $y = \dfrac{b}{a}x$
- x-intercepts: $-a$ and a
- y-intercepts: They do not exist.
- It opens to the right and left.
- It is not a function.

Properties of a hyperbola that opens right and left and is centered at a point other than the origin.

- Standard form: $\dfrac{(x - h)^2}{a^2} - \dfrac{(y - k)^2}{b^2} = 1$ $\qquad$ $a \neq 0, b \neq 0$
- Center: (h,k)
- Vertices: $(h - a,k)$
  $\qquad\quad (h + a,k)$
- Lines of symmetry: $x = h$ and $y = k$
- Asymptotes: $y - k = \dfrac{b}{a}(x - h)$ and $y - k = -\dfrac{b}{a}(x - h)$
- It opens to the right and left.
- It is not a function.

Properties of a hyperbola that opens up and down, and is centered at the origin.

- Standard form: $\dfrac{y^2}{b^2} - \dfrac{x^2}{a^2} = 1$ $\qquad\qquad$ $a \neq 0, b \neq 0$
- Center: $(0,0)$
- Vertices: $(0,b)$
  $\qquad\quad (0,-b)$

LIST 182   (Continued)

- Lines of symmetry: $x = 0$ and $y = 0$
- Asymptotes: $y = -\dfrac{b}{a}\,x$ and $y = \dfrac{b}{a}\,x$
- x-intercepts: They do not exist.
- y-intercepts: b and $-b$
- It opens up and down.
- It is not a function.

Properties of a hyperbola which opens up and down, and is centered at a point other than the origin.

- Standard form: $\dfrac{(y - k)^2}{b^2} - \dfrac{(x - h)^2}{a^2} = 1$ $a \neq 0,\ b \neq 0$
- Center: (h,k)
- Vertices: $(h, k + b)$
  $(h, k - b)$
- Lines of symmetry: $x = h$ and $y = k$
- Asymptotes: $y - k = \dfrac{b}{a}\,(x - h)$ and $y - k = -\dfrac{b}{a}\,(x - h)$
- It opens up and down.
- It is not a function.

LIST 183   PROPERTIES OF COMPLEX NUMBERS

A complex number is any number of the form a + bi where a and b are real numbers and $i^2 = -1$. The set of all complex numbers a + bi with b = 0 is the set of real numbers. In a complex number of the form a + bi, a is called the *real* part and b is called the *imaginary* part. If a = 0, then the complex number of the form a + bi is called *pure imaginary*.

Equality is defined as follows:

a + bi = c + di   if and only if   a = c and b = d.

Many of the properties of real numbers are also properties of complex numbers. In the properties of complex numbers listed below, w, y and z are complex numbers.

Closure	w + y is a unique complex number.
	w · y is a unique complex number.
Commutative Laws	w + y = y + w
	x · y = y · w
Associative Laws	w + (y + z) = (w + y) + z
	w(yz) = (wy)z
Identity Laws	w + 0 = w
	w · 1 = w
Distributive Laws	w(y + z) = wy + wz
Additive Inverse	w + (−w) = 0
Multiplicative Inverse	$w \cdot w^{-1} = 1$, w ≠ 0

LIST 184   OPERATIONS WITH COMPLEX NUMBERS

Operations with complex numbers can be compared to corresponding operations for polynomials.

In the operations below, a + bi and c + di are complex numbers. c is any real number.

Addition: Add the real parts and add the imaginary parts.

$$(a + bi) + (c + di) = (a + c) + (b + d)i$$

Subtraction: Subtract the real parts and subtract the imaginary parts.

$$(a + bi) - (c + di) = (a - c) + (b - d)i$$

Distributivity: Multiply the real part by c and multiply the imaginary part by c.

$$c(a + bi) = ca + cbi$$

Multiplication: Carry out the multiplication as if the numbers were binomials and replace i^2 by -1.

$$(a + bi)(c + di) = (ac - bd) + (ad + bc)i$$

Division: Multiply both the numerator and denominator of the fraction by the conjugate of the denominator. See List 185, "Conjugate Complex Numbers."

$$\frac{a + bi}{c + di} = \frac{a + bi}{c + di} \cdot \frac{\overline{c + di}}{c + di} = \frac{ac + bd}{c^2 + d^2} + \frac{bc - ad}{c^2 + d^2}i$$

$$c + di \neq 0 + 0i$$

The Math Teacher's Book of Lists, © 1995 by Prentice Hall

LIST 185 CONJUGATE COMPLEX NUMBERS

Conjugate complex numbers, which are also called complex imaginaries, are complex numbers that are identical except that the pure imaginary terms have opposite signs or are both zero.

a + bi and a − bi are conjugate complex numbers, where a and b are real numbers and $i^2 = -1$, bi and −bi are the pure imaginary terms.

The conjugate of a complex number is denoted by $\overline{}$. $\overline{a + bi}$ is read "the conjugate of a + bi and equals a − bi."

Important properties of conjugates follow:

- $\overline{a}$ = a where a is a real number because (a = a + 0i and a = a − 0i = a).

- $z \cdot \overline{z} = (a + bi)(a - bi) = a^2 - b^2$ where z = a + bi.

- $\overline{z + w} = \overline{z} + \overline{w}$. The conjugate of a sum is the sum of the conjugates. (z and w represent complex numbers.)

- $\overline{zw} = \overline{z} \cdot \overline{w}$. The conjugate of a product is the product of the conjugates. (z and w represent complex numbers.)

- $\overline{z^n} = (\overline{z})^n$ where z is a complex number and n is a positive integer.

- $\overline{\left(\dfrac{z}{w}\right)} = \dfrac{\overline{z}}{\overline{w}}$ where z and w represent complex numbers, w ≠ 0 + 0i.

LIST 186   VECTORS

Quantities that involve both magnitude (size) and direction are described mathematically by vectors.

Geometrically, a vector is a directed line segment, often described by a line segment with an arrow at one end.

Algebraically, it is described by the coordinates of the initial and terminal points of the directed line segment. Mathematicians are usually more concerned with the direction and length of the line segment rather than its initial and terminal points. This is especially true of magnitude and force.

Below are some definitions and notations about vectors.

- Vector—an ordered pair (a_1, a_2) of numbers.
- Components of a vector—the numbers a_1 and a_2.
- $\overrightarrow{PQ}$—the vector associated with the directed line segment with initial point $P = (x_0, y_0)$ and terminal point $Q = (x_1, y_1)$. This vector has components $x_1 - x_0$ and $y_1 - y_0$.
- Equal vectors—vectors (a_1, a_2) and (b_1, b_2) are equal if $a_1 = b_1$ and $a_2 = b_2$.
- Vector notation—Vectors are denoted by lower-case boldface letters, starting at the beginning of the alphabet. This is used to distinguish vectors from numbers which are sometimes called "scalars." Since it is difficult to write a boldfaced letter by hand, vectors are usually written as a lower-case letter with an arrow over it.
- Zero vector—$(0,0)$ is noted by $\mathbf{0}$.
- Length (or norm) of a vector—$||\mathbf{a}|| = \sqrt{a_1^2 + a_2^2}$
- Unit vector—a vector having length 1. $\mathbf{i} = (1,0)$ and $\mathbf{j} = (0,1)$ are unit vectors.
- Combination of vectors—$\mathbf{a} = (a_1, a_2)$ and $\mathbf{b} = (b_1, b_2)$

  $\mathbf{a} + \mathbf{b} = (a_1 + b_1,\ a_2 + b_2)$

  $\mathbf{a} - \mathbf{b} = (a_1 - b_1,\ a_2 - b_2)$

  $c\mathbf{a} = (ca_1, ca_2)$ where c is a number.
- Properties—

  $\mathbf{0} + \mathbf{a} = \mathbf{a} + \mathbf{0} = \mathbf{a}$

  $0\mathbf{a} = \mathbf{0}$

  $\mathbf{a} + (\mathbf{b} + \mathbf{c}) = (\mathbf{a} + \mathbf{b}) + \mathbf{c}$

  $\mathbf{a} - \mathbf{b} = \mathbf{a} + (-1)\mathbf{b}$

  $\mathbf{a} + \mathbf{b} = \mathbf{b} + \mathbf{a}$

  $1\mathbf{a} = \mathbf{a}$

  $c(\mathbf{a} + \mathbf{b}) = c\mathbf{a} + c\mathbf{b}$
- Expressing any vector—$\mathbf{a} = (a_1, a_2)$ as a combination of unit vectors $\mathbf{i}$ and $\mathbf{j}$.

  $\mathbf{a} = a_1\mathbf{i} + a_2\mathbf{j}$

  $||a_1\mathbf{i} + a_2\mathbf{j}|| = \sqrt{a_1^2 + a_2^2}$

  $(a_1\mathbf{i} + a_2\mathbf{j}) + (b_1\mathbf{i} + b_2\mathbf{j}) = (a_1 + b_1)\mathbf{i} + (a_2 + b_2)\mathbf{j}$

  $(a_1\mathbf{i} + a_2\mathbf{j}) - (b_1\mathbf{i} + b_2\mathbf{j}) = (a_1 - b_1)\mathbf{i} + (a_2 - b_2)\mathbf{j}$

  $c(a_1\mathbf{i} + a_2\mathbf{j}) = ca_1\mathbf{i} + ca_2\mathbf{j}$
- $||c\mathbf{a}|| = |c|\ ||\mathbf{a}||$

The Math Teacher's Book of Lists, © 1995 by Prentice Hall

LIST 187   MATRICES

A matrix is a set of quantities arranged in rows and columns to form a rectangular array, usually enclosed in parentheses. Matrices do not have a numerical value; they are used to represent relations between quantities. A plane vector can be represented by a single column with two numbers in which the upper number represents its component parallel to the x-axis; the lower number represents the component parallel to the y-axis. Matrices may also be used to represent and solve simultaneous equations.

- If there are m rows and n columns the matrix is an m x n matrix. This is called the order of the matrix.
- Matrices are named by capital letters.
- Individual members in a matrix are called elements (or entries) of the matrix.
- Particular elements may be identified by the horizontal row and vertical column to which they belong. a_{ij} denotes the element in the ith row and jth column of matrix A.
- Two matrices are equal if they are the same size and if all the corresponding elements are the same.
- To add matrices, add corresponding elements together to obtain another matrix of the same order.
- Only matrices of the same order may be added.
- To subtract matrices, subtract corresponding elements to obtain another matrix of the same order.
- Only matrices of the same order may be subtracted.
- To multiply a matrix by a number (also called a scalar), multiply each element by the scalar.
- To multiply matrices, multiply row by column and add.

    For example,

$$\begin{bmatrix} 1 & 2 & 3 \\ 4 & 5 & 6 \end{bmatrix} \times \begin{bmatrix} 8 & 11 & 14 \\ 9 & 12 & 15 \\ 10 & 13 & 16 \end{bmatrix} = \begin{bmatrix} 56 & 72 & 92 \\ 137 & 182 & 227 \end{bmatrix}$$

$$1 \times 8 + 2 \times 9 + 3 \times 10 = 56$$
$$1 \times 11 + 2 \times 12 + 3 \times 13 = 72$$
$$1 \times 14 + 2 \times 15 + 3 \times 16 = 92$$
$$4 \times 8 + 5 \times 9 + 6 \times 10 = 137$$
$$4 \times 11 + 5 \times 12 + 6 \times 13 = 182$$
$$4 \times 14 + 5 \times 15 + 6 \times 16 = 227$$

- Two matrices A and B may be multiplied only if the number of columns in A is the same as the number of rows in B. Multiplication is not commutative.

LIST 187   (Continued)

- The determinant is a function of a square matrix derived by multiplying and adding the elements together to obtain a single number.

—The determinant of a 1×1 matrix $[a_1]$ is its element.

—The determinant of a 2×2 matrix $\begin{bmatrix} a_1 & b_1 \\ a_2 & b_2 \end{bmatrix} = a_1 b_2 - a_2 b_1$

—The determinant of a 3×3 matrix $\begin{bmatrix} a_1 & b_1 & c_1 \\ a_2 & b_2 & c_2 \\ a_3 & b_3 & c_3 \end{bmatrix} =$

$$a_1 b_2 c_3 + a_2 b_3 c_1 + a_3 b_1 c_2 - a_1 b_3 c_2 - a_2 b_1 c_3 - a_3 b_2 c_1$$

- For any square matrix A, A has an inverse denoted A^{-1} if and only if the determinant of A does not equal zero.

LIST 188   TYPES OF MATRICES

Below are types of matrices and their distinguishing characteristics.

- Square Matrix—a matrix that has the same number of rows and columns. The diagonal from the top left to the bottom right is the leading diagonal (or principal diagonal). The sum of the elements in this diagonal is called the trace, or spur, of the matrix.
- Row Matrix—a matrix with only one row.
- Column Matrix—a matrix with only one column.
- Zero Matrix (Null Matrix)—a matrix in which all the elements are equal to zero.
- Unit Matrix (Identity Matrix)—a square matrix in which all the elements in the leading diagonal are one and the other elements are equal to zero.
- Diagonal Matrix—a square matrix in which all the elements are zero except those in the leading diagonal.
- Triangular Matrix—a square matrix in which either all the elements above the leading diagonal are zero, or all the elements below the leading diagonal are zero.
- Conformable Matrices—two matrices in which the number of columns in one is the same as the number of rows in the other.
- Transpose of a Matrix—the matrix that results from interchanging the rows and columns.
- The Negative of a Matrix—the matrix whose elements are the opposite of each corresponding element of the original matrix.

The Math Teacher's Book of Lists, © 1995 by Prentice Hall

TRIGONOMETRY AND CALCULUS

LIST 189   RIGHT TRIANGLE DEFINITION OF TRIGONOMETRIC FUNCTIONS

The six functions that collectively apply to right triangles are sine, cosine, tangent, cotangent, secant, and cosecant. The following formulas will help you in calculating the values of the trigonometric functions.

△ABC is a right triangle. ∠C is a right angle. c is the hypotenuse, b is the adjacent side with respect to ∠A. a is the opposite side with respect to ∠A.

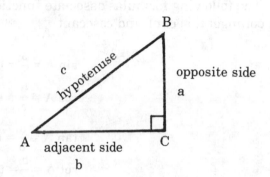

sine A = sin A
$$= \frac{\text{length of opposite side}}{\text{length of hypotenuse}} = \frac{a}{c}$$

cosine A = cos A
$$= \frac{\text{length of adjacent side}}{\text{length of hypotenuse}} = \frac{b}{c}$$

tangent A = tan A
$$= \frac{\text{length of opposite side}}{\text{length of adjacent side}} = \frac{a}{b}$$

cotangent A = cot A
$$= \frac{\text{length of adjacent side}}{\text{length of opposite side}} = \frac{b}{a}$$

secant A = sec A
$$= \frac{\text{length of hypotenuse}}{\text{length of adjacent side}} = \frac{c}{b}$$

cosecant A = csc A
$$= \frac{\text{length of hypotenuse}}{\text{length of opposite side}} = \frac{c}{a}$$

Sin A, cos A, tan A, cot A, sec A, and csc A don't depend on the lengths of the sides of the triangle but only on angle A. This is because ∠A could be in many similar right triangles; thus the ratios of the lengths of any two corresponding sides are identical.

Each of the trigonometric values is non-negative.

LIST 190   TRIGONOMETRIC FUNCTIONS OF COMPLEMENTARY ANGLES

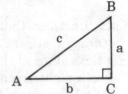

The acute angles of any right triangle are complementary. In the example, $\angle A$ and $\angle B$ are complementary angles, $m\angle A + m\angle B = 90°$.

The following formulas associate functions in pairs: sine and cosine, tangent and cotangent, secant and cosecant.

$$\sin A = \frac{a}{c} = \cos B$$

$$\cos A = \frac{b}{c} = \sin B$$

$$\tan A = \frac{a}{b} = \cot B$$

$$\cot A = \frac{b}{a} = \tan B$$

$$\sec A = \frac{c}{b} = \csc B$$

$$\csc A = \frac{c}{a} = \sec B$$

Each function of a pair is called a *cofunction* of the other. Any function of an acute angle is equal to the corresponding cofunction of the complement of the angle.

The Math Teacher's Book of Lists, © 1995 by Prentice Hall

LIST 191   HOW TO EXPRESS ANGLES IN CIRCULAR MEASURE

The familiar units used to measure angles are the degrees, minutes, and seconds. One complete circular revolution is partitioned into 360 equal units called degrees. Each degree is subdivided into 60 equal units called minutes. Each minute is further subdivided into 60 equal units called seconds. ° is the symbol for degree, ' is the symbol for minutes and " is the symbol for seconds.

1° = 60' and 1' = 60"

39°14'28" is read "39 degrees, 14 minutes, and 28 seconds."

An alternate system of measuring angles is the use of a unit called a radian. A radian (rad) is the measure of the central angle subtended by an arc of a circle whose length equals the radius of the circle. Any circle contains a total of 2 π radians. A straight angle which cuts off a semicircle, has a measure of π radians.

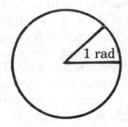

1 radian = 180/π degrees ≈ 57.296° ≈ 57°17'45"

1 degree = π/180 radians ≈ 0.01745 rad

Conversions

- To convert radians to degrees, multiply the number of radians by 57.296 or divide them by 0.01745.

- To convert degrees to radians, multiply the number of degrees by 0.01745 or divide them by 57.296.

It is customary to omit the unit "radian." Therefore we write $1° = \dfrac{\pi}{180}$. Below are the radian measures of the common angles.

Some Important Equivalents

$0° = 0$	$90° = \dfrac{\pi}{2}$	$180° = \pi$
$15° = \dfrac{\pi}{12}$	$105° = \dfrac{7\pi}{12}$	$225° = \dfrac{5\pi}{4}$
$30° = \dfrac{\pi}{6}$	$120° = \dfrac{2\pi}{3}$	$270° = \dfrac{3\pi}{2}$
$45° = \dfrac{\pi}{4}$	$135° = \dfrac{3\pi}{4}$	$315° = \dfrac{7\pi}{4}$
$60° = \dfrac{\pi}{3}$	$150° = \dfrac{5\pi}{6}$	$360° = 2\pi$
$75° = \dfrac{5\pi}{12}$	$165° = \dfrac{11\pi}{12}$	

LIST 192   CIRCULAR FUNCTION DEFINITION
OF TRIGONOMETRIC FUNCTIONS

The circular definition of trigonometric functions is used in physics, electronics, and biology where the periodic nature of the functions is emphasized. The circular function definition allows angles with measures greater than 90°, greater than 360°, or less than 0°. These angles were not defined by right triangle definition.

In the circular definition $\ominus$ is any angle in *standard position*. This means that the angle is imposed on the coordinate plane in such a way that the vertex of the angle is aligned with the origin. Its *initial side* coincides with the x-axis. The other side of the angle is called the *terminal side*. The direction that indicates rotation from the initial side of the angle to the terminal side of the angle is shown by the arrow. (x,y) is a point on the terminal ray of the angle. $r = \sqrt{x^2 + y^2}$.

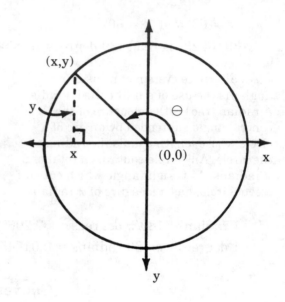

$$\sin \ominus = \frac{y}{r} \qquad\qquad \csc \ominus = \frac{r}{y}$$

$$\cos \ominus = \frac{x}{r} \qquad\qquad \sec \ominus = \frac{r}{x}$$

$$\tan \ominus = \frac{y}{x} \qquad\qquad \cot \ominus = \frac{x}{y}$$

The following trigonometric reciprocals result from the definitions:

$$\csc \ominus = \frac{1}{\sin\ominus} \qquad\qquad \sin \ominus = \frac{1}{\csc\ominus}$$

$$\sec \ominus = \frac{1}{\cos\ominus} \qquad\qquad \cos \ominus = \frac{1}{\sec\ominus}$$

$$\cot \ominus = \frac{1}{\tan\ominus} \qquad\qquad \tan \ominus = \frac{1}{\cot\ominus}$$

$$\cot \ominus = \frac{\cos\ominus}{\sin\ominus} \qquad\qquad \tan \ominus = \frac{\sin\ominus}{\cos\ominus}$$

LIST 193 TRIGONOMETRIC FUNCTIONS OF QUADRANT ANGLES

Angles may be measured in radians or degrees. See List 191, "How to Express Angles in Circular Measure."

Quadrant angles are angles whose measure are:

$0°$ or 0 radians

$90°$ or $\dfrac{\pi}{2}$ radians

$180°$ or π radians

$270°$ or $\dfrac{3\pi}{2}$ radians

$360°$ or 2π radians

and any angles coterminal with them.

Coterminal angles are two angles which, when placed in standard form, have the same terminal side.

To Find Coterminal Angles of

- *angles measured in degrees,* add integer multiples of 360° to the degree measure of the given angle.

- *angles measured in radians,* add integer multiples of 2π to the degree measure of the given angle.

The following values of the quadrant angles were obtained from the definition of the trigonometric functions. In some cases, substitutions will result in a zero in the denominator so the functions are undefined for these values. Some texts use ∞ or $\pm\infty$ to indicate that the function is undefined.

In Radians	In Degrees	Sin	Cos	Tan	Cot	Sec	Csc
0	$0°$	0	1	0	∞	1	∞
$\dfrac{\pi}{2}$	$90°$	1	0	∞	0	∞	1
π	$180°$	0	-1	0	∞	-1	∞
$\dfrac{3\pi}{2}$	$270°$	-1	0	∞	0	∞	-1

- Sine and cosine are defined for all values.

- Remaining functions are not defined when their denominators are 0.

LIST 194   THE QUADRANT SIGNS OF
THE FUNCTIONS

In the circular function definition of the trigonometric functions, r, the radius of the circle, is always positive. The quadrant signs of x and y determine the signs of the various trigonometric functions.

An angle in the standard form that terminates in the first quadrant is called "a first-quadrant angle" or "in the first quadrant."

An angle in standard form that terminates in the second quadrant is called "a second-quadrant angle," or "in the second quadrant."

The definitions are similar for the other two quadrants.

The chart below summarizes the signs of the trigonometric functions in each quadrant.

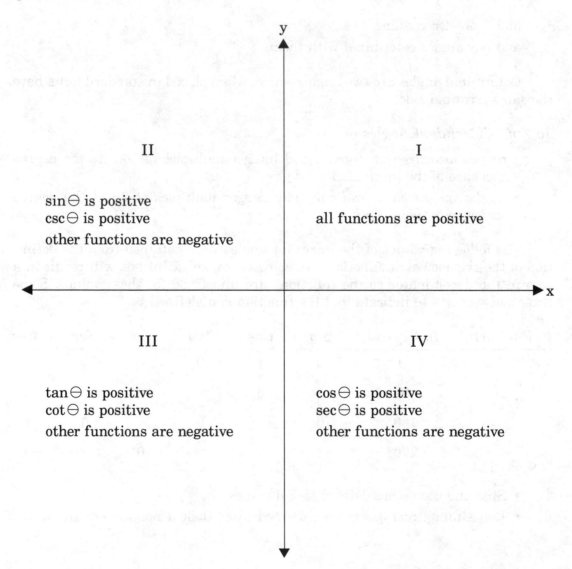

II

sin⊖ is positive
csc⊖ is positive
other functions are negative

I

all functions are positive

III

tan⊖ is positive
cot⊖ is positive
other functions are negative

IV

cos⊖ is positive
sec⊖ is positive
other functions are negative

LIST 195   VARIATIONS OF TRIGONOMETRIC FUNCTIONS

Each trigonometric function varies as $\ominus$ increases continuously from 0° to 360°. See List 192, "Circular Function Definition of Trigonometric Functions." Note how each of the trigonometric functions varies.

As $\ominus$ increases from	0° to 90° or 0 to $\frac{\pi}{2}$ rad	90° to 180° or $\frac{\pi}{2}$ rad to π rad	180° to 270° or π rad to $\frac{3\pi}{2}$ rad	270° to 360° or $\frac{3\pi}{2}$ rad to 2π rad
Sin $\ominus$	increases from 0 to 1	decreases from 1 to 0	decreases from 0 to −1	increases from −1 to 0
Cos $\ominus$	decreases from 1 to 0	decreases from 0 to −1	increases from −1 to 0	increases from 0 to 1
Tan $\ominus$	increases from 0 to +∞	increases from −∞ to 0	increases from 0 to +∞	increases from −∞ to 0
Cot $\ominus$	decreases from +∞ to 0	decreases from 0 to −∞	decreases from +∞ to 0	decreases from 0 to −∞
Sec $\ominus$	increases from 1 to +∞	increases from −∞ to −1	decreases from −1 to −∞	decreases from +∞ to 1
Csc $\ominus$	decreases from +∞ to 1	increases from 1 to +∞	increases from −∞ to −1	decreases from −1 to −∞

Summary:
- The sine and cosine take on values between −1 and 1 inclusive.
- The tangent and cotangent can take on any values.
- The secant and cosecant can take on any values except those between −1 and 1.

LIST 196   TRIGONOMETRIC FUNCTIONS OF SOME SPECIAL ANGLES

Some special angles have trigonometric function values that can be computed precisely, in terms of radicals. The following table summarizes those values.

Angle	Sin	Cos	Tan	Cot	Sec	Csc
$0° = 0$	0	1	0	∞	1	∞
$15° = \dfrac{\pi}{12}$	$\dfrac{\sqrt{2}}{4}(\sqrt{3}-1)$	$\dfrac{\sqrt{2}}{4}(\sqrt{3}+1)$	$2-\sqrt{3}$	$2+\sqrt{3}$	$\sqrt{2}(\sqrt{3}-1)$	$\sqrt{2}(\sqrt{3}+1)$
$30° = \dfrac{\pi}{6}$	$\dfrac{1}{2}$	$\dfrac{\sqrt{3}}{2}$	$\dfrac{\sqrt{3}}{3}$	$\sqrt{3}$	$\dfrac{2\sqrt{3}}{3}$	2
$45° = \dfrac{\pi}{4}$	$\dfrac{\sqrt{2}}{2}$	$\dfrac{\sqrt{2}}{2}$	1	1	$\sqrt{2}$	$\sqrt{2}$
$60° = \dfrac{\pi}{3}$	$\dfrac{\sqrt{3}}{2}$	$\dfrac{1}{2}$	$\sqrt{3}$	$\dfrac{\sqrt{3}}{3}$	2	$\dfrac{2\sqrt{3}}{3}$
$75° = \dfrac{5\pi}{12}$	$\dfrac{\sqrt{2}}{4}(\sqrt{3}+1)$	$\dfrac{\sqrt{2}}{4}(\sqrt{3}-1)$	$2+\sqrt{3}$	$2-\sqrt{3}$	$\sqrt{2}(\sqrt{3}+1)$	$\sqrt{2}(\sqrt{3}-1)$
$90° = \dfrac{\pi}{2}$	1	0	∞	0	∞	1
$105° = \dfrac{7\pi}{12}$	$\dfrac{\sqrt{2}}{4}(\sqrt{3}+1)$	$-\dfrac{\sqrt{2}}{4}(\sqrt{3}-1)$	$-(2+\sqrt{3})$	$-(2-\sqrt{3})$	$-\sqrt{2}(\sqrt{3}+1)$	$\sqrt{2}(\sqrt{3}-1)$
$120° = \dfrac{2\pi}{3}$	$\dfrac{\sqrt{3}}{2}$	$-\dfrac{1}{2}$	$-\sqrt{3}$	$-\dfrac{\sqrt{3}}{3}$	-2	$\dfrac{2\sqrt{3}}{3}$
$135° = \dfrac{3\pi}{4}$	$\dfrac{\sqrt{2}}{2}$	$-\dfrac{\sqrt{2}}{2}$	-1	-1	$-\sqrt{2}$	$\sqrt{2}$
$150° = \dfrac{5\pi}{6}$	$\dfrac{1}{2}$	$-\dfrac{\sqrt{3}}{2}$	$-\dfrac{\sqrt{3}}{3}$	$-\sqrt{3}$	$-\dfrac{2\sqrt{3}}{3}$	2
$165° = \dfrac{11\pi}{12}$	$\dfrac{\sqrt{2}}{4}(\sqrt{3}-1)$	$-\dfrac{\sqrt{2}}{4}(\sqrt{3}+1)$	$-(2-\sqrt{3})$	$-(2+\sqrt{3})$	$-\sqrt{2}(\sqrt{3}-1)$	$\sqrt{2}(\sqrt{3}+1)$
$180° = \pi$	0	-1	0	∞	-1	∞
$\vdots$						
$270° = \dfrac{3\pi}{2}$	-1	0	∞	0	∞	-1
$\vdots$						
$360° = 2\pi$	0	1	0	∞	1	∞

LIST 197 FUNDAMENTAL PERIODS OF TRIGONOMETRIC FUNCTIONS

Each of the six trigonometric functions is periodic, which means that, geometrically, the graph repeats itself over a period. The *fundamental period* is the smallest possible positive number with this property.

Stated formally: if f is a function defined by the equation $y = f(x)$ and there is a positive number a such that $f(x + a) = f(x)$ for all real numbers for which the function is defined, then f is a periodic function, and a is called the period of the function. Furthermore, if a is the smallest positive number with this property, then a is called "the fundamental period of the function."

Below is a summary of the six trigonometric functions and their fundamental periods. x is any real number for which the function is defined. See List 198, "Trigonometric Functions: Their Domains, Ranges, and Periods."

n is an integer.

$$\left.\begin{array}{l} \sin x = \sin(x + 2\pi n) \\ \cos x = \cos(x + 2\pi n) \end{array}\right\} \text{Fundamental period is } 2\pi$$

$$\left.\begin{array}{l} \tan x = \tan(x + \pi n) \\ \cot x = \cot(x + \pi n) \end{array}\right\} \text{Fundamental period is } \pi$$

$$\left.\begin{array}{l} \sec x = \sec(x + 2\pi n) \\ \csc x = \csc(x + 2\pi n) \end{array}\right\} \text{Fundamental period is } 2\pi$$

LIST 198 TRIGONOMETRIC FUNCTIONS: THEIR DOMAINS, RANGES, AND PERIODS

An important aspect of any function is the values for which it is defined. Below are the domains and ranges of the trigonometric functions, as well as the fundamental periods. Restrictions on the domains are noted. n is any integer.

Function	Domain	Range	Period
$y = \sin x$	all real numbers	$-1 \leq y \leq 1$	2π
$y = \cos x$	all real numbers	$-1 \leq y \leq 1$	2π
$y = \tan x$	all real numbers except $\dfrac{\pi}{2}$ plus integer multiples of π. $\left(x \neq \dfrac{\pi}{2} + n\pi\right)$	all real numbers	π
$y = \cot x$	all real numbers except integer multiples of π. $(x \neq n\pi)$	all real numbers	π
$y = \sec x$	all real numbers except $\dfrac{\pi}{2}$ plus integer multiples of π. $\left(x \neq \dfrac{\pi}{2} + n\pi\right)$	$|y| \geq 1$	2π
$y = \csc x$	all real numbers except integer multiples of π. $(x \neq n\pi)$	$|y| \geq 1$	2π

The Math Teacher's Book of Lists, © 1995 by Prentice Hall

LIST 199 GRAPHS OF THE TRIGONOMETRIC FUNCTIONS

The graphs of the trigonometric functions below have interesting features. Note the domain, range, and period of each. This accompanies List 197, "Fundamental Periods of the Trigonometric Functions" and List 198, "Trigonometric Functions: Their Domains, Ranges, and Periods."

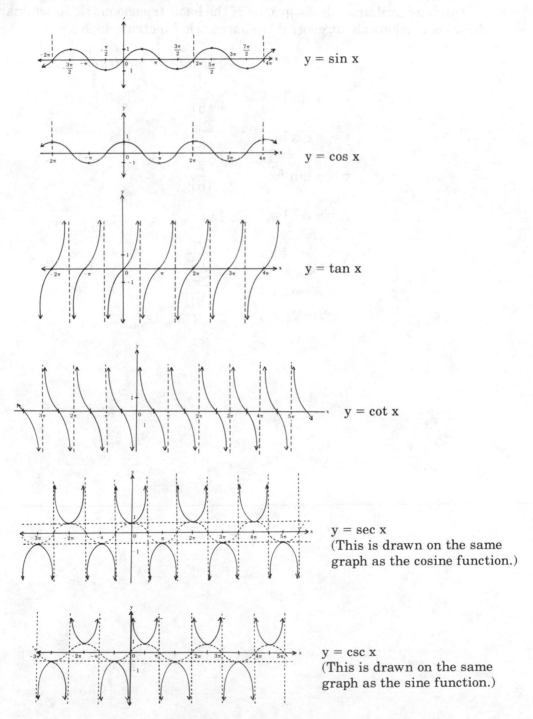

y = sin x

y = cos x

y = tan x

y = cot x

y = sec x
(This is drawn on the same graph as the cosine function.)

y = csc x
(This is drawn on the same graph as the sine function.)

LIST 200   GENERAL TRIGONOMETRIC FUNCTIONS: THEIR PERIODS AND AMPLITUDES

The amplitude of the sine (or cosine) function is defined to be half of the difference between its maximum and minimum values. Since the graph of $y = \sin x$ shows $\frac{1}{2}[1 - (-1)] = 1$, the amplitude of the sine (or cosine) function is 1.

Being familiar with the graphs of the basic trigonometric functions, you can draw conclusions about general trigonometric functions such as:

	Period	*Amplitude*
$y = a \sin bx$	$\dfrac{2\pi}{|b|}$	$|a|$
$y = a \cos bx$	$\dfrac{2\pi}{|b|}$	$|a|$
$y = a \tan bx$	$\dfrac{\pi}{|b|}$	—
$y = a \cot bx$	$\dfrac{\pi}{|b|}$	—
$y = a \sec bx$	$\dfrac{2\pi}{|b|}$	—
$y = a \csc bx$	$\dfrac{2\pi}{|b|}$	—

LIST 201 EIGHT BASIC TRIGONOMETRIC IDENTITIES

A trigonometric identity is an equation that is valid for all the values of the variable for which every expression in the equation is defined. Admissible values are values of the variable for which the trigonometric identity is defined.

While there are other trigonometric identities, below are eight basic identities which should be learned in order to simplify trigonometric expressions and verify identities.

Reciprocal Relationships

$$\csc \propto = \frac{1}{\sin \propto}$$

$$\sec \propto = \frac{1}{\cos \propto}$$

$$\cot \propto = \frac{1}{\tan \propto}$$

Quotient Relationships

$$\tan \propto = \frac{\sin \propto}{\cos \propto}$$

$$\cot \propto = \frac{\cos \propto}{\sin \propto}$$

Pythagorean Relationships

$$\sin^2 \propto + \cos^2 \propto = 1$$
$$1 + \tan^2 \propto = \sec^2 \propto$$
$$1 + \cot^2 \propto = \csc^2 \propto$$

LIST 202   ANGLE-SUM AND
ANGLE-DIFFERENCE FORMULAS

Addition formulas for the sine and cosine are formulas that express $\sin(\alpha + B)$ and $\cos(\alpha + B)$ in terms of $\sin\alpha$, $\sin B$, $\cos\alpha$, and $\cos B$. Equivalent forms result from substituting α for B and using $\cos(-B) = \cos B$ and $\sin(-B)$ for $-\sin B$.

$$\sin(\alpha + B) = \sin\alpha\cos B + \cos\alpha\sin B$$
$$\cos(\alpha + B) = \cos\alpha\cos B - \sin\alpha\sin B$$
$$\sin(\alpha - B) = \sin\alpha\cos B - \cos\alpha\sin B$$
$$\cos(\alpha - B) = \cos\alpha\cos B + \sin\alpha\sin B$$

Addition formulas for other functions may be derived from those for sine and cosine. The two most important derivations are the formulas for the tangent.

$$\tan(\alpha + B) = \frac{\tan\alpha + \tan B}{1 - \tan\alpha\tan B} \qquad \tan\alpha\tan B \neq 1$$

$$\tan(\alpha - B) = \frac{\tan\alpha - \tan B}{1 + \tan\alpha\tan B} \qquad \tan\alpha\tan B \neq -1$$

Following are the formulas for the cotangent.

$$\cot(\alpha + B) = \frac{\cot B \cot\alpha - 1}{\cot B + \cot\alpha} \qquad \cot B \neq -\cot\alpha$$

$$\cot(\alpha - B) = \frac{\cot B \cot\alpha + 1}{\cot B - \cot\alpha} \qquad \cot B \neq \cot\alpha$$

LIST 203   DOUBLE-ANGLE FORMULAS AND HALF-ANGLE FORMULAS

The following double-angle formulas result when $\alpha = B$ in the sum formulas. The half-angle formulas are derived from the double-angle formulas.

Double-Angle Formulas

$$\sin 2\alpha = 2 \sin\alpha\cos\alpha = \frac{2\tan\alpha}{1 + \tan^2\alpha}$$

$$\cos 2\alpha = \cos^2\alpha - \sin^2\alpha = 1 - 2\sin^2\alpha = 2\cos^2\alpha - 1 = \frac{1 - \tan^2\alpha}{1 + \tan^2\alpha}$$

$$\tan 2\alpha = \frac{2\tan\alpha}{1 - \tan^2\alpha}$$

$$\cot 2\alpha = \frac{\cot^2\alpha - 1}{2\cot\alpha}$$

Half-Angle Formulas

$$\sin\frac{1}{2}\alpha = \begin{cases} \sqrt{\dfrac{1 - \cos\alpha}{2}} & \text{if } \sin\frac{1}{2}\alpha \geq 0 \\[2ex] -\sqrt{\dfrac{1 - \cos\alpha}{2}} & \text{if } \sin\frac{1}{2}\alpha < 0 \end{cases}$$

$$\cos\frac{1}{2}\alpha = \begin{cases} \sqrt{\dfrac{1 + \cos\alpha}{2}} & \text{if } \cos\frac{1}{2}\alpha \geq 0 \\[2ex] -\sqrt{\dfrac{1 + \cos\alpha}{2}} & \text{if } \cos\frac{1}{2}\alpha < 0 \end{cases}$$

$$\tan\frac{1}{2}\alpha = \frac{\sin\alpha}{1 + \cos\alpha} = \frac{1 - \cos\alpha}{\sin\alpha}$$

$$\cot\frac{1}{2}\alpha = \frac{\sin\alpha}{1 - \cos\alpha} = \frac{1 + \cos\alpha}{\sin\alpha}$$

LIST 204 MULTIPLE-ANGLE FORMULAS, PRODUCT FORMULAS, AND SUM AND DIFFERENCE FORMULAS

The lists below are formulas for multiple-angles (including the general formula), formulas for the product of the sine and cosine functions, and sum and difference formulas.

Multiple-Angle Formulas

$\sin 3\alpha = 3\sin\alpha - 4\sin^3\alpha$

$\sin 4\alpha = 4\sin\alpha\cos\alpha - 8\sin^3\alpha\cos\alpha$

$\sin n\alpha = 2\sin(n-1)\alpha\cos\alpha - \sin(n-2)\alpha$

$\cos 3\alpha = 4\cos^3\alpha - 3\cos\alpha$

$\cos 4\alpha = 8\cos^4\alpha - 8\cos^2\alpha + 1$

$\cos n\alpha = 2\cos(n-1)\alpha\cos\alpha - \cos(n-2)\alpha$

$\tan 3\alpha = \dfrac{3\tan\alpha - \tan^3\alpha}{1 - 3\tan^2\alpha}$

$\tan 4\alpha = \dfrac{4\tan\alpha - 4\tan^3\alpha}{1 - 6\tan^2\alpha + \tan^4\alpha}$

$\tan n\alpha = \dfrac{\tan(n-1)\alpha + \tan\alpha}{1 - \tan(n-1)\alpha\tan\alpha}$

Product Formulas

$\sin\alpha\sin B = \dfrac{1}{2}\cos(\alpha - B) - \dfrac{1}{2}\cos(\alpha + B)$

$\cos\alpha\cos B = \dfrac{1}{2}\cos(\alpha - B) + \dfrac{1}{2}\cos(\alpha + B)$

$\cos\alpha\sin B = \dfrac{1}{2}\sin(\alpha + B) - \dfrac{1}{2}\sin(\alpha - B)$

$\sin\alpha\cos B = \dfrac{1}{2}\sin(\alpha + B) + \dfrac{1}{2}\sin(\alpha - B)$

Sum and Difference Formulas

$\sin\alpha + \sin B = 2\sin\left(\dfrac{\alpha + B}{2}\right)\cos\left(\dfrac{\alpha - B}{2}\right)$

$\sin\alpha - \sin B = 2\cos\left(\dfrac{\alpha + B}{2}\right)\sin\left(\dfrac{\alpha - B}{2}\right)$

$\cos\alpha + \cos B = 2\cos\left(\dfrac{\alpha + B}{2}\right)\cos\left(\dfrac{\alpha - B}{2}\right)$

$\cos\alpha - \cos B = -2\sin\left(\dfrac{\alpha + B}{2}\right)\sin\left(\dfrac{\alpha - B}{2}\right)$

The Math Teacher's Book of Lists, © 1995 by Prentice Hall

LIST 205   REDUCTION FORMULAS

Using these identities, a circular function of any arc may be expressed in terms of a circular function of an arc between 0 and $\pi/4$.

$$\sin \left(\frac{\pi}{2} - \alpha\right) = \cos \alpha$$

$$\cos \left(\frac{\pi}{2} - \alpha\right) = \sin \alpha$$

$$\tan \left(\frac{\pi}{2} - \alpha\right) = \cot \alpha$$

$$\sin \left(\frac{\pi}{2} + \alpha\right) = \cos \alpha$$

$$\cos \left(\frac{\pi}{2} + \alpha\right) = -\sin \alpha$$

$$\tan \left(\frac{\pi}{2} + \alpha\right) = -\cot \alpha$$

$$\sin (\pi - \alpha) = \sin \alpha$$

$$\cos (\pi - \alpha) = -\cos \alpha$$

$$\tan (\pi - \alpha) = -\tan \alpha$$

$$\sin (\pi + \alpha) = -\sin \alpha$$

$$\cos (\pi + \alpha) = -\cos \alpha$$

$$\tan (\pi + \alpha) = \tan \alpha$$

$$\sin \left(\frac{3\pi}{2} - \alpha\right) = -\cos \alpha$$

$$\cos \left(\frac{3\pi}{2} - \alpha\right) = -\sin \alpha$$

$$\sin \left(\frac{3\pi}{2} + \alpha\right) = -\cos \alpha$$

$$\cos \left(\frac{3\pi}{2} + \alpha\right) = \sin \alpha$$

$$\sin (2\pi - \alpha) = -\sin \alpha$$

$$\cos (2\pi - \alpha) = \cos \alpha$$

LIST 206   GENERAL GUIDELINES FOR VERIFYING IDENTITIES

There are several ways of verifying proposed identities. Usually you will need more than one method for verification. Below are some guidelines.

Before You Begin:

1. Know the eight basic trigonometric identities and recognize alternate forms of each.
2. Know procedures for adding and subtracting fractions, reducing fractions, and writing equivalent fractions.
3. Know factoring and special product techniques.

The General Plan:

1. Begin with the side that appears more complicated and try to transform it into the form on the other side.
2. Use substitution and simplification procedures that allow you to work on one side of the equation.
3. Transform each side of the equation independently into the same form.

Hints:

1. Avoid substitutions that involve radicals.
2. Use substitutions to change all trigonometric functions into expressions involving only sine and cosine. Then simplify.
3. Clear any fractions in the proposed identity. This may involve multiplying the numerator and denominator of a fraction by the conjugate of each other.
4. Simplify the square root of a fraction by using conjugates to transform it into the quotient of perfect squares.

LIST 207   THE TRIGONOMETRIC FUNCTIONS
IN TERMS OF ONE ANOTHER

A hint for verifying trigonometric identities is to express the trigonometric functions in terms of only sine and cosine. The list below expresses each trigonometric function, not only in terms of the sine and cosine, but each other as well.

$$\sin \alpha = \pm \sqrt{1 - \cos^2 \alpha}$$

$$= \frac{\tan \alpha}{\sqrt{1 + \tan^2 \alpha}}$$

$$= \frac{1}{\sqrt{1 + \cot^2 \alpha}}$$

$$= \frac{\sqrt{\sec^2 \alpha - 1}}{\sec \alpha}$$

$$= \frac{1}{\csc \alpha}$$

$$\tan \alpha = \frac{\sin \alpha}{\sqrt{1 - \sin^2 \alpha}}$$

$$= \frac{\sqrt{1 - \cos^2 \alpha}}{\cos \alpha}$$

$$= \frac{1}{\cot \alpha}$$

$$= \sqrt{\sec^2 \alpha - 1}$$

$$= \frac{1}{\sqrt{\csc^2 \alpha - 1}}$$

$$\sec \alpha = \frac{1}{\sqrt{1 - \sin^2 \alpha}}$$

$$= \frac{1}{\cos \alpha}$$

$$= \pm \sqrt{1 + \tan^2 \alpha}$$

$$= \frac{\sqrt{1 + \cot^2 \alpha}}{\cot \alpha}$$

$$= \frac{\csc \alpha}{\sqrt{\csc^2 \alpha - 1}}$$

$$\cos \alpha = \sqrt{1 - \sin^2 \alpha}$$

$$= \frac{1}{\sqrt{1 + \tan^2 \alpha}}$$

$$= \frac{\cot \alpha}{\sqrt{1 + \cot^2 \alpha}}$$

$$= \frac{1}{\sec}$$

$$= \frac{\sqrt{\csc^2 \alpha - 1}}{\csc \alpha}$$

$$\cot \alpha = \frac{\sqrt{1 - \sin^2 \alpha}}{\sin \alpha}$$

$$= \frac{\cos \alpha}{\sqrt{1 - \cos^2 \alpha}}$$

$$= \frac{1}{\tan \alpha}$$

$$= \frac{1}{\sqrt{\sec^2 \alpha - 1}}$$

$$= \sqrt{\csc^2 \alpha - 1}$$

$$\csc \alpha = \frac{1}{\sin \alpha}$$

$$= \frac{1}{\sqrt{1 - \cos^2 \alpha}}$$

$$= \frac{\sqrt{1 + \tan^2 \alpha}}{\tan \alpha}$$

$$= \sqrt{1 + \cot^2 \alpha}$$

$$= \frac{\sec \alpha}{\sqrt{\sec^2 \alpha - 1}}$$

The sign depends upon the quadrant of the angle.

LIST 208   TRIGONOMETRIC IDENTITIES AND OBLIQUE TRIANGLES

The following identities are true for any triangle but are most often used to find missing sides and angles of oblique triangles. An oblique triangle is a triangle that does not contain a right angle; it may have three acute angles or two acute angles and one obtuse angle. The notation of denoting the lengths of the sides by small letters and corresponding angles by capital letters is used.

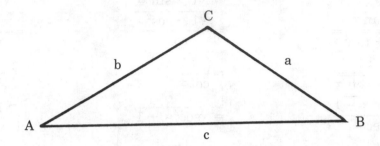

- Law of Sines: $\dfrac{a}{\text{Sin } A} = \dfrac{b}{\text{Sin } B} = \dfrac{c}{\text{Sin } C}$

  This identity is used if you are given

  —two angles and the side opposite one of them.

  —two angles and the included side.

  —two sides and the angle opposite one of them. (In this case there may be no solution for the angle, one solution, or two solutions.)

- Law of Cosines: $a^2 = b^2 + c^2 - 2bc \cos A$

  $b^2 = c^2 + a^2 - 2ca \cos B$

  $c^2 = a^2 + b^2 - 2ab \cos C$

  This identity is used if you are given

  —two sides and the included angle.

  —3 sides.

- Law of Tangents: $\dfrac{b - c}{b + c} = \dfrac{\tan \frac{1}{2}(B - C)}{\tan \frac{1}{2}(B + C)}$

  $\dfrac{a - b}{a + b} = \dfrac{\tan \frac{1}{2}(A - B)}{\tan \frac{1}{2}(A + B)}$

  $\dfrac{c - a}{c + a} = \dfrac{\tan \frac{1}{2}(C - A)}{\tan \frac{1}{2}(C + A)}$

The Math Teacher's Book of Lists, © 1995 by Prentice Hall

LIST 208 (Continued)

This identity may be used if you are given

—two sides and the included angle, especially if the computations involve logarithms.

- Newton's Formulas: $\dfrac{b + c}{a} = \dfrac{\cos \frac{1}{2}(B - C)}{\sin \frac{1}{2}A}$

$$\frac{c + a}{b} = \frac{\cos \frac{1}{2}(C - A)}{\sin \frac{1}{2}B}$$

$$\frac{a + b}{c} = \frac{\cos \frac{1}{2}(A - B)}{\sin \frac{1}{2}C}$$

- Mollweide's Formulas: $\dfrac{b - c}{a} = \dfrac{\sin \frac{1}{2}(B - C)}{\cos \frac{1}{2}A}$

$$\frac{c - a}{b} = \frac{\sin \frac{1}{2}(C - A)}{\cos \frac{1}{2}B}$$

$$\frac{a - b}{c} = \frac{\sin \frac{1}{2}(A - B)}{\cos \frac{1}{2}C}$$

Both Newton's Formulas and Mollweide's Formulas are used to check solutions.

LIST 209   INVERSE TRIGONOMETRIC FUNCTIONS

Since each of the trigonometric functions is periodic, none has an inverse. However, if the domain of each of these functions is restricted to a suitable interval, then each of the functions has an inverse. These inverse functions are called *inverse trigonometric functions*. Each may be denoted in two ways—the inverse of the sine function is the arcsin function or $\sin^{-1}x$. (Note: the same notation is used for the other five trigonometric functions.)

Below is a list of the inverse trigonometric functions, their definitions, domains, and ranges. Note that "iff" means "if and only if."

Inverse Function	*Domain of Inverse*	*Principal Range of Inverse*
$y = \sin^{-1} x$ iff $\sin y = x$ $= \arcsin x$	$-1 \le x \le 1$	$-\dfrac{\pi}{2} \le y \le \dfrac{\pi}{2}$
$y = \cos^{-1} x$ iff $\cos y = x$ $= \arccos x$	$-1 \le x \le 1$	$0 \le y \le \pi$
$y = \tan^{-1} x$ iff $\tan y = x$ $= \arctan x$	x is any real number	$-\dfrac{\pi}{2} < y < \dfrac{\pi}{2}$
$y = \cot^{-1} x$ iff $\cot y = x$ $= \text{arccot } x$	x is any real number	$0 < y < \pi$
$y = \sec^{-1} x$ iff $\sec y = x$ $= \text{arcsec } x$	$|x| \ge 1$	$-\pi \le y \le 0,\ y \ne -\dfrac{\pi}{2}$
$y = \csc^{-1} x$ iff $\csc y = x$ $= \text{arccsc } x$	$|x| \ge 1$	$-\dfrac{\pi}{2} \le y \le \dfrac{\pi}{2},\ y \ne 0$

LIST 210   RELATIONS BETWEEN INVERSE TRIGONOMETRIC FUNCTIONS

The inverse trigonometric functions—$\sin^{-1}x$, $\cos^{-1}x$, $\tan^{-1}x$, $\cot^{-1}x$, $\sec^{-1}x$, $\csc^{-1}x$—are the inverses of $\sin x$, $\cos x$, $\tan x$, $\cot x$, $\sec x$, and $\csc x$ respectively. The relationships between the inverse functions to each other are listed below, assuming principal values are used.

$$\sin^{-1}x + \cos^{-1}x = \frac{\pi}{2}$$

$$\tan^{-1}x + \cot^{-1}x = \frac{\pi}{2}$$

$$\sec^{-1}x + \csc^{-1}x = \frac{\pi}{2}$$

$$\csc^{-1}x = \sin^{-1}\left(\frac{1}{x}\right)$$

$$\sec^{-1}x = \cos^{-1}\left(\frac{1}{x}\right)$$

$$\cot^{-1}x = \tan^{-1}\left(\frac{1}{x}\right)$$

$$\sin^{-1}(-x) = -\sin^{-1}x$$

$$\cos^{-1}(-x) = \pi - \cos^{-1}x$$

$$\tan^{-1}(-x) = -\tan^{-1}x$$

$$\cot^{-1}(-x) = \pi - \cot^{-1}x$$

$$\sec^{-1}(-x) = \pi - \sec^{-1}x$$

$$\csc^{-1}(-x) = -\csc^{-1}x$$

LIST 211   GRAPHS OF THE INVERSE TRIGONOMETRIC FUNCTIONS

The graphs of the inverse trigonometric relations are those of the corresponding trigonometric functions, except that the roles of x and y are interchanged.

For example, the graph of y = arcsin x is the graph of x = sin y and differs from the graph of y = sin x in that the roles of x and y are interchanged. The graph of y = arcsin x is a sine curve drawn on the y-axis.

The graphs below show the graphs of the inverse relations. When the domain is restricted to a suitable interval, as in List 209, "Inverse Trigonometric Functions," the graph is a function. The graph of the principal values of the inverse functions are shown in bold.

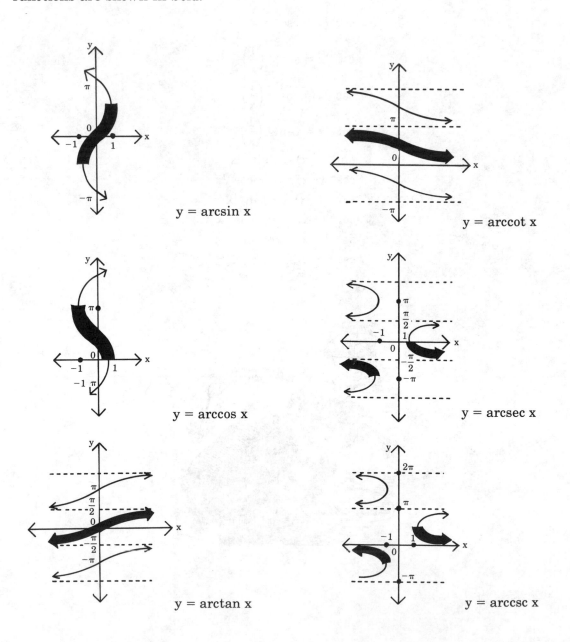

y = arcsin x

y = arccot x

y = arccos x

y = arcsec x

y = arctan x

y = arccsc x

The Math Teacher's Book of Lists, © 1995 by Prentice Hall

LIST 212   LIMITS

The notion of a limit is fundamental to the study of calculus. In everyday life we use expressions such as "the speed limit," "my patience is limited," and "the only limits to your potential are those you impose yourself." These expressions suggest that a limit is a type of boundary which may, on some occasions be reached, but on some others may be exceeded.

In calculus, a limit is defined: If f(x) becomes arbitrarily close to a single number L as x approaches c from either side, then we write

$$\lim_{x \to c} f(x) = L$$

and say that the *limit* of f(x) as x approaches c is L.

Note that "x approaches c" means that no matter how close x comes to the value c, there is another value of x (different from c) in the domain of f that is even closer to c.

One-Sided Limits

The definition of the limit $\lim_{x \to c} f(x) = L$ requires that x approach c from the right as well as the left.

$x \to c^-$ is read "x approaches c from the left."

$x \to c^+$ is read "x approaches c from the right."

Each limit obtained from the one-sided approach has a special name:

- $\lim_{x \to c^-} f(x)$ is called the *limit from the left*.

- $\lim_{x \to c^+} f(x)$ is called the *limit from the right*.

Properties of Limits

The properties hold for real numbers b and c. n is a positive integer.

- $\lim_{x \to c} b = b$

- $\lim_{x \to c} x = c$

- $\lim_{x \to c} x^n = c^n$

- $\lim_{x \to c} \sqrt[n]{x} = \sqrt[n]{c}, \ c > 0$

LIST 213   OPERATIONS WITH LIMITS

In order for the limit of a function to exist as $x \to c$, it must be true that both one-sided limits exist and are equal. Formally stated: if f is a function and c and L are real numbers, then

$$\lim_{x \to c} f(x) = L$$

if and only if

$$\lim_{x \to c^-} f(x) = L \text{ and } \lim_{x \to c^+} f(x) = L$$

If f and g are two functions, we can produce several new functions: their sum, $f + g$, difference, $f - g$, product, fg, and quotient, f/g. The limits of these functions as $x \to c$ can easily be determined once we know the limit of f at c and the limit of g at c.

Rules governing the limits of functions are listed below. b and c are real numbers. n is a positive integer. If the limits of $f(x)$ and $g(x)$ exist as x approaches c, then:

- Constant Multiple: $\lim_{x \to c} [bf(x)] = b [\lim_{x \to c} f(x)]$

- Addition: $\lim_{x \to c} [f(x) + g(x)] = \lim_{x \to c} f(x) + \lim_{x \to c} g(x)$

- Subtraction: $\lim_{x \to c} [f(x) - g(x)] = \lim_{x \to c} f(x) - \lim_{x \to c} f(x)$

- Multiplication: $\lim_{x \to c} [f(x)g(x)] = [\lim_{x \to c} f(x)][\lim_{x \to c} g(x)]$

- Division: $\lim_{x \to c} \dfrac{f(x)}{g(x)} = \dfrac{\lim_{x \to c} f(x)}{\lim_{x \to c} g(x)}$ if $\lim_{x \to c} g(x) \neq 0$

- Power: $\lim_{x \to c} [f(x)]^n = [\lim_{x \to c} f(x)]^n$

- Radical: $\lim_{x \to c} \sqrt[n]{f(x)} = \sqrt[n]{\lim_{x \to c} f(x)}$, $\lim_{x \to c} f(x) > 0$

LIST 214   CONTINUITY

In mathematics, the term "continuous" means the same as it does in everyday usage. If someone talks continuously, it means that there is no stopping in the chatter. In math, a function is continuous at x = c if there is no interruption of the graph of f at c. There are no holes, jumps, or gaps. The graph of a function is continuous (on an interval) if its graph (on the interval) can be traced without lifting the pencil from the paper.

Here are some useful definitions:

- Continuity at a Point—a function is said to be continuous at c if the following conditions are met:

    f(c) is defined.

    $\lim\limits_{x \to c} f(x)$ exists.

    $\lim\limits_{x \to c} f(x) = f(c)$

- Continuity on an Open Interval—a function is said to be continuous on an interval (a,b) if it is continuous at each point in the interval.

- Continuity on a Closed Interval—if f is continuous on the open interval (a,b) and

    $\lim\limits_{x \to a^+} f(x) = f(a)$ and $\lim\limits_{x \to b^-} f(x) = f(b)$

then f is *continuous on [a,b]* and we say f is continuous from the right at a and continuous from the left at b (provided that f is defined on [a,b]).

LIST 215   PROPERTIES OF CONTINUOUS FUNCTIONS

Because continuity is defined in terms of limits, continuous functions and limits share many of the same properties. In the list below f and g are continuous at c and k is a real number.

The following functions are also continuous at c.

- Sum: f + g
- Difference: f − g
- Constant Multiple: kf
- Product: fg
- Quotient: f/g g(c) ≠ 0
- Composition f ∘ g (x) where f is continuous at g(c)
- Polynomial function is continuous at every number.
- Rational function is continuous at every number in its domain.
- f(x) = $\sqrt[n]{x}$, n is a positive integer is continuous at every number if n is odd; continuous at every positive number if n is even.

The Math Teacher's Book of Lists, © 1995 by Prentice Hall

LIST 216   DIFFERENTIATION RULES

Differentiation is the process for finding the rate at which one quantity changes with respect to another. The rules needed to differentiate any algebraic function are listed below. u and v are differentiable functions of x, and y is a differentiable function of u. c is a constant. n is a real number.

- Constant Rule: $\dfrac{d}{dx}[c] = 0$

- Constant Multiple Rule: $\dfrac{d}{dx}[cu] = c\dfrac{du}{dx}$

- Sum Rule: $\dfrac{d}{dx}[u + v] = \dfrac{du}{dx} + \dfrac{dv}{dx}$

- Difference Rule: $\dfrac{d}{dx}[u - v] = \dfrac{du}{dx} - \dfrac{dv}{dx}$

- Product Rule: $\dfrac{d}{dx}[uv] = u\dfrac{dv}{dx} + v\dfrac{du}{dx}$

- Quotient rule: $\dfrac{d}{dx}\left[\dfrac{u}{v}\right] = \dfrac{v\dfrac{du}{dx} - u\dfrac{dv}{dx}}{v^2}$

- Power Rules: $\dfrac{d}{dx}[x^n] = nx^{n-1}$

  $\dfrac{d}{dx}[u^n] = nu^{n-1}\dfrac{du}{dx}$

- Chain Rule: $\dfrac{dy}{dx} = \dfrac{dy}{du} \cdot \dfrac{du}{dx}$

The following rules are special cases of the Power Rule or combinations of the Constant Multiple and Power Rules:

$$\frac{d}{dx}[x] = 1$$

$$\frac{d}{dx}[cx^n] = cnx^{-1}$$

$$\frac{d}{dx}[cx] = c$$

The Math Teacher's Book of Lists, © 1995 by Prentice Hall

LIST 217   HIGHER-ORDER DERIVATIVES

Since the derivative of a function is a function, you may find the derivative of the derivative (called the second derivative). By repeating this process you can obtain higher-order derivatives.

To find the higher-order derivatives of f(x)—

1) Find the derivative of a function. This is called finding the first derivative. It is denoted f'(x) and is read "f prime of x."

2) Find the derivative of the first derivative. This is called finding the second derivative, and is denoted f"(x). It is read "f double prime of x."

3) Find the derivative of the second derivative, which is called finding the third derivative. It is denoted f'''(x) and is read "f triple prime of x."

4) Continue this process provided each successive derivative is differentiable.

Commonly used notation for higher-order derivatives are listed below:

First Derivative	Second Derivative	Third Derivative	Fourth Derivative	nth Derivative
$f'(x)$	$f''(x)$	$f'''(x)$	$f^{(4)}(x)$	$f^{(n)}(x)$
y'	y''	y'''	$y^{(4)}$	$y^{(n)}$
$\dfrac{dy}{dx}$	$\dfrac{d^2y}{dx^2}$	$\dfrac{d^3y}{dx^3}$	$\dfrac{d^4y}{dx^4}$	$\dfrac{d^ny}{dx^n}$
$\dfrac{d}{dx}[f(x)]$	$\dfrac{d^2}{dx^2}[f(x)]$	$\dfrac{d^3}{dx^3}[f(x)]$	$\dfrac{d^4}{dx^4}[f(x)]$	$\dfrac{d^n}{dx^n}[f(x)]$
$Dx(y)$	$Dx^2(y)$	$Dx^3(y)$	$Dx^4(y)$	$Dx^n(y)$

- In the context of higher derivatives, the derivative of f is called the *first derivative*.
- The prime notation is usually dropped after the third derivative. Parentheses are placed around the order of the derivative instead.

The Math Teacher's Book of Lists, © 1995 by Prentice Hall

LIST 218   CURVE DRAWING—APPLICATION OF HIGHER-ORDER DERIVATIVES

A function y = f(x) is increasing if its graph moves up as x moves to the right. It is decreasing if its graph moves down as x moves to the right. This can be determined by finding the first derivative of the function, provided the function is differentiable.

- If the first derivative is positive, then the value of the original function is increasing.
- If the first derivative is negative, then the value of the original function is decreasing.
- If the first derivative is 0, then the original curve has a horizontal tangent at that point.

The second derivative (provided it exists) is used to determine concavity and point of inflection. A point of inflection is the point where the graph of a continuous function possesses a tangent line and its concavity changes from upward to downward, or downward to upward.

- If the second derivative is positive, then the original curve is concave upward (shaped like a $\cup$).
- If the second derivative is negative, then the original curve is concave downward (shaped like a $\cap$).
- If the second derivative is 0, then the original curve has a point of inflection, provided that the second derivative is positive on one side of the point and negative on the other.

The first and second derivatives (if they exist) may be used to test for relative minimum and relative maximum. Relative minimum and relative maximum are the lowest and highest points on a given interval.

- If the first derivative is 0 and—
  a) the second derivative is positive, the point is a relative minimum.
  b) the second derivative is negative, the point is a relative maximum.
  c) the second derivative is 0, the test fails.

LIST 219   NOTATION FOR ANTIDERIVATIVES

The process of determining the original function from its derivative is called antidifferentiation.

- A function F is called an *antiderivative* of a function f if for every x in the domain of f F'(x) = f(x).
- F(x) is an antiderivative of f(x). It is used synonymously with F is an antiderivative of f.
- The antidifferentiation process is also called integration.
- ∫ is called the integral sign.
- ∫f(x) dx is called the indefinite integral of f(x) and denotes a family of antiderivatives of F(x).
- ∫f(x) dx = F(x) + C means that F is an antiderivative of f. That is F'(x) = f(x) for all x in the domain of f. f(x) is called the *integrand*. C is the *constant of integration*.

LIST 220   INTEGRATION RULES

Because integration and differentiation are inverse relations, integration formulas may be obtained directly from differentiation formulas. They are summarized below.

Constant Rule: $\int k\,dx = kx + c$

Constant Multiple Rule: $\int kf(x)\,dx = k\int f(x)\,dx$

Sum Rule: $\int [f(x) + g(x)]\,dx = \int f(x)\,dx + \int g(x)\,dx$

Difference Rule: $\int [f(x) - g(x)]\,dx = \int f(x)\,dx - \int g(x)\,dx$

Power Rule: $\int x^n\,dx = \dfrac{x^{n+1}}{n+1} + c,\ n \neq {}^-1$

General Power Rule: $\int u^n \dfrac{du}{dx}\,dx = \dfrac{u^{n+1}}{n+1} + c,\ n \neq {}^-1$

u is a differentiable function of x.

LIST 221   DEFINITE INTEGRALS

Definite integrals are integrals which have upper and lower limits.

- $\int_a^b f(x)\,dx$ is called the *definite integral from a to b* where—

    a is the lower limit of integration,

    b is the upper limit of integration.

- The Fundamental Theorem of Calculus describes a means for evaluating a definite integral. It is stated below:

    If a function f is continuous on the interval [a,b], then

    $\int_a^b f(x)\,dx = F(b) - F(a)$

    where F is any function such that $F'(x) = f(x)$ for all x in [a,b].

- Properties of definite integrals are listed below. f and g are integrable on [a,b].

    $\int_a^b kf(x)dx = k\int_a^b f(x)dx$ k is a constant

    $\int_a^b [f(x) + g(x)]dx = \int_a^b f(x)dx + \int_a^b g(x)dx$

    $\int_a^b [f(x) - g(x)]dx = \int_a^b f(x)dx - \int_a^b g(x)dx$

    $\int_a^b f(x)dx = \int_a^c f(x)dx + \int_c^b f(x)dx$ if $a < c < b$

    $\int_a^b f(x)dx = \int_a^c f(x)dx + \int_c^b f(x)dx$ regardless of the order of a, b, and c.

    If k is any constant, then $\int_a^b kdx = k(b - a)$

    $\int_a^a f(x)dx = 0$

    $\int_a^b f(x)dx = -\int_b^a f(x)dx$

- The definite integral $\int_a^b f(x)\,dx$ is a number whereas the indefinite integral $\int f(x)\,dx$ is a family of functions.

LIST 222   EXPONENTIAL FUNCTIONS

Many functions that have been studied involve a variable raised to a constant power such as $f(x) = x^2$, $k(x) = \sqrt{x} = x^{\frac{1}{2}}$, $g(x) = x^{-1}$. If the roles are interchanged and a constant is raised to a variable power, then a group of functions called *exponential functions* results. Some examples are $f(x) = 2^x$, $k(x) = \frac{1}{2}^x$, $g(x) = 3^{-x}$. You can use any positive base except 1 for exponential functions.

- Stated mathematically: if $a > 0$ and $a \neq 1$, then the exponential function with base a is given by $y = a^x$.
- In calculus the choice for the base is e, an irrational number whose decimal approximation is $e \approx 2.71828\ldots$
- e is defined by a limit definition—

$$e = \lim_{x \to 0} (1 + x)^{\frac{1}{x}}$$

- Properties of exponetial functions

$$e^0 = 1$$
$$e^a \cdot e^b = e^{a+b}$$
$$e^a \div e^b = e^{a-b}$$
$$(e^a)^b = e^{ab}$$

- Derivatives of exponential functions—

$$\frac{d}{dx}[e^x] = e^x \quad \text{and} \quad \frac{d}{dx}[e^u] = e^u \frac{du}{dx}$$

where u is a differentiable function of x
- Integrals of exponential functions—

$$\int e^x dx = e^x + c$$
$$\int e^u \frac{du}{dx} dx = e^u + c$$

where u is a differentiable function of x.

LIST 223   NATURAL LOGARITHMIC FUNCTIONS

The exponential function $f(x) = e^x$ is both increasing and continuous. It possesses an inverse called the *natural logarithmic function,* defined as follows:

- $\ln x = b$ if and only if $e^b = x$ ($\ln x$ is read "the natural log of x.")
- Inverse properties of $\ln x$ and e^x—

    $\ln e^x$ and $e^{\ln x} = x$

- Properties of logarithms—

    $\ln 1 = 0$

    $\ln xy = \ln x + \ln y$

    $\ln \dfrac{x}{y} = \ln x - \ln y$

    $\ln x^y = y \ln x$

- Derivatives of natural logarithmic functions—

    $\dfrac{d}{dx}[\ln x] = \dfrac{1}{x}$ and $\dfrac{d}{dx}[\ln u] = \dfrac{1}{u}\dfrac{du}{dx}$

    u is a differentiable function of x.

- Log rule for integration—

    $\int \dfrac{1}{u}\dfrac{du}{dx}dx = \int \dfrac{1}{u}du = \ln|u| + c$

    u is a differentiable function of x.

LIST 224   DERIVATIVES AND INTEGRALS OF TRIGONOMETRIC FUNCTIONS

The six trigonometric functions were defined in List 189, "Right Triangle Defintion of Trigonometric Functions" and List 192, "Circular Function Definition of Trigonometric Functions."

The derivatives and the corresponding integrals are listed below.

$$\frac{d}{dx}[\sin u] = \cos u \frac{du}{dx} \qquad\qquad \int \cos u\; du = \sin u + C$$

$$\frac{d}{dx}[\cos u] = -\sin u \frac{du}{dx} \qquad\qquad \int \sin u\; du = -\cos u + C$$

$$\frac{d}{dx}[\tan u] = \sec^2 u \frac{du}{dx} \qquad\qquad \int \sec^2 u\; du = \tan u + C$$

$$\frac{d}{dx}[\cot u] = -\csc^2 u \frac{du}{dx} \qquad\qquad \int \csc^2 u\; du = -\cot u + C$$

$$\frac{d}{dx}[\sec u] = \sec u \tan u \frac{du}{dx} \qquad\qquad \int \sec u \tan u\; du = \sec u + C$$

$$\frac{d}{dx}[\csc u] = -\csc u \cot u \frac{du}{dx} \qquad\qquad \int \csc u \cot u\; du = -\csc u + C$$

The integrals of the six basic trigonometric functions follow.

$$\int \sin u\; du = -\cos u + C \qquad\qquad \int \cot u\; du = \ln|\sin u| + C$$

$$\int \cos u\; du = \sin u + C \qquad\qquad \int \sec u\; du = \ln|\sec u + \tan u| + C$$

$$\int \tan u\; du = -\ln|\cos u| + C \qquad\qquad \int \csc u\; du = \ln|\csc u - \cot u| + C$$

The Math Teacher's Book of Lists, © 1995 by Prentice Hall

section 6

MATH IN OTHER AREAS

LIST 225   DESCRIPTIVE STATISTICS

Descriptive statistics is a method of collecting, organizing, analyzing, and utilizing numerical data. Suppose a group of test scores of a class of 10 students was 80, 70, 90, 100, 50, 100, 100, 90, 70, and 60. The group can be described statistically, as noted below.

- Data—Facts and figures collected on the same characteristics of a population or sample. In this case, one or more of the scores.
- Population—All of the members of a particular group or item. In the example above, the population is all 10 scores.
- Frequency—The number of times a score or group of scores occurs. The frequency of 50 is 1; 60 is 1; 70 is 2; 80 is 1; 90 is 2, and 100 is 3.
- Mean—The average of all scores, denoted by $\overline{x}$. Adding the scores and dividing by 10 gives a mean of 81.
- Median—The number in the middle when the numbers are ordered from least to greatest or greatest to least. (A good way to remember median is to think of the "median" of a highway, the divider in the center that separates the highway into opposite lanes.) For the test scores of the example, the median is shown as:

  50, 60, 70, 70, 80, 90, 90, 100, 100, 100

  Since there is no "middle" number, take the average of the fifth and sixth numbers. $(80 + 90) \div 2 = 85$. Thus, 85 is the median.
- Mode—The number that appears most often in a group. 100 is the mode of the example because it occurs three times, which is the most of any number.
- Range—The highest score minus the lowest score. $100 - 50 = 50$.

Measures of Central Tendency

Mean, median, and mode are often referred to as the measures of central tendencies. While it is hard to determine which is the most important to use when describing specific data, here are some general guidelines:

- The mode is usually most appropriate for evaluating the quality of a program or situation.
- The median is usually used when the sample is small and the data extreme.
- The mean is usually used when the sample is large.
- Both mode and median are usually unaffected by extreme data.

LIST 226   TYPES OF GRAPHS, DISPLAYS, AND TABLES

We live in a world where we are bombarded by data. One of the best ways to organize and represent information is graphically.

Artistic Graph—displays information pictorially. Unlike a pictograph, which represents data in the form of symbols, an artistic graph uses an illustration to show information.

Bar Graph—uses the lengths of bars to compare data. Bars are separated by spaces. There are single bar graphs and double bar graphs.

Box-and-whisker Plot—displays the median of a set of data, the median of each half of the data, and the least and greatest values of the data. Box-and-whisker plots are used to compare sets of data.

Circle Graph—represents data expressed as parts of a whole. The circle equals 100%. Each part of a circle graph is called a sector. Circle graphs are also known as pie graphs.

Frequency Polygon—a line graph used to represent frequencies. It is made by connecting the midpoints of the tops of the bars of a histogram.

Frequency Table—a table used for organizing a set of data. Frequency tables show the number of times each item of the set occurs.

Histogram—a special kind of bar graph that displays the frequency of data that has been organized into equal distributions.

Line Graph—displays data as points that are connected by line segments. There are single and double line graphs.

Line Plot—a vertical graph that displays information on a number line.

Pictograph—a graph in which a symbol is used to represent data. Values are approximations.

Scattergram—displays relationships between data. Information is represented by unconnected points. A given number may have more than one point on either scale. Points seldom lie in a line.

Stem-and-leaf Plot—represents data where each number is displayed by a stem and a leaf. Stem-and-leaf plots show the value for each piece of data. They may be single or back-to-back.

Trend Line—a line that can be drawn near the points on a scattergram. A trend line is used to make predictions.

LIST 227   PERMUTATIONS

Permutations are arrangements of things in a particular order. The symbolic representation of the total number of arrangements of n things taken r at a time is $_nP_r$.

Permutation Formulas and Applications

- A factorial is a product of all whole numbers less than or equal to a number and is represented as n!

- $n! = n(n - 1)(n - 2)(n - 3) \ldots (3)(2)(1)$.

  For example $6! = (6)(5)(4)(3)(2)(1) = 720$

- $0! = 1$

- $1! = 1$

- To find the total number of arrangements of n things taken r at a time use the formula

$$_nP_r = \frac{n!}{(n-r)!}$$

Application: Suppose you wanted to rearrange the letters of the word "MATH" to form other four-letter arrangements. How many are there? You could list them and get 24 arrangements:

MATH	AMTH	TMAH	HMAT
MAHT	AMHT	TMHA	HMTA
MTAH	ATHM	TAMH	HAMT
MTHA	ATMH	TAHM	HATM
MHAT	AHMT	THAM	HMTA
MHTA	AHTM	THMA	HMAT

Or you could use the formula $_nP_r$ where n = 4 and r = 4. (4 letters taken 4 at a time.)

$$_4P_4 = \frac{4!}{(4-4)!} = \frac{4 \cdot 3 \cdot 2 \cdot 1}{0!} = 24$$

- P_c is the total number of all circular permutations of n things arranged in a circle.

$$P_c = (n - 1)!$$

- Application: Suppose you wanted to arrange the letters of "MATH" in a circle. In a circle there is no first, second, or third position, etc. If one position is fixed as a reference point, then the other three letters may be permutated around it. By making a list there are 6 arrangements.

```
    M           M           M           M           M           M
  A   H       T   H       H   T       A   T       T   A       H   A
    T           A           A           H           H           T
```

LIST 227   (Continued)

Or you could use the formula $P_c = (n - 1)!$ where $n = 4$

$$P_c = (4 - 1)! = 3! = (3)(2)(1) = 6$$

- P_a is the total number of indistinguishable permutations possible for n things when n_1 are alike, n_2 are all alike, and so on.

$$P_a = \frac{n!}{n_1! \, n_2! \, \ldots}$$

- Application: Suppose you want to find all possible arrangements of the letters in the word "THAT." Two letters are indistinguishable: the two Ts. You could make a list:

THAT	HATT	ATHT
THTA	HTAT	ATTH
TAHT	HTTA	AHTT
TATH		
TTAH		
TTHA		

- Or you could use the formula $P_a = \dfrac{n!}{n_1! n_2! \, \ldots}$ where $n = 4$ and $n_1 = 2$

$$P_a = \frac{4!}{2!} = \frac{4 \cdot 3 \cdot 2 \cdot 1}{2 \cdot 1} = 12$$

The Math Teacher's Book of Lists, © 1995 by Prentice Hall

LIST 228   COMBINATIONS

Combinations are a grouping of items without regard to order. The symbolic representation of the total combinations of n things taken r at a time is $_nC_r$.

Combinations Formulas and Applications

- $_nC_r = \dfrac{n!}{r!(n-r)!}$ Note: $n! = n(n-1)(n-2) \ldots (3)(2)(1)$

- $_nC_r = \dfrac{_nP_r}{r!}$ Note: $_nP_r = \dfrac{n!}{(n-r)!}$

- $_nC_n = \dfrac{n!}{n!} = 1$

Here's an example. How many ways may groups of 3 students be chosen from a group of 10? The grouping of three students is important and order is not. In this case, n = 10 and r = 3.

You may use the following formula:

$$_nC_r = \frac{n!}{r!(n-r)!} = \frac{10!}{3!(10-3)!} = \frac{10 \cdot 9 \cdot 8}{3 \cdot 2 \cdot 1} = \frac{720}{3} = 120$$

Or use the following formula which relates combinations to permutations.

$$_nC_r = \frac{_nP_r}{r!} = \frac{\dfrac{10!}{(10-3)!}}{3!} = \frac{10 \cdot 9 \cdot 8}{3 \cdot 2 \cdot 1} = 120$$

Following are intergroup combination formulas.

- $N = {}_{n_1}C_{r_1} \cdot {}_{n_2}C_{r_2} \cdot \ldots \cdot {}_{n_k}C_{r_k}$ is the total number of joint selections possible from k different sets of $n_1, n_2, \ldots n_k$ things taken $r_1, r_2 \ldots r_k$ at a time respectively.
- $N = n_1 n_2 n_3 \ldots n_k$ is a special case where $r_1 = r_2 = r_k = 1$
- $N = n^k$ is a special case where $n_1 = n_2 = \ldots n_k = n$

To apply the intergroup combination formulas, try this question. How many groups of three students may be chosen from four members of Room 101 and five members of Room 102?

In this case, $n_1 = 4$ (possibilities from Room 101)

$n_2 = 5$ (possibilities from Room 102)

$r_1 = r_2 = 3$ (because you are forming groups of three members).

$$N = {}_{n_1}C_{r_1} \cdot {}_{n_2}C_{r_2} = {}_4C_3 \cdot {}_5C_3 = \frac{4!}{3!(4-3)!} \cdot \frac{5!}{3!(5-3)!} = \frac{4}{1} \cdot \frac{5 \cdot 4}{2 \cdot 1} = 40$$

- $M = {}_1C_k + {}_2C_k + \ldots {}_kC_k = 2^k - 1$ where M is the sum of all possible combinations of k things taken 1, 2, 3, . . . and any other number up to and including k, at a time.

    For example, how many different selections can be made of one or more books from a shelf of five books? K = 5 (because you are choosing from 5 books).

$$M = 2^k - 1 = 2^5 - 1 = 32 - 1 = 31$$

LIST 229   PROBABILITY AND ODDS

Throughout the day, we speak in terms of probabilities. "It's probably going to rain," "I'll probably go to a movie tonight," "I'll probably ace the probability test because I studied" are some examples. When stated like this, the speaker believes that the event is likely to happen. If we feel that something is not likely to happen, the event is improbable.

Probability theory is the branch of mathematics that deals with the chances of specific events happening. By assigning measures which can be computed and compared, it tries to take the randomness out of prediction.

Definitions

Experiment—a procedure that has the same possible outcomes every time it is repeated. No single outcome is predictable.

   Example: If you pick a card randomly from a deck of cards, you know you will choose a card, but it is impossible to predict what particular card.

Sample Space—the set of all possible outcomes.

   Example: In the deck of cards the sample space for picking one card is 52, because a complete deck consists of 52 cards.

Event—a subset of a sample space.

   Example: In choosing a card from a deck of 52 cards, an event is picking the two of hearts.

Independent Events—two separate events such that the outcome of one does not affect the outcome of the other.

   Example: If you choose the ace of spades, return it to the deck, and then choose the six of hearts, the events are independent.

Dependent Events—two separate events such that the outcome of one does affect the outcome of the other.

   Example: Choosing the ace of spades, returning it and choosing a card of the same suit. (The suit of the second card depends on the suit of the first.)

Mutually Exclusive Events—two events that cannot both occur at the same time.

   Example: Choosing an ace of spades and a two of hearts when you are only picking *one* card.

Probability Laws

• Probability of A

$$P(A) = \frac{\text{the number of outcomes of Event A}}{\text{the number of possible Outcomes}}$$

The Math Teacher's Book of Lists, © 1995 by Prentice Hall

LIST 229   (Continued)

as long as all outcomes are equally likely.

Example: $P \text{ (ace of spades)} = \dfrac{1}{52} = \dfrac{1 \text{ card}}{\text{total outcomes in the sample space}}$

- Probability of A not occurring

$$P(\text{not A}) = 1 - P(\text{A})$$

as long as all outcomes are equally likely.

Example: The probability of not picking an ace of spades is $1 - \dfrac{1}{52} = \dfrac{51}{52}$.

- $0 \leq$ probability of Event A ≤ 1.
- All the probabilities in any experiment must total 1.
- Probability of A or B

$$P(\text{A or B}) = P(\text{A}) + P(\text{B}) - P(\text{A and B})$$
$$= P(\text{A}) + P(\text{B}) \text{ if A and B are mutually exclusive events}$$

Example: The probability of picking an ace of spades or a two of hearts is
$\dfrac{1}{52} + \dfrac{1}{52} = \dfrac{2}{52} = \dfrac{1}{26}$

- Probability of A and B

$$P(\text{A and B}) = P(\text{A, given B})P(\text{B})$$
$$= P(\text{A})P(\text{B}) \text{ if A and B are independent events}$$

Example: The probability of choosing an ace of spades, returning it, and then picking a two of hearts is $\frac{1}{52} \cdot \frac{1}{52} = \frac{1}{2704}$ because the events are independent.

- Odds of Event A

$$\frac{P(\text{A})}{P(\text{not A})}$$

Example: The odds of choosing an ace of spades is

$$\frac{P(\text{choosing the ace of spades})}{P(\text{not choosing the ace of spades})} = \frac{\dfrac{1}{52}}{\dfrac{51}{52}} = \frac{1}{51}$$

LIST 230   ODDS IN POKER

We are all familiar with the shrewd poker player who bluffs his opponents and wins the big hand. Without question, bluffing is a major part of the game; but poker is, above all else, a game of chance. Every time a game of poker is played, a player may receive any one of a possible 2,598,960 hands. The odds of being dealt a particular hand are a result of mathematics. Knowing the odds helps a player decide when to up the pot or fold.

The following hands are listed in descending order. A full house, for example, beats a flush, but does not beat four of a kind.

Hand	*Definition*	*Odds Against*
Royal Flush	sequence of ten to ace in the same suit	649,739 to 1
Straight Flush	sequence of five cards in the same suit	72,192 to 1
Four of a Kind	four of the same card; four 8s for example	4,164 to 1
Full House	three of a kind and one pair	693 to 1
Flush	five cards of the same suit but not in sequence	508 to 1
Straight	five cards in sequence but of mixed suit	254 to 1
Three of a Kind	three of the same card; for example three 10s	46 to 1
Two Pairs	two sets of the same cards; two queens and two 5s	20 to 1
One Pair	two of the same card; two 9s	1.37 to 1
Empty Hand	no winners	1 to 1

The Math Teacher's Book of Lists, © 1995 by Prentice Hall

LIST 231   ODDS IN DICE

People have been playing dice for thousands of years. Dice are small cubes, which have one, two, three, four, five, or six dots on their six faces. The dots indicate the numbers one through six.

One of the best known dice games is craps. The thrower makes a money bet, which is matched, or covered, by one or more opponents. The thrower then tosses two dice. If he or she throws a 7 or 11, the thrower wins. If the thrower tosses 2, 3, or 12, he or she loses. If any other number results, that number becomes the thrower's point and he or she continues to throw until the same number is thrown, which wins. If the thrower tosses a 7, he or she loses the bet as well as the toss.

Following are the odds on dice for one throw.

Dice Total	Odds Against
2	35 to 1
3	17 to 1
4	11 to 1
5	8 to 1
6	31 to 5
7	5 to 1
8	31 to 5
9	8 to 1
10	11 to 1
11	17 to 1
12	35 to 1

LIST 232   THE CHANCES ARE . . .

Have you ever wondered what the odds are that you might be struck by lightning? Or that you might win the lottery? Or you might be involved in a car accident? Or one day become a movie star? Following are your chances for a variety of occurrences.

Event	Odds
Being struck by lightning	1 in 600,000
Starring in a movie	1 in 385,000
Winning a major lottery	1 in 5,200,000
Dying in a plane crash	1 in 10,000,000
Dying in a train accident	less than 1 in 1,000,000
Being hurt in a car accident	1 in 75
Wearing glasses or contacts at some time in your life	1 in 2
Someday believing you saw a UFO	1 in 10
Having your marriage end in divorce	1 in 2
Someday having a too high cholesterol level	1 in 4
Someday having high blood pressure	2 in 5
As a smoker, finding that you are able to quit on your own	1 in 4
Having a supernatural experience	1 in 15
The chances of your new business still being in business after five years	1 in 2
If you're a golfer, sinking a hole-in-one	1 in 10,700
If you are a baseball pitcher, pitching a no-hitter	1 in 1,300
If you're a pregnant woman, your chances of giving birth to twins	1 in 50

LIST 233 WAYS PEOPLE ARE PAID

People are paid in various ways for the work they do (although of course never enough). The following list provides the ways people are compensated for their work. While bartering, developed during prehistoric times, was probably one of the first methods of exchange, some of the other methods have been around almost as long.

Salary—a fixed rate of payment for services on a regular basis. A salary may be paid weekly, biweekly (two times per month), or monthly.

Commission—payment based on a percentage of sales.

Salary plus commission—payment that is a combination of a set amount (salary), and a percentage of sales (commission).

Hourly wage—a fixed payment based on the amount of hours worked.

Overtime—payment for work done in addition to one's regular hours.

Fee—a fixed payment based on a particular job. For example, a fee for painting a house.

Bonus—an extra payment for a job well done, or a job effort that surpasses what is considered adequate. Sometimes bonuses are given before a major holiday.

Merit pay—similar to a bonus, merit pay is payment for reaching a specific goal or plateau.

Piecework—payment for the number of products completed.

Differential piecework—a payment plan similar to piecework, except that workers are paid more as they move to higher levels of production.

Tip—a small amount of money given in recognition of a service rendered. Also called a gratuity. For many services, a standard tip amounts to 15% of the bill for the service.

Royalties—a share paid to an author or composer out of the proceeds resulting from the sale or performance of the work; also the share paid to an inventor or proprietor for the use of his invention or services. Grantors of mineral leases may be paid in royalties for the use of their land.

Bartering—an exchange of services or products agreed upon by two people. No money changes hands.

LIST 234   DEDUCTIONS

When you are paid by check for the work you do on your job, the amount you receive is always less than the amount you earned. The amount earned is your *gross pay*. The amount you actually receive is called your *net pay* (or take-home pay). The difference is a result of payroll deductions, which are listed below.

Federal Income Withholding Tax—a method by which the U.S. government collects a portion of the income tax that it anticipates you will owe, based on your salary and the number of dependents you claim on your W-4 Withholding form. When more dependents are claimed, less money is withheld. When fewer dependents are claimed, more money is withheld.

Social Security Tax (F.I.C.A.)—the tax levied to sustain the Social Security System.

State Income Tax—for those who live in a state that levies an income tax.

City Income Tax—for those who live in a city that levies an income tax.

Other Possible Deductions—

- Employee's contribution to health, life, and/or disability insurance premiums.
- Savings Bonds.
- Credit Union Dues.
- Union or Agency Dues.
- Savings Plans or Stock Plans.
- Pension Loans.
- Employee's Portion of Unemployment Insurance.

Less Typical Deductions—

- Lost Work Time.
- Court Liens.

To Determine That Your Net Pay Is Correct—

1. Write down the amount of each deduction.
2. Make sure the deduction applies to your check.
3. Add to get a total deduction.
4. Subtract this from your gross pay for the given pay period.

The Math Teacher's Book of Lists, © 1995 by Prentice Hall

LIST 235   HOW TO WRITE AND ENDORSE A CHECK

Checks are a common method of monetary payment, generally accepted in the place of cash. There are specific steps to writing and endorsing checks properly, as the following list shows.

How to Write a Check

- General guidelines:
  - —Use pen.
  - —Write clearly.
  - —Don't leave any blank spaces.
  - —Don't cross out or change any part of the check.
  - —Record the check in the check register (or on the stub).
  - —Make sure you have enough money in the account or the check will not be honored by the bank.
- Fill out the information on the front (or face) of the check.
  - —*Date.* Write the date the check is written.
  - —*Payee's name.* Write the person's name to whom the check is written after "Pay to the order of."
  - —*Amount in numbers.* Write the dollar value close to the dollar sign. Change should be written after a decimal point, for example, $10.95.
  - —*Amount in words.* This is the line below the payee's name. Begin at the extreme left of the line. Start with a capital letter and write out the dollar value of the check. To show change, use the word "and," then the value over 100, for example, "Ten and $\frac{95}{100}$. If any space remains to right, draw a line up to the words or numbers so that no blank space is left.

Ten and $\frac{95}{100}$ _____

LIST 235   (Continued)

—*Memo*. This is optional. You may write what the check is for in this space.

—*Signature*. This is where you write your name. Don't print.

How to Endorse (or Cash) a Check

- To endorse a check payable to you, turn the check over. Write your name, as it appears on the check, on the back at the top of the far left end. (Usually, the words "Endorse here" will be there.)

- Include your checking or savings account number below your name.

- Endorsing allows you to cash, deposit, or transfer to someone else a check made payable to you.

The Math Teacher's Book of Lists, © 1995 by Prentice Hall

LIST 236   HOW TO COMPLETE A CHECK REGISTER

Check registers, forms of check stubs where you can record to whom you write your checks, vary. Some are included at the left of the check, while others are not actually stubs but are a part of a register that contains a record of checks written, fees, deposits, and interest earned. Although they may be different, they all provide you with a place to keep accurate records about your checks, and they all include the same general information.

To Complete a Check Register for Checks

- *Check number.* This is the number of the written check.
- *To.* This is the name of the person, company, or organization to whom the check was written.
- *Date.* The date the check was written.
- *For.* What the check was for.
- *Amount.* The amount of the check. To keep a running tally of how much money is in your account, subtract the current check from the previous balance.

A Note about Fees

- Bank service fees are subtracted from the balance in your account.
- They vary from bank to bank. Some banks charge the following fees on checking accounts—
  —Per check fee.
  —Monthly service fee.
  —A charge for new checks.
  —A penalty fee if your balance drops below a specific amount.
  —A fee for the use of an ATM (automatic teller machine).

A Note about Deposits

- A deposit is an amount you add to your account.
- Deposits are added to the previous balance.
- When you make a deposit, record the date and the amount of the deposit in your check register.
- Keep a receipt of your deposit for your records. (Even banks sometimes make mistakes.)

A Note about Interest-Bearing Checking Accounts

- Some checking accounts pay interest on money in the account.
- The interest will be recorded on the bank statement you receive each month. Add it to your previous balance.

LIST 237   HOW TO BALANCE A CHECKBOOK

Once a month the bank sends a statement which tells you the balance of your checking account. The statement contains a listing of all the checks that have been cashed and deposits you have made, as of the date of the statement. Because banks sometimes make errors, it is a good practice to balance your account according to your check register or check stubs and compare it to the bank's statement. The first step is organization.

Getting Organized

- Checks.
  - —Arrange, in numerical order, the checks that you received with your statement.
  - —Mark, in your register, each one that has cleared (been honored by the bank).
  - —Be sure the amount on the check matches the amount of the check on the statement, as well as the amount of the check recorded in the check register.
  - —On the bank statement, or a separate sheet of paper, list any checks that have not been returned.
  - —If your bank charges a fee for each check you write, multiply the fee by the number of checks returned and deduct this from your balance.
- Be sure all withdrawals and ATM transactions are recorded.
- Check your register and statement to make sure that all deposits appear on each.

Finding Errors

- You're a rare individual if your check register always matches the statement you receive from the bank.
- If your register and bank statement don't agree, here's what to do.
  - —Review your account. Has it been credited correctly? This is where your deposit receipts are vital.
  - —Review your account and make sure it has been debited correctly. Review the check amounts and fees. Has each check been properly paid?
  - —Redo your addition and subtraction.
  - —Make certain that you have copied the balance correctly to start a new page in your register.
- If you made the mistake, recheck everything from that point forward. One error will throw off the rest of the balance.
- If the bank made the mistake, notify the bank. You may need to provide copies of deposit receipts or cashed checks to prove that you're right.

LIST 237   (Continued)

A Few Suggestions on Doing the Math

- Start with the balance shown on the statement.
- Add deposits made since the last statement.
- Subtract any outstanding checks from the statement that have not been honored by your bank. Note that these will not yet be debited from the statement.
- Subtract any checks you've written since the time of the statement. Note that these will not yet be debited.
- Subtract any check fees.
- Add any interest. (Some checking accounts offer interest if a minimal balance is maintained.)
- The balance on the statement should equal the balance in your register.

LIST 238   LOANS AND INTEREST

Unless you borrow money from a generous friend or relative, you will have to repay the loan with interest. Following are some facts about loans and interest.

- A *loan* is a sum of money that is lent at interest. When you borrow money, the money you borrowed becomes a loan.

- *Interest* is the cost to you of using someone else's money. It is a fee that banks, for example, charge for lending money.

- Interest rates vary, based on the economy and the type of loan. Generally, the longer you take a loan, the more interest you will pay.

- Loans can be repaid over time. For small purchases, a loan might last a year or two. When you buy a car, you might take a loan for between one and five years, but when you buy a house, your loan (called a mortgage) might be for 15, 20, 25, or 30 years.

- The typical loan is repaid in monthly payments. As you repay the loan, you will be paying off the amount of money you borrowed, plus the interest. (When you borrow money that is to be repaid with interest, you always pay back more than you borrowed.)

- Since interest is calculated on the amount of money you borrow, it is helpful to "put down" as much of your own money as you can to reduce the amount of the loan. The lower the amount of the loan, the less total interest you will pay (given the same interest rate and time).

The following formula may be used to calculate the monthly payment necessary to repay borrowed money at interest.

$$M = \frac{A\left(\dfrac{r}{12}\right)\left(1 + \dfrac{r}{12}\right)^n}{\left(1 + \dfrac{r}{12}\right)^n - 1}$$

M = monthly payment, A = amount borrowed, r = annual rate of interest, n = the number of months of the loan

The Math Teacher's Book of Lists, © 1995 by Prentice Hall

LIST 239   STEPS TO MAKING A BUDGET

A budget is an excellent tool for keeping track of your money. A good budget contains your sources of income and your expenses.

1. Decide if you need a weekly or monthly budget. If you choose a weekly budget, you will work with income and expenses for the week. If you choose a monthly budget, your income and expenses will be calculated over a four-week period. For most people a monthly budget is more practical.

2. Take a sheet of paper. Label the left side "Income" and the right side "Expenses."

3. List all of your sources of income. Include money you earn from jobs, allowances, and gifts. (If a source of income varies, or if you are unsure about it, underestimate its amount.)

4. Add up the total amount of money you receive.

5. List all of your expenses.

   • Include all fixed expenses such as bills, the cost of food, lunches, clothing, entertainment, recreation, etc. (Some people like to include money committed to savings as an expense. This way they are certain to budget for it.)

   • Estimate miscellaneous expenses for such things as sports equipment, special events, gifts, replacement parts for equipment that might break down and need repair, etc.

6. Add up all of your expenses, and subtract the total from your total income.

   • If your income equals your expenses, your budget is balanced.

   • If your income exceeds your expenses, you have a profit. You may save the extra money or keep it handy for unexpected expenses.

   • If your expenses exceed your income, you must spend less or find new sources of income.

LIST 240   THE COSTS OF RUNNING MAJOR APPLIANCES

There are many different appliances in our homes. Since they all require electricity to operate, the number of appliances you have, and the hours they are used, can add up to big electric bills.

You can easily figure out how much it costs you to run your major appliances with the help of the list below. First, you must find out how much your electric company charges for electricity per kilowatt hour. (A kilowatt hour is a thousand watts per hour, and is a standard in computing electrical usage.) This information is on your monthly bill. Multiply the kilowatts the appliance requires times the hours it is used. This gives you the total kilowatt hours for the use of the appliance, which you then multiply by the cost of electricity.

kilowatts × hours used × cost = cost per month

Suppose your air-conditioner uses 1.5 kilowatts, it was used 80 hours in July, and your electric company charges you 14¢ per kilowatt hour. Using the formula above:

1.5 × 80 × .14 = $16.80

Your air-conditioner cost $16.80 to operate during July.

The following list shows the kilowatt requirements of several appliances. Exact information about the energy consumption for specific models is usually included in the owner's manual. Your costs will be affected by your model and how much you use it.

Appliance	Kilowatts Required
air-conditioner	1.5
blow dryer for hair	1.5
coffee maker	1.1
dishwasher	1.3
dryer	4.5
hot water heater	4.5
iron	1.3
microwave oven	0.9
refrigerator	0.5
space heater	1.5
stove	0.5
toaster	1.2
TV (color)	0.3
washing machine	0.5

The Math Teacher's Book of Lists, © 1995 by Prentice Hall

LIST 241   ITEMS ON SALE

Everybody likes to buy things on sale. Sales always give you a good deal. Or do they? Sale signs or notices may express the value of the sale by telling you the dollar savings off the original price, or they may offer only the percent savings, in which case you'll need to do some fast figuring to see how much you'll really save.

The following list offers some important words you'll need to know to understand the true value of a sale, as well as some formulas you can use to see how good your buy actually is.

Regular price (or marked price)—the price of an item when it is not on sale.

Sale price—the price of an item that is on sale.

Discount—the dollar amount saved (off the regular price.)

Rate of discount (percent off)—the fraction of the original price that is saved when an item is bought on sale.

Common Formulas for Discount and Sale Price

Discount = Regular Price − Sale Price

or

Discount = Rate of Discount × Regular Price

Sale Price = (1 − Rate of Discount) × Regular Price

It is also possible to calculate the values of any of the four terms above if you are given two other values. The following abbreviations are used in the formulas below:

R = Regular Price

S = Sale Price

D = Discount

P = Rate of Discount (expressed as a fraction or decimal)

To Find	Given	Use
Sale Price	Regular Price and Discount	$S = R - D$
	Regular Price and Rate of Discount	$S = (1 - P)R$
	Rate of Discount and Discount	$S = (D \div P) - D$
Discount	Regular Price and Sale Price	$D = R - S$
	Rate of Discount and Regular Price	$D = PR$
	Rate of Discount and Sale Price	$D = [S \div (1 - P)] - S$
Rate of Discount	Regular Price and Sale Price	$P = 1 - \dfrac{S}{R}$
	Regular Price and Discount	$P = 1 - \dfrac{R - D}{R}$
	Sale Price and Discount	$P = 1 - \dfrac{S}{S + D}$
Regular Price	Sale Price and Original	$R = S + D$
	Sale Price and Rate of Discount	$R = S \div (1 - P)$
	Discount and Rate of Discount	$R = D \div P$

LIST 241   (Continued)

Examples:

1. To find the sale price given a regular price of $50 and a discount of $10, use the formula

$$S = R - D$$
$$= 50 - 10$$
$$= 40$$

2. To find the regular price given the discount of $10 and the rate of discount of 20%, use the formula

$$R = D \div P$$
$$= 10 \div .2$$
$$= 50$$

Here's a shortcut for mental calculations to estimate the discount. It works only with percents that can be reduced to fractions with numerators of 1.

> Example: 25% off the original price of $29.95. Round $29.95 to $30. Since 25% = ¼, divide $30 by 4, which equals $7.50. Your savings would be about $7.50.

Additional examples to find the discount.

50% off. 50% = ½. Divide the original price by 2.

33⅓% off. 33⅓% = ⅓. Divide the original price by 3.

20% off. 20% = ⅕. Divide the original price by 5.

10% off. 10% = ¹⁄₁₀. Divide the original price by 10.

5% off. 5% = ¹⁄₂₀. Divide the original price by 20.

LIST 242   HOW MUCH TO TIP

When others render a service—for example, a waiter taking an order and bringing food—the customer "tips" him. For many people in the service industry, tips are a major source of their income. The standard tip for most services is 15% of the bill. If you've been given superior service, you might tip up to 20%, but if you are dissatisfied, you might leave only 10%. Not every service requires a percentage tip, however. After all, you wouldn't tip a parking attendant 15% of your dinner bill for parking your car. The following list shows common tip amounts.

- At the barbershop—15% of the bill.
- A bartender—15%–20% of the bill.
- At the beauty salon—15–20% for the stylist; $1–$2 for the person who shampoos your hair.
- Bellboy—$1 per bag; an extra dollar for opening the door to your room or opening the window.
- Bus tour guide—at least $1 per half-day.
- A caterer—15%–20% of the bill.
- Chambermaid—$2 per day.
- Coat check—$1 per coat.
- Doorman at a hotel—$1 for each bag he carries into the hotel for you.
- Drivers of hired limousines—10% of the bill.
- Manicurist—15%–20%.
- Parking attendant—$1–$2 for parking your car.
- Pedicurist—15%–20%.
- Pet groomer—15% of the cost for grooming your pet.
- Restroom attendant—50¢–$1 for handing you a towel.
- Taxis—15%–20% of the fare.
- Valet at a hotel—$2–$3 for performing special services for you.
- Waiter or waitress—15%–20% of the bill.
- Wine steward—10% of the wine check.

LIST 243 TIP SHEET

A standard tip, or gratuity, is 15%. Unless they have a calculator handy, people usually try to estimate 15% of their bill, doing some fast mental math. The list below provides those calculations for tips on bills up to $100.00. Reviewing the list not only shows the amount of a 15% tip, it also shows a useful application of percent. (Note: the bills are rounded off for practicality.)

Bill	15%	Bill	15%
$ 1.00	$ .15	$32.00	$ 4.80
2.00	.30	33.00	4.95
3.00	.45	34.00	5.10
4.00	.60	35.00	5.25
5.00	.75	36.00	5.40
6.00	.90	37.00	5.55
7.00	1.05	38.00	5.70
8.00	1.20	39.00	5.85
9.00	1.35	40.00	6.00
10.00	1.50	41.00	6.15
11.00	1.65	42.00	6.30
12.00	1.80	43.00	6.45
13.00	1.95	44.00	6.60
14.00	2.10	45.00	6.75
15.00	2.25	46.00	6.90
16.00	2.40	47.00	7.05
17.00	2.55	48.00	7.20
18.00	2.70	49.00	7.35
19.00	2.85	50.00	7.50
20.00	3.00		
21.00	3.15	Increases now in tens	
22.00	3.30	60.00	9.00
23.00	3.45		
24.00	3.60	70.00	10.50
25.00	3.75		
26.00	3.90	80.00	12.00
27.00	4.05		
28.00	4.20	90.00	13.50
29.00	4.35		
30.00	4.50	100.00	15.00
31.00	4.65		

LIST 244   STOCK MARKET WORDS

The stock market is the foundation of America's economy. It is the arena where stocks (shares of ownership in a company) and bonds (long term debts) are traded. For businesses, the stock market is a place where they can raise money to operate and expand their enterprises. For people who wish to invest money, the stock market offers a chance to buy shares in a company and benefit from the company's growth. The following list contains the words you'll need to become a savvy investor.

Bear—an investor who expects stock prices to fall.

Bear Market—a period of generally falling stock prices.

Bid—the price a dealer says he will pay for stocks or bonds at a given time.

Blue Chips—stocks of companies that are industry leaders.

Board of Governors—the officials of the New York Stock Exchange who oversee the trading of stocks and bonds.

Bond—a certificate, written and sold by the government or a company, that promises to repay, with interest, borrowed money.

Bondholder—an individual or institution that owns a bond or bonds.

Bull—an investor who expects stock prices to rise.

Bull Market—a period of generally rising stock prices.

Call—an option to buy stock at a pre-set price until a given date.

Commission—the fee a stockbroker receives from a customer for buying or selling a stock.

Common Stock—the typical method by which a company divides its ownership. Owners of common stock have the right to vote at stockholders' meetings and receive dividends (if the company distributes dividends after payments are made to any preferred stockholders and bondholders.)

Corporation—a group of people who obtain a charter or certificate of incorporation, which gives them specific legal rights in the operation of their business.

Director—the principal official of a company; he or she is elected by the stockholders to oversee the management of the company. Directors choose the officers who manage the company.

Dividend—money a corporation pays to its stockholders.

Dow-Jones Averages—the average price of 65 important stocks traded on the New York Stock Exchange. Investors often judge the general performance of the overall market based on the Dow-Jones Average.

Earnings—the profits of a company.

LIST 244   (Continued)

Floor Brokers—brokers who trade stocks and bonds on the exchange floor for member firms. They are also called commission brokers.

Go Public—the action of a private company deciding to sell stock to the public.

Incorporate—the act of starting a corporation.

Institutional Investors—Organizations that invest money which has been entrusted to them by others.

Interest—payment for the use of money.

Investor—an individual who buys stocks or bonds with the hopes of earning a profit.

Margin—an investment method in which an investor buys stocks or bonds partly on credit, borrowing some of the amount due for the purchase from his broker.

Market Price—the current price of stocks or bonds.

Municipal Bonds—Bonds issued by units of government other than the federal government. Interest on municipal bonds paid to investors usually is exempt from federal tax.

Mutual Funds—companies that invest money entrusted to them by others.

Odd Lots—a purchase or sale of stock less than the normal unit of trading, usually less than 100 shares.

Odd-Lot Dealers—brokers who specialize in buying and selling odd lots.

Offer—the price for which a dealer will sell stock at a given time.

Offering—the initial public sale of stock by an underwriter.

Officer—a company official who is elected by the Board of Directors. A company's officers typically include a president, vice-president, secretary, and treasurer.

Options—contracts that permit investors to buy or sell stocks at a prearranged price during a given time period.

Over-the-Counter Broker—a broker who buys and sells over-the-counter stocks.

Over-the-Counter Market—stocks that are not traded on a stock exchange.

Partnership—a company owned by two or more people.

Portfolio—the total list of stocks and bonds owned by an investor.

Preferred Stock—stock on which dividends must be paid first, before dividends can be paid to owners of common stock.

Profit—the money earned by a company.

LIST 244   (Continued)

Prospectus—a booklet that contains information about a company that issues stocks and bonds to the public.

Quote—the current price of a stock or bond.

Rate of Return—the percentage of interest or dividends earned on money that is invested.

Regional Exchange—a stock exchange located at a place other than in New York City.

Registered Representative—the representative of a brokerage house who offers financial advice to customers and buys and sells stocks and bonds for them.

Seat—membership in a stock exchange.

Securities and Exchange Commission (SEC)—the agency of the federal government that is responsible for regulating the buying and selling of securities.

Securities—stocks, bonds, and notes bought and sold on the stock exchanges.

Single Proprietorship—a business owned by one person.

Speculator—an individual who invests in risky ventures and stocks in hopes of realizing high profits.

Stockbroker—an individual who is a member of the stock exchange and can buy and sell stocks on the exchange.

Stock Certificate—a certificate that shows the number of shares an investor owns.

Stockholder—an individual who owns stock in a corporation.

Ticker Tape—a ribbon-like tape on which a ticker machine prints stock prices.

Underwriter—an investment bank that buys new stocks from a corporation for the purpose of reselling them to brokers who represent investors.

Warrant—an option that allows investors to buy a given number of common shares of stock at a given price during a specific period of time.

Yield—the amount of interest or dividends an investment earns.

LIST 245   READING A FINANCIAL PAGE

The listing of stock prices on a financial page may look complicated, but it's not as confusing as it may first seem. Here's how to do it.

- Read the information from left to right. Remember that the prices of stocks are quoted in fractions of a dollar, such as 23¼ or 23½.

- "Hi" gives the highest price of the stock over the last 52 weeks. A new high for the year is indicated by an arrow to the left pointing up.

- "Lo" gives the lowest price of the stock over the last 52 weeks. A new low for the year is indicated by an arrow to the left pointing down.

- "Stock" tells you the company's name. Names are abbreviated.

- "Sym" indicates the official symbol of the stock. This is the same symbol that appears on the ticker tape. The symbols "pf" or "pr" tell you if the stock is preferred. If these letters are absent, you know that the stock is common stock. The symbol "Wt" after a company's name means that the quotation is for a warrant. A warrant allows its owner to buy a specific amount of common stock at a pre-set price for a certain amount of time. The letter "S" means that the stock has been split (or divided) recently, and "N" means that the stock is new, having been issued during the last 52 weeks.

- "Div" tells you the cash dividend per share. A dividend is the money from its profits that a company pays to its stockholders. A blank in this column means that the company hasn't paid dividends.

- "Yld %" states the company's yield. This is the stock's return on the stockholder's investment. You can determine the yield of a stock by dividing the dividend by the closing price. When you divide, work your answer out in decimals and round off to hundredths. Change your decimal answer to its percent equivalent; this will be the yield.

- "PE" is the P-E Ratio (price-earnings ratio). It tells you the relationship between the price of the stock and the company's annual earnings. A P/E of 15 means that the price of the stock is 15 times that of the company's earnings per share over the last four quarters. Stocks that are highly sought by investors usually have high P/E Ratios while those that are unpopular usually have low ones.

- "Vol 100s" provides information on the volume of shares of the stock traded on the previous day. Take the number in the column and multiply it by 100 to find how many shares were traded yesterday. The letter "z" before the number means that you should not multiply by 100, because the number that appears is the total.

LIST 245 (Continued)

- "Hi" provides the stock's highest price yesterday.

- "Lo" provides the stock's lowest price yesterday.

- "Close" provides the stock's closing price of yesterday.

- "Net Chg," net change, shows the difference between the closing price for the day and the day before. A minus (−) sign tells you that the closing price is lower today than it was yesterday; a plus (+) sign tells you that it is higher. Bold type on these numbers means that the price of the stock changed 5% or more.

Note: The above information describes listings on the New York Stock Exchange. Listings for over-the-counter stocks vary somewhat. The listings may also vary a little in local newspapers, but all provide the important information.

LIST 246   HOW TO READ THE NEW FOOD LABEL

Reading the labels that accompany the foods you buy can help you select foods for a healthy diet, which may reduce your risks for developing certain diseases. Too much sodium (salt), for instance, causes high blood pressure in some people; in others, too much cholesterol may eventually lead to a heart attack. The following list spells out how to read a food label.

SERVING SIZE

This tells you how much of the food is usually served at one meal. All of the amounts of nutrients, fats, and sodium are calculated upon a single serving. If you eat twice as much as the serving size on the label, you must double the values. If you eat about half of the serving size noted, you'll need to divide the values by 2.

CALORIES

Knowing the amount of calories you consume each day can help you to lose or gain weight.

TOTAL FAT

Most people should reduce the amount of fat they consume. Try to select foods in which the number of calories from fat are significantly less than the total calories.

SATURATED FAT

Saturated fat plays a major role in raising blood cholesterol and your risk for heart disease. Look for foods low in saturated fat.

CHOLESTEROL

Cholesterol also has been linked to heart disease. For many people, the more cholesterol they have in their blood, the greater their chances for suffering a heart attack. Most doctors recommend limiting cholesterol to less than 300 mg each day.

SODIUM

Sodium is another name for salt. For some people too much can lead to high blood pressure, which in turn has been linked to heart disease and strokes. Try keeping your sodium intake between 2,400 and 3,000 mg (or less) each day.

TOTAL CARBOHYDRATE

Carbohydrates are an important source of nutrients for your body. Foods high in carbohydrates are a good choice for most people.

The Math Teacher's Book of Lists, © 1995 by Prentice Hall

LIST 246   (Continued)

PROTEIN

Most Americans eat diets high in protein. While protein is important to good health, most of us eat more protein than we need. Most sources of animal protein also contain fat and cholesterol.

VITAMINS AND MINERALS

Vitamins and minerals are essential for good health. By eating a variety of foods, you should be able to achieve 100% of the vitamins and minerals you need each day.

DAILY VALUE

This helps to put the numbers in perspective. The Daily Value is based on people who eat 2,000 calories each day. If you eat more, your personal Daily Value may be higher; if you eat less, it may be lower.

KEY WORDS ON FOOD LABELS

Fat Free—contains less than 0.5 gram of fat per serving.

Low Fat—contains 3 or less grams of fat per serving.

Lean—contains less than 10 grams of fat, 4 grams of saturated fat, and 95 milligrams of cholesterol per serving.

Light or Lite—contains less calories or no more than ½ the fat of the version of the food with more calories and more fat, or no more than ½ the sodium of the higher-sodium version.

Cholesterol Free—contains less than 2 milligrams of cholesterol and 2 grams or less of saturated fat per serving.

The Math Teacher's Book of Lists, © 1995 by Prentice Hall

Nutrition Facts

Serving Size ½ cup (114g)
Servings Per Container 4

Amount Per Serving

Calories 90   Calories from Fat 30

	% Daily Value*
Total Fat 3g	5%
Saturated Fat 0g	0%
Cholesterol 0mg	0%
Sodium 300mg	13%
Total Carbohydrate 13g	4%
Dietary Fiber 3g	12%
Sugars 3g	
Protein 3g	

Vitamin A	80%	•	Vitamin C	60%
Calcium	4%	•	Iron	4%

* Percent Daily Values are based on a 2,000 calorie diet. Your daily values may be higher or lower depending on your calorie needs:

		Calories 2,000	2,500
Total Fat	Less than	65g	80g
Sat Fat	Less than	20g	25g
Cholesterol	Less than	300mg	300mg
Sodium	Less than	2,400mg	2,400mg
Total Carbohydrate		300g	375g
Fiber		25g	30g

Calories per gram:
Fat 9 • Carbohydrate 4 • Protein 4

More nutrients may be listed on some labels.

LIST 247   THE CHOLESTEROL CONTENT OF POPULAR FOODS

The fat in the diets of Americans has been linked to greater risks for heart disease and a variety of cancers. Most researchers believe that the fat in a person's diet should be less than 30%. For most people, that's a hard goal to reach because many of the foods we enjoy, especially processed ones, are high in fat.

While there are different kinds of fat, the one most diets attempt to control is cholesterol. Foods low in cholesterol also tend to be low in saturated fats, which have been implicated in disease. Avoiding foods high in cholesterol generally reduces the overall amount of fat in a person's diet.

As you look through the list, you'll see that fish, poultry, fruits, and vegetables usually have less fat than other foods. It is for this reason that nutritionists urge people to eat more of these foods.

Both calories and the amount of cholesterol in milligrams are provided in the following list. "—" means that the amount of cholesterol is negligible.

Food	Calories	Cholesterol (mg)
Meat and Dairy Products		
3 oz haddock	134	63
3 oz halibut	155	52
3 oz baked cod	152	63
3 oz salmon	145	54
3 oz bluefish	132	63
3 oz canned tuna	168	54
3 oz chicken (no skin)	169	54
3 oz cooked turkey	170	67
3 oz roast turkey	200	67
3 oz lean roast veal	194	81
3 oz veal cutlet	186	81
4 oz roast lamb	256	84
1 egg (boiled)	78	165
1 egg (omelet)	106	165
1 egg (scrambled)	106	165
2 slices of bacon	98	20
1 hot dog	126	55
1 beef hamburger	102	76
3 oz round beef	198	76
3 oz liver	177	270
3 oz sirloin tip roast (fat trimmed)	156	69
3 oz pork tenderloin	142	26
3 oz spareribs (lean)	285	121
2 slices of ham	172	63
2 slices of bologna	124	60
2 slices of salami	165	55
2 sausages	312	67
4 oz lobster	104	240
4 oz shrimp	104	150

The Math Teacher's Book of Lists, © 1995 by Prentice Hall

LIST 247   (Continued)

Food	Calories	Cholesterol (mg)
6 oysters	101	500
3 oz crab	88	113
1 oz American cheese	82	16
1 oz Swiss cheese	107	26
1 oz Parmesan cheese	129	22
1 oz cheddar cheese	104	36
1 tsp butter	36	13
8 oz whole milk	146	11
1 cup of buttermilk	81	1
1 cup of nonfat milk	88	—
1 oz sour cream	61	12

Fruits and Juices

Food	Calories	Cholesterol (mg)
1 medium apple	87	—
1 peach	46	—
1 pear	63	—
2 plums	57	—
1 tangerine	50	—
½ grapefruit	75	—
1 orange	70	—
½ cantaloupe	60	—
¼ honeydew	42	—
½ cup of cherries	61	—
½ cup of grapes	54	—
½ cup of watermelon	28	—
½ cup of apricots	54	—
½ cup of raspberries	35	—
½ cup of strawberries	28	—
½ cup apple juice	63	—
½ cup grapefruit juice	66	—

Vegetables

Food	Calories	Cholesterol (mg)
3 celery stalks	9	—
1 pepper	17	—
1 cucumber	6	—
6 mushrooms	7	—
3 asparagus spears	11	—
1 baked potato	139	—
½ cup of mashed potatoes	94	—
1 tomato	22	—
½ cup of tomatoes	23	—
½ cup of tomato juice	25	—
3 lettuce leaves	20	—
½ cup of broccoli	22	—
½ cup of Brussels sprouts	31	—

LIST 247   (Continued)

Food	Calories	Cholesterol (mg)
½ cup of beets	34	—
½ cup of carrots	22	—
½ cup of green beans	14	—
½ cup of cabbage	12	—
½ cup of peas	73	—
½ cup of spinach	23	—

Breads and Cereals

1 slice of white bread	62	—
1 slice of whole wheat	56	—
½ cup of oatmeal	74	—
½ cup of cornflakes	50	—
½ cup of branflakes	58	—
½ cup of puffed wheat	21	—
½ cup of noodles	54	—

Spreads and Dressings

1 tsp margarine	36	—
1 tbsp jelly	50	—
1 tbsp peanut butter	92	—
1 tsp butter	36	13
1 tbsp mayonnaise	110	—
1 tbsp Italian	69	—
1 tbsp Russian	76	—
1 tbsp French	67	—
1 tbsp blue cheese	77	—

Snacks and Desserts

1 oz milk chocolate	145	6
1 doughnut	210	20
1 doughnut (glazed)	235	21
1 oz potato chips	147	0
1 oz corn chips	155	25
4 chocolate chip cookies	185	18
1 piece of cream pie	450	8
1 piece of cake	110	64
1 cup of ice cream	270	59

A few additional notes: The serving sizes above are basics. People often eat more than the portions listed. Also realize that the caloric content and amount of cholesterol in foods may increase because of the way they are cooked or served. For example, chicken is considered to be a low-fat, low-cholesterol food. Chicken fried in fat is not. While a baked potato has a negligible amount of cholesterol, once it's topped with butter the cholesterol increases significantly.

The Math Teacher's Book of Lists, © 1995 by Prentice Hall

LIST 248   A BASIC, LOW-FAT MEAL PLAN

Most doctors and researchers agree that a low-fat diet that controls cholesterol and limits the amount of saturated fat is good for a person's health. By following a diet-plan like the one below you'll reduce your risk of heart disease and
some types of cancer.

Breakfast

1 serving of fruit or juice
1 serving of cereal with nonfat milk
2 servings of bread (with margarine or jelly)
1 serving of coffee, tea, or nonfat milk

Lunch

1 serving of fish or poultry
1 serving of potato
1 serving of cooked vegetable
1 serving of raw vegetable
1 serving of bread (with margarine if preferred)
1 serving of fruit
1 serving of nonfat milk or juice

Dinner

1 serving of meat, fish, or poultry
1 serving of potato, rice, or noodles
1 serving of cooked vegetable
1 serving of raw vegetables (in a salad with light dressing if preferred)
1 serving of bread (with margarine if preferred)
1 serving of coffee, tea, or nonfat milk
1 serving of fruit

Snacks

any serving of fruits
any serving of nonfat or low-fat snacks

(Note: Many snack foods are high in fats.)

LIST 249   FATTY FAST FOOD

Almost everybody likes fast food. What could be more convenient than cruising into a fast-food restaurant, placing your order, and getting a tasty meal at a reasonable price? You can even have it your way. It's too bad that most fast foods are loaded with fat. That's one of the reasons they taste so good, and the major reason why you should eat them in moderation. The following list, which provides the calories and total fat in grams, is based on an average of the foods served at various fast food chains.

Food	Calories	Total Fat (gm)
Regular hamburger	255	9.8
Large hamburger	425	21.5
Regular cheeseburger	310	14.3
Double hamburger	560	32.0
Fish sandwich	400	16.0
Regular hot dog	270	15.0
Large hot dog	518	30.0
Fried chicken (drumstick)	136	8.0
Fried chicken (wing)	151	10.5
Fried chicken (thigh)	276	19.0
Taco	185	8.0
French fries	214	10.0
Pizza	500	14.5

For most people, just one fast-food meal provides them with more than their daily requirement of fat.

The Math Teacher's Book of Lists, © 1995 by Prentice Hall

LIST 250   PHYSICAL ACTIVITIES AND CALORIE EXPENDITURE

Just about everyone knows that physical activity burns calories. But how much depends on the activity and the individual. The following list contains estimates of the amount of calories you'd burn each hour for each pound you weigh, as you took part in various activities. You'll need to compute your caloric expenditures based on your weight.

Here's the computation:

$$\text{Your Weight} \times \text{Time} \times \text{Cal./hr./lb.} = \text{Total Calories}$$

Suppose you weigh 120 pounds and play tennis (singles) for 2 hours. Multiply $120 \times 2 \times 2.9$, which equals 696 calories. This means that you expended 696 calories during those 2 hours.

Activity	Cal./hr./lb. (Calories per hour per pound)
Ballroom Dancing	1.6
Chopping Wood (ax)	2.3
Cycling	2.5
Disco Dancing	2.6
Gardening	3.2
Golf (walking)	2.3
Housecleaning	1.6
Jogging	4.2
Jumping Rope	3.8
Mowing the Lawn	2.7
Racquetball	4.0
Raking Leaves	1.5
Rowing Machine	3.1
Shoveling Snow	3.9
Skating	2.6
Skiing (cross-country)	3.7
Skiing (downhill)	2.5
Soccer	3.7
Swimming	3.8
Tennis (singles)	2.9
Tennis (doubles)	1.8
Volleyball	2.2
Walking (briskly)	2.4
Weight Training	1.9

LIST 251   FINDING YOUR EXERCISE
HEART RATE

While exercise is important for good health, overdoing exercise can be dangerous. One of the best ways to find out if you're doing too much is to know the safe levels of your heart rate during exercise, commonly referred to as your exercise heart-rate range. It is based on the number of beats your heart makes in one minute. (Note: If you've been a couch potato much of your life, are overweight, or suffer from a chronic illness, consult your doctor before undertaking any exercise program. When you begin an exercise program, go slow and gradually build up your endurance and strength.)

The American College of Sports Medicine (ACSM) recommends that you find both 55% and 90% of your maximum safe heart rate. These numbers will serve as the low and high points of your exercise range.

You can find your safe heart-rate range by doing the following:

1. Start with 220, which is the maximum recommended heart rate.

2. Subtract your age. This gives you *your* predicted safe maximum heart rate.

3. To find 55% of your safe maximum heart rate, multiply your safe maximum heart rate (Step 2) by .55. This answer will be the low point of your exercise heart-rate range.

4. To find 90% of your safe maximum heart rate, multiply your safe maximum heart rate (Step 2) by .9. This answer will be the high point of your exercise heart-rate range.

5. During exercise or immediately afterward, measure your heart rate by taking your pulse. Here's how—

    • Take your first two fingers (not your thumb), and press lightly on the carotid artery just beneath your chin. It's almost in a straight line down from the corner of your eye. You may also use the pulse close to your thumb or wrist if you wish.

    • Count the number of beats for 10 seconds.

    • Multiply by six, which will adjust the number for the length of a minute. Your pulse should be within the high and low points of your range. If it is too high, slow down; if it is too low and you are not winded or tired, work a little harder.

    • Periodically check your pulse rate throughout your workouts. Pay close attention to signs that you're overdoing it. Symptoms such as dizziness, faintness, having trouble catching your breath, excessive sweating, or a pounding in your chest are your body's way of telling you to slow down.

The Math Teacher's Book of Lists, © 1995 by Prentice Hall

LIST 252   THE NUMBERS IN POPULAR SPORTS

We often take numbers for granted, seldom realizing how important they are to our lives. Consider sports. Few sports could be played and enjoyed without numbers. How would the score be kept? How could statistics be compiled? How could field sizes be made standard? The following examples show just how important numbers are to many of the sports we watch and play. (For fun, see how many math words and numbers you can find in the following list.)

Baseball

- The game is played on a level field. The infield is called a diamond but it's really a square with sides 90 feet long. Starting with home plate, at each corner is a base. Each corner is a 90° angle.

- The outfield is flat. Foul lines extend from the first and third baselines to foul poles. Within these lines is fair territory; outside of them is foul territory.

- The distance from home plate to the outfield varies according to park. The area in foul territory also varies. When the distance to the outfield wall is short, the field is sometimes called a "hitter's park" because it is easier to hit home runs there than in other parks. When the distance is long and there is plenty of foul territory, the field is a "pitcher's park." Balls that would be homers in other parks become long fly outs, and fielders have lots of room to catch foul pops.

- In a standard game, there are nine fielders. Rosters vary according to league. Professional teams usually carry 25 players.

- The standard baseball is between 9 and 9¼ inches in diameter and weighs between 5 and 5¼ ounces. Bats are long and rounded, made of wood or aluminum. (Only wooden bats may be used in professional baseball.)

- Professional games are nine innings long, with six outs per inning, three for each side. The team that scores the most runs wins.

Football

- American football is played on a field 120 yards long, including the end zones, and 53 yards wide. It is 100 yards from goal line to goal line. The field is divided every five yards by a line.

- At the end lines are goal posts. They may be two parallel uprights extending at least 20 feet from the ground and connected by a crossbar; or as in professional football, the goal posts are one upright post, 10 feet high and topped by a horizontal crossbar from the ends of which extend two vertical uprights.

- Points are tallied in several ways: touchdowns—7 points, extra points after touchdowns—1 point when kicked through the uprights, or 2 when passed or carried across the goal line, field goals—3 points, or safeties—2 points.

- Each team fields 11 players. There is usually a team for offense and a team for defense.

LIST 252   (Continued)

- The professional and college game is played in four 15-minute quarters.
- A football is a prolate spheroid. Its circumference is between 28 and 28½ inches at its long axis and 21¼ to 21½ inches at its short axis. It weighs between 14 and 15 ounces.

Basketball

- A basketball court is a rectangle, no more than 94 feet by 50 feet, and no less than 74 feet by 42 feet.
- The court is divided in half by a center line.
- At center court is the center court circle used to start the game with a jump ball. The circle is actually two concentric circles. The inside circle has a radius of two feet and the outside one has a radius of six feet.
- At both ends of the court are vertical backboards, usually six feet by four feet. Attached to the backboards are baskets, 10 feet above the floor. Each basket is 18 inches in diameter and consists of a horizontal hoop of cloth or thin-chain mesh.
- Fifteen feet from the backboard is the foul line; players shoot foul shots from behind the line.
- Each basketball team fields five players on the court, although teams may have rosters of 12 or more, depending on the league.
- In the pros, games are 48 minutes long, divided into four periods of 12 minutes each. In college, games are 40 minutes long, divided into two halves of 20 minutes each.
- A basketball is a rubber- or leather-covered sphere with a circumference of 30 inches. It weighs 20 to 22 ounces.
- Points are scored when the ball is put through the opponents' basket. Field goals are worth 2 points, and foul shots count as 1. Long shots from behind the three-point line count as 3 points.

Soccer

- Soccer, known as football in many parts of the world, is played on a rectangular field not more than 130 yards long by 100 yards wide, and not less than 100 yards by 50 yards.
- At either end of the field is a goal, which is made of a pair of upright posts, eight feet high and 24 feet apart. A horizontal crossbar runs from the top of one pole to the other. Netting backs the goal.
- A soccer team fields 11 players, although rosters vary.
- Games are 90 minutes long, divided into two halves of 45 minutes each.
- A soccer ball is a sphere 27 to 28 inches in circumference, weighing 14 to 16 ounces.
- Points are scored by kicking or "heading" the ball into the opponents' net. Each goal counts as 1 point.

The Math Teacher's Book of Lists, © 1995 by Prentice Hall

LIST 252   (Continued)

Ice Hockey

- Ice hockey is generally considered to be the fastest of all team sports. It is played on natural or artificial ice on an oval rink. The standard rink is 200 feet long by 98 feet wide. It is enclosed by a board wall about four feet high.
- A goal with a net, four feet high and six feet wide, is situated 10 feet from each end of the rink.
- Two blue lines divide the rink into three equal zones. In the pros, a center line also divides the rink.
- Each team puts six players on the ice at the same time, although roster sizes vary by league.
- Professional games are divided into three 20-minute periods.
- The puck is a hard rubber disk, one inch thick and three inches in diameter.
- Players control the puck with wooden sticks. Shafts may be no longer than 53 inches, and the blade may be no wider than three inches or longer than 14½ inches.
- Points are scored when the puck goes into the opponents' net.

Field Hockey

- Field hockey is usually played on a grassy field, 100 yards long and between 55 and 60 yards wide. The field is divided into four 25-yard zones.
- Goals are located at the center of each goal line, at opposite ends of the field. Each goal is four yards wide, goal posts are seven feet high, and joined by a crossbar at the top.
- The ball is about 9¼ inches in circumference and weighs no more than 5¾ ounces.
- Players use wooden sticks that weigh between 12 and 18 ounces. The sticks are curved at one end and flattened on the left side.
- Games are divided into two halves of 35 minutes each.
- Teams play with 11 players each, although rosters vary according to league.
- Points are scored by hitting the ball into the opponents' net.

Lacrosse

- Lacrosse is played on a field 110 yards long, including 15 yards of a clear area behind each goal. Lacrosse fields are between 60 and 70 yards wide.
- Goals are located at opposite ends of the field and are formed by two six-foot poles connected by a six-foot long crossbar along the top.
- The typical men's team consists of 10 players, while the typical women's team has 12.
- The ball is between 7¾ and 8 inches in circumference and weighs between 5 and 5¼ ounces. A lacrosse stick is between five and six feet long. They are hooked on top with strings attached to form a net.

LIST 252 (Continued)

- A game lasts 60 minutes. Points are scored when the ball is hit into the opponents' net.

Tennis

- The standard tennis court is 78 feet long and 27 feet wide, and is expanded to 36 feet in width for doubles play. The court is divided into two equal parts by a net. Each half court is further divided into service courts.
- The ball is made of inflated rubber overlaid with a wool composition. It is between 2½ and 2⅝ inches in diameter, and weighs between 2 and 2¹⁄₁₆ ounces. The typical tennis racket weighs between 14 and 16 ounces, and is made of wood, steel, or aluminum. It has a rounded head, usually strung with gut or nylon.
- Scoring in tennis is calculated in a sequence of four points, specified as 15, 30, 40 and game. No points is called "love." A tie at 40 is called "deuce." After deuce, a game is won by two points. Points are scored when an opponent fails to return a ball hit by the server.

Racquetball

- This fast-moving game is played on an indoor court that is 40 feet long, 20 feet wide, and has front and side walls 20 feet high. The back wall is at least 12 feet high. A shortline, so named because the served ball must cross over it on a fly, is 20 feet from the front wall and divides the court in half. The service line is 15 feet from the front wall.
- The hollow, hard rubber ball is between 2¼ and 2½ inches in diameter and weighs about 1 ounce. Rackets are slightly smaller than tennis rackets and are usually made of composite metals, steel, or fiberglass. The rounded head is strung tightly with strong nylon.
- Points are scored when a player fails to return a shot of the server.

Volleyball

- Volleyball is played on a court 60 feet long by 30 feet wide. The court is divided into two equal parts by a net. Indoor rules call for clearance of at least 26 feet above the entire court.
- A volleyball net is 32 feet long, 3 feet wide, and is composed of 4 inch square mesh of black or dark brown linen. The top of the net is set 8 feet for men, 7½ feet for women, and 7 feet or lower for children.
- The volleyball is an inflated sphere between 25 and 27 inches in circumference, and weighs 9 to 10 ounces.
- The typical team consists of 6 players, although rosters vary.
- Points are scored when the opposing team fails to return a hit by the serving team.

LIST 253   FINDING STATISTICS IN BASEBALL

Numbers and statistics play a greater role in the understanding and enjoyment of baseball than in any other sport. The details of every game are recorded, from the first pitch to the final out. But it's the numbers that describe a player's performance that are most interesting to the fans.

Players are compared by their "stats." Any baseball fan knows the value of a .300 hitter compared to one who bats .190. Likewise, any pitcher whose ERA is over 7.00 is going to win fewer games than the ace whose ERA is under 2.00. Note that most baseball statistics are given in decimal form in hundredths or thousandths. Following are the ways the most important baseball statistics are calculated.

A Team's Winning Percentage—This is the percent of the games a team wins compared to the total number of games it has played. To find a team's winning percentage, divide the total number of wins by the total number of games played. Work the answer out to thousandths.

- Here's the math: A team has won 12 and lost 8. 12 divided by 20 = .600. The team has a winning percentage of .600.
- A winning percentage of .600 is often good enough for first place.

Batting Average—A batting average is the measure of how often a batter gets a hit. A batting average is found by dividing the number of hits by the number of official at-bats. (Walks, being hit by a pitch, and sacrifices are not counted as official at-bats. Getting on base on a fielder's choice or an error is counted as an at-bat but not a hit.)

- Here's the math: 1 hit in 4 at-bats. 1 divided by 4 = .250.
- An average of .300 is considered good; an average of .400 is rare. The last player to hit .400 for a season was Ted Williams of the Boston Red Sox in 1941, .406.

On-Base Average—The on-base average (sometimes referred to as the on-base "percentage") measures how often a batter gets on base. The on-base average is found by dividing the number of times a player reaches base by the number of times he comes to the plate. (The on-base average includes walks, being hit by a pitch, and sacrifices, which are considered to be plate appearances.)

- Here's the math: In 4 plate appearances, a player has 1 hit, 1 walk, 1 sacrifice, and 1 ground-out. He reached base 2 times in four appearances, therefore 2 divided by 4 is .500.
- A player's on-base average is always higher than his batting average. An on-base average of .400 over the course of a season is excellent.

Slugging Average—The slugging average (sometimes referred to as the slugging "percentage") measures a batter's power-hitting. It is found by taking the total number of bases the batter reaches, divided by the number of official at-bats. Obviously, the more home runs, triples, and doubles a batter has, the higher his slugging percentage will be.

LIST 253   (Continued)

- Here's the math: In 5 at-bats, a batter hits a single and double. The single is worth 1 base, and the double is worth 2, giving him 3 total bases. 3 (total bases) divided by 5 (at-bats) = .600 (slugging average).

- In the major leagues, a slugging average over .500 is the mark of a true power-hitter.

RBIs—RBIs (Runs Batted In) are the total number of runs that score when a batter gets a hit, base on balls, is hit with a pitch, sacrifices (either a bunt or fly), grounds out with less than two outs, or reaches base on an infield out. If the batter reaches base because of an error, grounds into a double-play or what would have been a double-play except for an error, no RBI is credited. A batter reaching the 100-RBI plateau in a season has had a fine year.

ERA—ERA (Earned Run Average) represents the number of runs given up by a pitcher during a 9-inning game. The ERA does not include runs scored because of an error or the baserunner initially reaching first base because of an error. You can find a pitcher's ERA by multiplying the number of earned runs scored by 9, then dividing by the total number of innings pitched. Because innings have three outs, fractions (thirds) play a part in calculating a pitcher's ERA.

- Here's the math: A starting pitcher has pitched 125⅔ innings (125.66 innings) and has given up 35 earned runs. First multiply 35 times 9, which equals 315. Now divide 315 by 125.66, which equals 2.5067642, rounded off to 2.51. This pitcher gives up about 2½ earned runs every 9 innings.

- An ERA under 3.00 is considered good, an ERA under 2.00 is outstanding.

Fielding Percentage—The fielding percentage is a measurement of a fielder's ability to make plays cleanly, without errors. It is found by dividing the number of successful fielding plays by the number of opportunities.

- Here's the math: A second basemen has 150 fielding chances and makes 10 errors. That means he has fielded 140 balls cleanly. Divide 140 by 150 which equals a fielding percentage of .933.

- A fielder whose fielding percentage approaches .900 is nearing a Gold Glove.

The Math Teacher's Book of Lists, © 1995 by Prentice Hall

LIST 254 GEOMETRY AND NATURE

Examples and applications of the different branches of mathematics can be found throughout the world. No branch, however, rivals geometry in its countless representations. The following list offers just some examples of geometry in nature.

diatoms—circles

snowflakes—hexagons

chambered nautilus (snail)—spirals

tourmaline (a mineral)—internal structure made of triangles

common starfish—pentagons

honeycomb—hexagons

earthworms—cylinders

salt—cubic crystals

diamond—octahedron

quartz—hexagons

sulfur—rhombic prism

morning glory buds—spirals

daisy head—spirals

pine-cone scales—spirals

stalks of many flowers—lines or gentle arcs

tree trunks—lines or cylinders

human beings—show remarkable symmetry: two ears, two eyes, two arms, two hands, two legs, two feet, four fingers and one thumb on each hand, five toes on each foot

other animals—symmetry similar to that of humans

stars—gaseous spheres

planets—solid spheres (in most cases)

moons—solid spheres

galaxies—spirals and ellipticals (some are irregular with no specific shape)

orbits of planets—generally circular (with slight variations)

orbits of comets—elliptical or parabolic

LIST 255   YOUR WEIGHT ON OTHER PLANETS

If you want to weigh less, take a trip to the moon and get on a scale. If instead you want to gain a few pounds, rocket over to Jupiter and you'll weigh about 2½ times what you weigh on Earth. Because of the different masses of the planets, their surface gravity varies from that of Earth. Although your body mass remains the same, the force of gravity pulling down on you is different on other planets. The result—your weight would change.

To find how much you'd weigh on another planet in our solar system, use this formula:

Your Earth Weight × Surface Gravity of Planet = Your Weight on the Planet

The following list makes the math easy.

The Surface Gravity of the Planets Compared to Earth

Earth = 1.00

Earth's Moon = 0.17

Mercury = 0.37

Venus = 0.88

Mars = 0.38

Jupiter = 2.51

Saturn = 1.07

Uranus = 0.93

Neptune = 1.23

Pluto = 0.05

A quick question: If you were in space, and there was no gravity, how much would you weigh?

Answer: Nothing. You would be weightless, although you'd still have the same mass.

The Math Teacher's Book of Lists, © 1995 by Prentice Hall

LIST 256   SOME MATHEMATICAL FACTS ABOUT SPACE

Should we ever meet beings from other worlds, one of the ways we might communicate with them is through mathematics. Unquestionably, mathematics is a universal language. Travelers from distant stars will surely have concepts of direction, distance, and geometric shapes—after all, every star and planet is a sphere—and this would be a starting point on which to begin communication.

The following list offers some interesting facts about the universe we live in. First, some information about our solar system.

- Because distances even in our solar system are so long, astronomers use a measure called an astronomical unit (AU). It is equivalent to the average distance between the Earth and our sun, about 93,000,000 miles or 150,000,000 kilometers.
- Our solar system consists of our sun, the nine planets, and countless asteroids, comets, and meteoroids.
- Our sun, an average star, is a huge, glowing ball of gases. It is about 4.5 billion years old, and is expected to shine for at least 4.5 billion more. While at its center, the temperatures approach 27,000,000°F, the sun's surface is a mere 10,000°F. The sun's diameter is about 109 times that of the Earth's.
- The general orbits of the planets, with a little variation, are circular.
- A planet's year is based on its revolution around the sun.
- A planet's day is based on its rotation, or how fast it spins on its axis.
- While the Earth has one moon, some planets have many and others have none.

Following is a chart that provides additional information about the planets.

Average Distance from Sun (AU) and Miles (millions)			Period of Revolution*	Period of Rotation**	Number of Moons
Mercury	0.4	36.0	88.0 D	58.7 D	0
Venus	0.7	67.2	224.7 D	243.0 D	0
Earth	1.0	92.9	365.3 D	23.9 H	1
Mars	1.5	141.6	687.0 D	24.6 H	2
Jupiter	5.2	483.3	11.9 Y	9.9 H	16
Saturn	9.5	886.2	29.5 Y	10.7 H	18
Uranus	19.2	1783.0	84.0 Y	17.2 H	15
Neptune	30.1	2794.0	164.8 Y	17.0 H	8
Pluto	39.5	3670.0	248.5 Y	6.4 D	1

*The period of revolution is given in Earth time. D = Days and Y = Years. Thus, Venus circles the sun in a little over a half of the Earth's year. Pluto, being so far from the sun, takes over 247 Earth years to circle the sun.

**The period of rotation is given in Earth time. D = Days and Y = Years. Some planets spin on their axis faster than others. How fast they spin entirely around determines their days. On the Earth, a day is about 24 hours long. On Venus, which spins very slowly, one day is equivalent to 243 Earth days. (Talk about a long day!)

LIST 256   (Continued)

While we use astronomical units to measure distances within our solar system, once beyond Pluto the distances become too great even for that. To measure the distances between the stars astronomers use *light years*.

A light year is the distance light travels in one year, about 6 trillion miles or 9.5 trillion kilometers.

To work out the math yourself, take the speed of light, about 186,282 miles per second, and multiply it by—

60 seconds in a minute, then 60 minutes in an hour, then 24 hours in a day, then 365.25 days in a year.

Here are some additional facts.

- Our solar system is less than one light "day" across.
- Alpha Centauri is the star nearest our sun. It is 4.3 light years away, about 25 trillion miles.
- With our present technology, the fastest ship we could build would take about 94,000 years to reach Alpha Centauri.
- The North Star, Polaris, is 782 light years from Earth.
- Our galaxy, the Milky Way, is a group of some 400 billion stars. It is a spiral galaxy, moving through space like a gigantic pinwheel.
- The Milky Way is about 10,000 light years wide at its center and about 100,000 light years across.
- The Milky Way is one of an estimated billions of galaxies in the observable universe. No one has yet seen to the edge of the universe, if there is an edge.
- The next nearest spiral galaxy to the Milky Way is Messier 31. It is about 2 million light years away.
- The farthest galaxies are several billion light years from Earth.

The Math Teacher's Book of Lists, © 1995 by Prentice Hall

LIST 257 RECYCLING CODES

Recycling is one of the best ways to conserve our natural resources and reduce the pollution of our environment. An important area of recycling involves
plastics. The Society of the Plastics Industry (SPI) has developed a voluntary cod-
ing system made up of numbers that makes it easier for consumers to identify
which plastic products can be recycled. The recycling symbols are found on the
bottoms of 16 oz. and higher plastic bottles, and 8 oz. and higher rigid plastic containers.

Only those plastics products labeled 1 or 2 *are recyclable.*

Symbol	Material

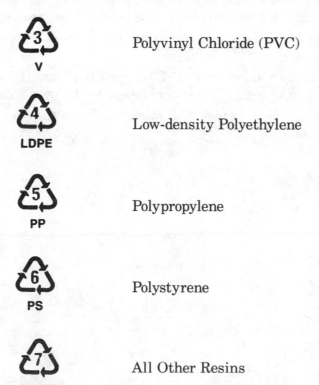

Polyethylene Terephthalate (PET)
(Examples: soda or liquor bottles, peanut jars,
pourable salad dressing bottles. The colors of the
containers are usually clear, green, or brown.)

High-density Polyethylene
(Examples: milk, juice, water bottles; detergent, soap,
bleach, antifreeze, or cleaning solution bottles.
Containers are usually translucent or lightly colored.)

The products marked with the following codes *are not* recyclable.

Polyvinyl Chloride (PVC)

Low-density Polyethylene

Polypropylene

Polystyrene

All Other Resins

LIST 258   CONSERVATION FACTS

The conservation of precious resources is vital if we are to maintain the earth for future generations. When facts are given about conservation, they usually include numbers. The following are a sampling.

- An average running faucet empties between 3 and 5 gallons of water down the drain every minute. Avoid leaving the faucet running while washing your face, brushing your teeth, or shaving.
- Washing the dishes with the tap running wastes up to 30 gallons of water.
- Attaching a low-flow faucet aerator to your faucet or showerhead can reduce the flow by up to 50%. Because air is mixed in with the flowing water, you won't notice the decrease in volume. It's estimated that if every American home installed faucet aerators, more than 250 million gallons of water would be saved daily.
- Every time you flush your toilet, you use 5 to 7 gallons of water. Nearly 40% of the water used in American homes is "flushed." By installing an inexpensive displacement device, available at most plumbing supply outlets, you can reduce the amount of water your toilet uses by 1 to 2 gallons.
- Nearly 50% of the garbage Americans produce each day is recyclable.
- Each day Americans throw out nearly 40 million newspapers, equal to about 70,000 trees. If every American recycled just 10% of the newspapers he or she reads, nearly 25 million trees would be saved each year.
- Using cloth diapers would save over 1 million metric tons of wood pulp each year.
- Recycling glass not only reduces the need for additional landfill space, it reduces the energy costs needed for making new glass by over 30%.
- Making aluminum cans from recycled aluminum reduces the energy costs needed for making new cans by 95%.

LIST 259   SOME HELPFUL FORMULAS

Scientists as well as mathematicians use formulas in their work. Following are some of the more common ones.

Area of a Circle: $A = \pi r^2$
A = area, r = length of the radius, $\pi \approx 3.14$ or $\dfrac{22}{7}$

Converting to Celsius from Fahrenheit: $C = \dfrac{5}{9}(F - 32)$

C = Celsius, F = Fahrenheit

Density: $D = M/V$
D = density, M = mass, V = volume

Distance: $d = rt$
d = distance, r = rate at which you travel, t = time spent traveling

Effort: $E = R/M.A.$
E = effort, R = resistance, M.A. = mechanical advantage

Energy: $E = mc^2$
E = energy, m = mass, c = the speed of light

Converting to Fahrenheit from Celsius: $F = \dfrac{9}{5}C + 32$

F = Fahrenheit, C = Celsius

Force: $F = MA$
F = force, M = mass, A = acceleration

Converting to Kelvin from Celsius: $K = C + 273.15$

Mean: $\bar{x} = \dfrac{\Sigma x}{n}$

$\bar{x}$ = mean, Σx = the sum of the individual numbers, n = the total numbers

Pressure: $P = F/A$
P = pressure, F = force, A = area

Area of a Rectangle: $A = lw$
A = area, l = length, w = width

Area of a Trapezoid: $A = \frac{1}{2}h(b_1 + b_2)$
A = area, h = height, b_1 = length of base 1, b_2 = length of base 2

Area of a Triangle: $A = \frac{1}{2}bh$
A = area, b = length of the base, h = height

Speed: $S = D/T$
S = speed, D = distance traveled, T = time

Velocity: $V = \frac{1}{2}at^2$
V = velocity, a = acceleration, t = time

LIST 259   (Continued)

Volume of a Cone: $V = \dfrac{\pi r^2 h}{3}$

V = volume, r = length of the radius, h = height, $\pi \approx 3.14$ or $\dfrac{22}{7}$

Volume of a Cylinder: $V = \pi r^2 h$

V = volume, r = length of the radius, h = height, $\pi \approx 3.14$ or $\dfrac{22}{7}$

Volume of a Rectangular Prism: $V = lwh$
V = volume, l = length, w = width, h = height

Volume of a Sphere: $V = \dfrac{4\pi r^3}{3}$

V = volume, r = length of the radius, $\pi \approx 3.14$ or $\dfrac{22}{7}$

Work: $W = FD$
W = work, F = force, D = distance

section 7

POTPOURRI

LIST 260   THE HISTORY OF MATHEMATICS

Mathematics is an evolving discipline. It is constantly expanding and changing. Although the ancient Greeks, for instance, began to develop number theory and made major contributions to geometry and logic, they had little inkling of probability, which wasn't formalized until the mid 1600s.

Following is a brief history of mathematics, according to topic and mathematician. Note that most dates are approximations as these individuals often worked years in furthering mathematics. Also, because so many people have contributed to mathematics throughout history, this list is quite subjective and we picked who we feel are some of the most significant contributors. Undoubtedly, you will be able to name several others that should be included here.

3000 B.C.—Egyptians and Babylonians begin the development of number systems and early bookkeeping. Simple problems of arithmetic and geometry necessary to a civilized society become commonplace.

700 B.C.—Ancient Greece starts to flourish. Greek thinkers contribute number theory, geometry, and logic to mathematics.

530 B.C.—Pythagoras, one of the most famous of the Greek mathematicians and philosophers, founds the Pythagorean movement.

300 B.C.—Euclid completes his writing of *Elements*, 13 volumes on mathematics.

100 A.D.—Astronomers begin to develop trigonometry.

170   —Ptolemy, mathematician and astronomer, declares that the earth is the center of the universe. This becomes the dominate view until the 17th century when Copernicus claims that the sun is the center of the solar system.

200   —Diophantus, a Greek mathematician, develops algebra. He is considered by many to be the father of that subject.

540   —Aryabhata, Hindu mathematician and astronomer, advances mathematics by solving the quadratic equation.

600   —Geometry, algebra, and numeral systems benefit from Hindu and Arabian thought. The idea of zero is introduced.

775   —The translation of Hindu mathematics to Arabic takes place.

830   —al-Khowârizmî, an Arabian, works with algebra, numeral systems, and equations.

1100   —Arabic and Hindu mathematics spread throughout Western Europe.

1200   —Leonardo of Pisa (Fibonacci), an Italian, works with equations, sequences, series, and Pi.

1478   —The first mathematics books are printed.

1489   —The signs of + and − are introduced.

1500   —Negative numbers and perspective are introduced.

1525   —Great work is done on solving equations.

The Math Teacher's Book of Lists, © 1995 by Prentice Hall

LIST 260   (Continued)

1540   —Imaginary numbers are explored.

1557   —Englishman Robert Record writes the first English algebra text.

1560   —The Italian Girolamo Cardano works with complex numbers, equations, and probability.

1580   —Decimals are introduced.

1614   —John Napier, Scottish mathematician, creates the first system of logarithms. He is the first to use the decimal point.

1630   —The coordinate system is developed.

1640   —René Descartes, French philosopher, scientist, and mathematician, works on systemizing analytic geometry. He also attempts to classify curves according to the types of equations that produce them.

1645   —Pierre de Fermat, French mathematician, studies various topics, including coordinates, polygons, probability, and the Pythagorean theorem.

1650   —Blaise Pascal, French philosopher, physicist, and mathematician, formulates one of the basic theorems of projective geometry, known as Pascal's theorem. He also invents the first adding machine.

1680   —The German Gottfried Wilhelm von Leibniz works on calculus, functions, and infinity.

1700   —Work on determinants is done.

1780   —Complex numbers are explored by several mathematicians.

1799   —The Metric System is introduced.

1800   —Theories on projection are developed. Number theory is explored.

1810   —Carl Friedrich Gauss, a German mathematician, expands the study of number theory.

1820   —The Russian Nikolai Ivanovich Lobachevsky works on geometry.

1840   —Various mathematicians work with matrices, vectors, and symbolic logic.

1870   —George Cantor works with infinite sets.

1905   —Albert Einstein develops the theory of relativity.

1910   —Various mathematicians, including Alfred North Whitehead and Bertrand Russell, study the logical foundations of mathematics.

1920   —Emmy Noether studies abstract algebra.

1945   —Various mathematicians and researchers work on computers.

1976   —Kenneth Appel and Wolfgang Haken find a solution of the Four Color Problem.

1977   —Robert Connelly finds a rigidity counterexample.

1993   —Andrew Wiles presents what he believes is the proof of the most famous problem in mathematics—Fermat's last theorem. At the time of this book's printing, Wiles' work has not been confirmed.

The Math Teacher's Book of Lists, © 1995 by Prentice Hall

LIST 261   FAMOUS MATHEMATICIANS THROUGH HISTORY

Throughout history countless men and women have made great contributions to mathematics. The following list identifies many, but certainly not all, of them. The list is arranged according to nationality and includes the individual's major areas of study. In some cases, a mathematician may have been born in one country and done his or her major work in another.

American

Howard Aiken (1900–1973)—Computers

Vannevar Bush (1890–1974)—Computers

R. Buckminster Fuller (1895–1983)—Polyhedra

Josiah Willard Gibbs (1839–1903)—Vectors

Herman Hollerith (1860–1929)—Computers

Charles F. Richter (1900–1985)—Logarithms

Eli Whitney (1765–1825)—Congruence

Frank Lloyd Wright (1860–1959)—Triangles

Arabian

Jamshid al-Kashî (about 1430)—Pi

Muhammed ibn Mûsâ al-Khowârizmî (about 780–850)—Algebra, Equations, Numeral Systems

Austrian

Kurt Gödel (1906–1979)—Mathematical Systems

George Joachim (1514–1576)—Algebra, Trigonometry

Chinese

Tsu Chung-chi (about 480)—Pi

An Wang (1920–1990)—Computers

Dutch

Luitzen E.J. Brouwer (1881–1967)—Logic

Maurits Cornelis Escher (1898–1971)—Geometry, Polygons, Symmetry

Willebrord Snell (1581–1626)—Pi

Adriaen Vlacq (about 1600–1667)—Logarithms

LIST 261 (Continued)

English

Charles Babbage (1792–1871)—Computers
George Boole (1815–1864)—Algebra, Logic, Sets
Henry Briggs (1561–1631)—Logarithms
Lord William Brouncker (1620–1684)—Pi
Henry Cavendish (1731–1810)—Algebra, Scientific Notation
Arthur Cayley (1821–1895)—Algebra
Augustus DeMorgan (1806–1871)—Infinity, Logic, Sets
Charles L. Dodgson (Lewis Carroll, 1832–1898)—Logic
Sir Arthur Eddington (1882–1944)—Infinity
Edmund Gunter (1581–1626)—Computer, Logarithms
Thomas Harriot (1560–1621)—Geometry, Inequalities
Lord Kelvin (William Thomson, 1824–1907)—Measurement
Lady Ada Byron Lovelace (1815–1852)—Computers
John Machin (1680–1751)—Pi
Thomas Malthus (1766–1834)—Sequences and Series
Sir Isaac Newton (1642–1727)—Algebra, Calculus, Infinity, Logic
William Oughtred (1574–1660)—Computers, Logarithms
Bertrand A. Russell (1872–1970)—Logic
William Shanks (1812–1882)—Pi
Brook Taylor (1685–1741)—Algebra
Alan Mathison Turing (1912–1954)—Computers
John Venn (1834–1923)—Sets
John Wallis (1616–1703)—Pi
Alfred North Whitehead (1861–1947)—Logic

Egyptian

Ahmes (about 1650 B.C.)—Circles, Fractions

Flemish

Gerhard Mercator (Kremer, 1512–1594)—Projection
Simon Stevin (1548–1620)—Decimals, Exponents, Fractions, Vectors

French

Jean le Rond d' Alembert (1717–1783)—Complex Numbers
Comte George Buffon (1707–1788)—Pi, Probability

LIST 261   (Continued)

Jean Buteo (about 1492–1565)—Exponents

Augustin-Louis Cauchy (1789–1857)—Proofs

Pierre Curie (1859–1906)—Exponents

Gérard Desargues (1591–1661)—Projection

René Descartes (1596–1650)—Coordinates, Exponents, Polyhedra, Sets, Signed Numbers

Pierre de Fermat (1601–1665)—Coordinates, Polygons, Probability, Pythagorean Theorem

Jean-Baptiste Joseph Fourier (1768–1830)—Trigonometry

Evariste Galois (1811–1832)—Equations

Sophie Germain (1776–1831)—Symmetry

Charles Hermite (1822–1902)—Algebra

Joseph l. Lagrange (1736–1813)—Calculus, Measurement

Pierre-Simon Laplace (1749–1827)—Calculus

Marin Mersenne (1588–1648)—Variation

Gaspard Monge (1746–1818)—Projection

Nicole Oresme (1323–1382)—Functions

Blaise Pascal (1623–1662)—Algebra, Computers, Probability, Projection

Jules Henri Pincaré (1854–1912)—Topology

Jean Victor Poncelet (1788–1867)—Projection

Francois Viète (1540–1603)—Decimals, Equations, Exponents, Pi

German

Georg Cantor (1845–1918)—Functions, Infinity, Pi, Probability, Sets

Ludolph van Ceulen (1540–1610)—Pi, Rational and Irrational Numbers

Ernest Chladni (1756–1827)—Symmetry

Zacharias Dase (1824–1861)—Pi

Richard Dedekind (1831–1916)—Infinity

Albrecht Dürer (1471–1528)—Projection

Albert Einstein (1879–1955)—Functions, Geometry, Infinity, Lines, Vectors

Gabriel Fahrenheit (1686–1736)—Measurement

Carl Friedrich Gauss (1777–1855)—Complex Numbers, Geometry, Polygons, Statistics, Topology

Hermann Günther Grassman (1809–1877)—Vectors

Werner Heisenberg (1901–1976)—Measurement

David Hilbert (1862–1943)—Infinity, Mathematical Systems, Sets

Johannes Kepler (1571–1630)—Calculus, Conic Sections, Polyhedra

LIST 261   (Continued)

Johann Heinrich Lambert (1728–1777)—Complex Numbers, Pi, Rational and Irrational Numbers

Gottfried Wilhelm von Leibniz (1646–1716)—Calculus, Computers, Functions, Infinity, Logic, Numeral Systems

Ferdinand Lindemann (1852–1939)—Pi

August Ferdinand Moebius (1790–1868)—Topology

Johann Müller (Regiomontanus, 1436–1476)—Algebra, Trigonometry

Emmy Noether (1882–1935)—Algebra

Georg Friedrich Bernhard Riemann (1826–1866)—Geometry

Christoff Rudolff (about 1500–1545)—Arithmetic Operations

Charles Steinmetz (1865–1923)—Complex Numbers

Michael Stifel (about 1486–1567)—Signed Numbers

Greek

Apollonius of Perga (262–190 B.C.)—Conic Sections

Archimedes of Syracuse (287–212 B.C.)—Angles, Calculus, Circles, Logarithms, Pi, Polyhedra

Archytas of Tarentum (about 400 B.C.)—Geometry

Aristotle (384–322 B.C.)—Geometry, Infinity, Logic

Diophantus of Alexandria (about 250)—Algebra, Equations

Eratosthenes of Cyrene (about 284–192 B.C.)—Numbers

Euclid of Alexandria (about 365–300 B.C.)—Geometry, Numbers, Planes

Eudoxus (408–355 B.C.)—Estimations, Geometry

Hipparchus of Alexandria (about 180–125 B.C.)—Trigonometry

Hypatia of Alexandria (370–415)—Conic Sections

Menelaus of Alexandria (about 100)—Trigonometry

Pappus (about 300)—Geometry

Plato (427–347 B.C.)—Polyhedra

Claudius Ptolemy of Alexandria (about 85–168)—Trigonometry

Pythagoras of Samos (about 585–507 B.C.)—Pythagorean Theorem, Triangles, Trigonometry, Variation

Hindu (Indian)

Āryabhata (476–550)—Pi

Bhaskara (1114–1185)—Pi, Pythagorean Theorem

Srinivasa Ramanujan (1887–1920)—Algebra

LIST 261 (Continued)

Hungarian

János Bolyai (1802–1860)—Geometry
John von Neumann (1903–1957)—Computers

Irish

William Rowan Hamilton (1805–1865)—Algebra, Complex Numbers, Vectors

Italian

Girolamo Cardano (1501–1576)—Complex Numbers, Equations, Probability, Signed Numbers
Pietro Cataldi (1548–1626)—Exponents
Bonaventura Cavalieri (1598–1647)—Geometry
Lodovico Ferrari (1522–1565)—Equations
Scipione del Ferro (1465–1526)—Equations
Antonio Maria Fior (about 1515)—Equations
Niccolò Fontana (about 1499–1557)—Equations
Galileo Galilei (1564–1642)—Algebra, Functions, Infinity
Leonardo of Pisa (Fibonacci, about 1170–1250)—Equations, Pi, Sequences and Series
Giuseppe Peano (1858–1932)—Logic
Cubastro Gregorio Ricci (1853–1925)—Vectors
Paolo Ruffini (1765–1822)—Equations
Girolamo Saccheri (1667–1733)—Geometry
Leonardo da Vinci (1452–1519)—Projection, Triangles

Japanese

Lady Murasaki (about 978–1031)—Permutations and Combinations

Norwegian

Niels Henrik Abel (1802–1829)—Equations
Caspar Wessel (1745–1818)—Complex Numbers

Persian

Omar Khayyám (about 1048–1123)—Geometry

LIST 261   (Continued)

Polish

Nicholas Copernicus (1473–1543)—Trigonometry

Marie Sklodovska Curie (1867–1934)—Exponents

Russian

Christian Goldbach (1690–1764)—Induction

Sonya Kovalevsky (1850–1891)—Sequences and Series

Nikolai Ivanovich Lobachevsky (1793–1856)—Geometry

Andrey Andreyevich Markov (1856–1922)—Probability

Scottish

James Gregory (1638–1675)—Calculus, Pi

Colin MacLaurin (1698–1746)—Geometry

J. Clerk Maxwell (1831–1879)—Statistics

John Napier (1550–1617)—Computers, Decimals, Logarithms

John Playfair (1748–1819)—Geometry

A. Henry Rhind (1833–1863)—Circles, Fractions, Numeral Systems

James Watt (1736–1819)—Lines

Swedish

Anders Celsius (1701–1744)—Measurement, Metric System

Swiss

Jean-Robert Argand (1768–1822)—Complex Numbers

Joost Bürgi (1552–1632)—Exponents, Logarithms

Gabriel Cramer (1704–1752)—Matrices

Leonhard Euler (1707–1783)—Functions, Pi, Polyhedra, Sets, Topology, Vectors

Marcel Grossman (1878–1936)—Vectors

The Math Teacher's Book of Lists, © 1995 by Prentice Hall

LIST 262 MATHEMATICAL QUOTES

Mathematics can be a demanding discipline. The following words may help to inspire and encourage.

"Imagination is more important than knowledge."

Albert Einstein

"There is no royal road to geometry."

Euclid

"Mathematics, rightly viewed, possesses not only truth, but supreme beauty—"

Bertrand Russell

"Mathematics is the queen of sciences."

Carl Friedrich Gauss

"No man may be so great that he cannot be proven wrong."

Aristotle

"Geometry is nothing if it be not rigorous . . ."

H.J.S. Smith

"There is no inquiry which is not finally reducible to a question of numbers."

Auguste Comte

"Mathematics is the science which draws necessary conclusions."

Benjamin Pierce

". . . it is written in the language of mathematics, and its characters are triangles, circles, and other geometrical figures . . ."

Galileo, speaking of understanding the universe

"Wherever there is a number, there is beauty."

Proclus

"Mathematics is the gate and key to science."

Roger Bacon

"It appears to me that if one wants to make progress in mathematics, one should study the masters and not the pupils."

N.H. Abel

"The science of pure mathematics, in its modern developments, may claim to be the most original creation of the human spirit."

Alfred North Whitehead

"God made the integers; all else is the work of man."

Leopold Kronecker

"The profound study of nature is the most fertile source of mathematical discoveries."

Joseph Fourier

"When we cannot use the compass of mathematics or the torch of experience . . . it is certain we cannot take a single step forward."

Voltaire

"I cannot believe that God plays dice with the world."

Albert Einstein

LIST 263   CAREERS IN MATH

When most students, and many adults, think about potential careers in mathematics, they usually think about professions and jobs that work directly with numbers—math teachers come immediately to mind. Yet, there are many occupations that rely on mathematics, as the following list shows.

Accountant
Actuary
Aerospace Engineer
Air-Traffic Controller
Appraiser
Architect
Astronomer
Attorney
Auditor
Bank Officer
Bookkeeper
Budget Officer
Cartographer
Casino Manager
Chemist
Computer Analyst
Computer-Applications Engineer
Computer Programmer
Computer Software Developer
Computer-Systems Engineer
Credit Manager
Cryptanalyst
Curator
Data-Processing Manager
Demographer
Director of Vital Statistics
Draftsman or Draftswoman
Economist
Efficiency Expert
Electrical Engineer
Electrician
Electronics Technician
Engineering Analyst
Environmental Planner

Financial Planner
Fund Raiser
Geologist
Geophysicist
Insurance Agent
Internal Revenue Agent
Market Research Analyst
Mathematical Technician
Math Text Editor
Medical Laboratory Technician
Meteorologist
Navigator
Nuclear Engineer
Nuclear Scientist
Opinion Researcher
Pharmacologist
Physicist
Product Manager
Professor of Mathematics
Purchasing Agent
Quality Control Supervisor
Radar Technician
Real Estate Agent
Sales Representative
Securities Trader
Seismologist
Statistician
Structural Engineer
Surveyor
Teacher of Mathematics
Technical Illustrator
Tool and Die Maker

LIST 264   BOOKS ABOUT CAREERS THAT REQUIRE MATHEMATICS

There are many careers that require a sound understanding of mathematics. Following is a list of sources.

Career Associates. *Career Choices for Students of Mathematics*. New York: Walker and Co., 1990.

Career Associates. *Career Choices for Students of Economics*. New York: Walker and Co., 1985.

CEIP Fund. *The Complete Guide to Environmental Careers*. Washington, DC: Island Press, 1989.

Downes, Paul, ed. *Chronicle Math and Science Occupations Guidebook*. Moravia, NY: Chronicle Guidance Publications, 1990.

Easton, Thomas A. *Careers in Science*. Chicago: National Textbook Co., 1984.

Gaylord, G., and G. Ried. *Careers in Accounting*. Homewood, IL: Dow Jones-Irwin, 1984.

Goldstein, Amy J., ed. *Peterson's Engineering, Science and Computer Jobs*. 11th ed. Princeton, NJ: Peterson's Guides, 1990.

Haef, Robert. *Success Guide for Accountants*. New York: McGraw-Hill, 1984.

Kaplan, Andrew. *Careers for Number Lovers*. Connecticut: The Millbrook Press, 1991.

King, Julie L. *Opportunities in Computer Science Careers*. Lincolnwood, IL: National Textbook Co., 1990.

Maples, Wallace R. *Opportunities in Aerospace Careers*. Lincolnwood, IL: National Textbook Co., 1990.

Medawar, P.B. *Advice to a Young Scientist*. New York: Harper & Row, 1979.

Rossbacher, Lisa A. *Career Opportunities in Geology and the Earth Sciences*. New York: Arco Publishing, 1983.

Schwartz, Lester, and Irv Brechuer. *Career Tracks*. New York: Ballantine Books, 1985.

Shanahan, William F. *Your Career in Engineering*. New York: Arco Publishing, 1981.

Sheffield, C., and C. Rosin. *Space Careers*. New York: William Morrow, 1983.

Sunichrast, Michael, and Dean Crist. *Opportunities in Financial Careers*. Chicago: National Textbook Co., 1985.

Weinstein, Robert V. *Jobs for the 21st Century*. New York: Collier Books, 1983.

Weinstein, Bob. *140 High-Tech Careers*. New York: Collier Books, 1985.

LIST 265   SOURCES ON MATH CAREERS

The following sources offer information for students about careers in the mathematical sciences. Some are free, while others require a fee. Since availability and prices of these items often change, we suggest that you contact the organization for an update of their available materials and costs before ordering.

Booklets and Pamphlets

- Booklet, "Mathematical Scientists at Work." Essays written by teachers and professionals in occupations that require mathematics. For middle school students. Contact: Mathematical Association of America (MAA), 1529 Eighteenth St., NW, Washington, DC 20036.

- Pamphlet, "More Careers in the Mathematical Sciences." Short autobiographies of authors who explain how math has helped them in their careers. For middle school students. Contact: Mathematical Association of America (MAA), 1529 Eighteenth St., NW, Washington, DC 20036.

- Booklet, "The Actuarial Profession." Describes the actuarial profession and the education and training necessary for such a career. For middle school students. Contact: Society of Actuaries (SOA), 475 North Martingale Rd., Schaumburg, IL 60173-2226.

- Booklet, "Computer and Mathematics-Related Occupations." Provides career information about accountants, auditors, actuaries, computer programmers, computer systems analysts, economists, engineers, data processors, mathematicians, and statisticians. For middle school students. Contact: Division of Occupational Outlook, U.S. Department of Labor, Bureau of Labor Statistics, Washington, DC 20212.

- Pamphlet, "Shape the Future: A Career as a Mathematics Teacher." Provides information about becoming a mathematics teacher. For students in high school. Contact: The National Council of Teachers of Mathematics (NCTM), 1906 Association Dr., Reston, VA 22091-1593.

- Booklet, "Careers That Count." Profiles 16 women with careers in math, including university and school teaching, industry, and government. For high school students. Contact: Association for Women in Mathematics, 4114 Computer and Science Bldg., University of Maryland, College Park, MD 20742.

- Pamphlet, "What is a Mechanical Engineer?" Describes a career as a mechanical engineer. For high school students. Contact: The American Society of Mechanical Engineers (ASME), 345 East 47th St., New York, NY 10017-2392.

- Pamphlet, "Careers in Electrical, Electronics, and Computer Engineering." Describes the preparation needed for careers in the fields of electronics noted in the title. For high school students. Contact: The Institute of Electrical and Electronic Engineers, Inc. (IEEE), 345 East 47th St., New York, NY 10017-2394.

LIST 265 (Continued)

Videos

- Video, "The Challenge: A Kid's Introduction to Engineering." This 33-minute video introduces students to engineering careers. For middle school students. Contact: National Action Council for Minorities in Engineering (NACME), 3 West 35th St., New York, NY 10001.

- Video, "Connecting the Past with the Future: Women in Math and Science." Details modern role models who use math that relates to the contributions of Ada Lovelace. For middle school students. Contact: Judith Olson, Department of Mathematics, Western Illinois University, Macomb, IL 61455.

- Video, "Futures." A series of 24, 15-minute programs designed to motivate students to study math and science, with an emphasis on careers. For students in grades 7 to 12. Contact: FASE Productions, 4801 Wilshire Blvd., Suite 215, Los Angeles, CA 90010.

LIST 266   BASIC CALCULATOR KEYS

Calculators are great assets in solving math problems. Sometimes, however, the calculators themselves present problems—especially when students don't know how to use them. Although there are many brands of calculators on the market, fortunately, most of them, like typewriters and computers, have similar keys. This list provides the basic keys.

ON/OFF—Turns the power on or shuts the power off.

CE or C—Clears the display of an entry.

+ —Adds.

− —Subtracts.

× —Multiplies.

÷ —Divides.

= —Completes the problem; works the problem out.

Numbers 0 through 9—Enters the number selected in the display.

M+—Adds an entry to the memory.

M−—Subtracts memory.

MRC or RCM—Recalls memory to the display.

STO—Stores the displayed value in memory.

2nd [d/c]—Enters mixed numbers and fractions. May also convert mixed numbers or fractions to decimal values.

.—Enters a decimal point.

%—Percent key. Different brands of calculators use it in different ways. Most enable you to find the percent of a number and discounts.

√—Square root key. Using it displays the square root of a number.

LIST 267 WORLD FIRSTS

The following list contains some first-place rankings of our world's natural wonders.

Highest Mountains by Continent

Mt. Everest, Nepal-Tibet, Asia . . . . 29,028 ft.
Aconcagua, Argentina, South America . . . . 22,834 ft.
Mt. McKinley, Alaska, North America . . . . 20,320 ft.
Kilimanjaro, Tanzania, Africa . . . . 19,340 ft.
Vinson Massif, Antarctica . . . . 16,864 ft.
Mont Blanc, France-Italy, Europe . . . . 15,771 ft.
Kosciusko, Australia . . . . 7,310 ft.

The Deepest Parts of the Oceans

Mariana Trench, Pacific, southwest of Guam . . . . 35,840 ft.
Puerto Rico Trench, Atlantic, near Puerto Rico . . . . 28,232 ft.
Java Trench, Indian, near Java . . . . 23,376 ft.
Eurasia Basin, Arctic, near Arctic Circle . . . . 17,881 ft.

Average Depths of Oceans

Pacific . . . . 12,925 ft.
Indian . . . . 12,598 ft.
Atlantic . . . . 11,730 ft.
Arctic . . . . 3,407 ft.

Principal Rivers of the World by Continent

Nile, Africa . . . . 4,160 mi.
Amazon, South America . . . . 4,000 mi.
Yangtze, Asia . . . . 3,400 mi.
Congo, Africa . . . . 2,270 mi.
Mississippi, North America . . . . 2,330 mi.
Murray, Australia . . . . 2,310 mi.

Principal Lakes of the World by Continent

Caspian Sea*, Asia-Europe . . . . 143,244 sq. mi.
Lake Superior, North America . . . . 31,700 sq. mi.
Victoria, Africa . . . . 26,828 sq. mi.
Maracaibo, South America . . . . 5,217 sq. mi.
Eyre, Australia . . . . 3,600 sq. mi.

*The Caspian Sea is a lake, despite its name. It is entirely bounded by land and fed by several rivers.

The Math Teacher's Book of Lists, © 1995 by Prentice Hall

LIST 267   (Continued)

Notable Waterfalls

Angel Falls, Venezuela .... 3,212 ft.
Tugela, South Africa...................................... 2,014 ft.
Cuquenan, Venezuela .... 2,000 ft.
King George Falls, Guyana .... 1,600 ft.
Krimmler, Austria.. 1,312 ft.
Takakkaw, Canada.. 1,200 ft.
Silver Strand Falls, USA (Calif.) .... 1,170 ft.
Wollomombi, Australia .... 1,100 ft.

LIST 268   TRICKY MATH PROBLEMS

Here are some problems that may tickle your math funny bone. For some questions, your reasoning must also be correct. When you are done, check your total against the rating scale.

1. Two U.S. coins total 55¢. One is not a nickel. What are they?

_____

2. A farmer has 20 cows. He sold all but 12. How many does he have left?

_____

3. A farmer takes 2 dozen oranges from 3 dozen. How many does he have?

_____

4. Julius Caesar was given a gold coin dated 48 B.C. He immediately knew it had to be counterfeit. Why?

_____

5. A rabbit, chased by a dog, ran from a carrot patch into a nearby woods. How far did he run into the woods?

_____

6. In the United States we celebrate the 4th of July. Do they have the 4th of July in Canada?

_____

7. Two students played checkers. Each played 3 games and won 3. There were no draws. Explain how this could be?

_____

8. Some months have 30 days. Others have 31. How many have 27?

_____

9. How much is 2 times 4 times 0 times 4 times 2?

_____

10. Does $\frac{1}{2}$ of 40 = 40 divided by $\frac{1}{2}$?

_____

Rating

9-10 correct—Very bright.
 7-8 correct—Still bright, but a little dimmer.
 5-6 correct—Fading, but okay.
 3-4 correct—Getting dark.
 1-2 correct—Very dark.
 0   correct—It's clear you've been living in a cave.

LIST 268   (Continued)

Answers Key:

1. A half-dollar and a nickel. The question said that one coin was not a nickel; the other is.
2. 12.
3. 2 dozen.
4. The notation B.C. came into use after the birth of Christ, 48 years later.
5. Halfway because then the rabbit would be running out of the woods.
6. Yes, but they don't celebrate it as a holiday.
7. They played against different people.
8. Every month has 27 days.
9. 0
10. No. $\frac{1}{2}$ of 40 = 20; 40 divided by $\frac{1}{2}$ = 80.

LIST 269   MATHEMATICAL PALINDROMES

Most people are familiar with palindromes in language. Words like "mom," "dad," and "wow" are palindromes because they are spelled the same forwards or backwards. Numbers can be palindromes, too. For example, the year 1991 is a palindrome, because read from front to back or back to front it is still 1991. The year 2002 is also a palindrome. While a mere list of palindromic numbers might have some interest, the real fun—or frustration—comes in when you work with palindromic sums.

If you take any number, reverse the digits, and add the numbers, continuing this process through as many steps as necessary, you will eventually find a number that is a palindrome. In some cases, you need only a few steps. In others, like the number 89, you need 24 steps before the sum becomes a palindrome of 13 digits.

Following are some numbers for which you'll find palindromic sums in just a few steps. We encourage you to try some on your own. (Just make sure the batteries in your calculator are charged!)

One Step: 18

$18 + 81 = 99$

Three Steps: 257

$257 + 752 = 1,009$; $1,009 + 9,001 = 10,010$; $10,010 + 01,001 = 11,011$

Four Steps: 372

$372 + 273 = 645$; $645 + 546 = 1,191$; $1,191 + 1,911 = 3,102$; $3,102 + 2,013 = 5,115$

Seven Steps: 485

$485 + 584 = 1,069$; $1,069 + 9,601 = 10,670$; $10,670 + 07,601 = 18,271$; $18,271 + 17,281 = 35,552$; $35,552 + 25,553 = 61,105$; $61,105 + 50,116 = 111,221$; $111,221 + 122,111 = 233,332$

LIST 270   ROMAN NUMERALS

The ancient Romans were master politicians, soldiers, and engineers. They conquered the world from the British Isles to North Africa and Asia Minor, spreading Roman civilization everywhere they went. Rome influenced much of Western Civilization that came after it. Despite all their achievements, the Romans never managed to develop a practical number system, and once Rome fell their numbers were supplanted by the Arabic system which we use today. That we still use Roman numerals—on some clocks, watches, movie and book copyright dates, formal outlines, and decorations—is a tribute to Rome's lasting influence.

Working with Roman numerals is not as hard as it is tedious. You read a Roman numeral from left to right. When a symbol of lesser value comes before a symbol of greater value, subtract the lesser from the greater. For example, IV = 4, or 1 taken from 5. When a symbol of lesser value follows a symbol of greater value, add the two values. Thus VI = 6, or 5 plus 1. The Romans had no symbol for zero.

Arabic	Roman	Arabic	Roman
1	I	21	XXI
2	II	22	XXII
3	III	23	XXIII
4	IV	24	XXIV
5	V	25	XXV
6	VI	26	XXVI
7	VII	27	XXVII
8	VIII	28	XXVIII
9	IX	29	XXIX
10	X	30	XXX
11	XI	40	XL
12	XII	50	L
13	XIII	60	LX
14	XIV	70	LXX
15	XV	80	LXXX
16	XVI	90	XC
17	XVII	100	C
18	XVIII	200	CC
19	XIX	500	D
20	XX	1,000	M

When they needed large numbers, the Romans sometimes used a bar (called a vinculum) over the number to multiply it by 1,000. For example, $\overline{V} = 5{,}000$, $\overline{X} = 10{,}000$, $\overline{XV} = 15{,}000$, $\overline{XXV} = 25{,}000$, $\overline{L} = 50{,}000$, $\overline{C} = 100{,}000$, and $\overline{M} = 1{,}000{,}000$.

LIST 270 (Continued)

Some Important Dates in Western History
(As the Romans Would Write Them!)

DCCLIII
753 B.C.
—According to legend, Romulus and his twin brother Remus found Rome. (Of course, there was no B.C. back then.)

CDLXXVI
476
—The Fall of the Roman Empire in the West. The Eastern Empire continued for several more centuries.

MLXVI
1066
—William the Conqueror, Duke of Normandy, invades and conquers England.

MCCXV
1215
—The Magna Carta is signed in England, codifying the principle that the king is subject to law.

MCDXCII
1492
—Columbus discovers America.

MDCCLXXXVII
1787
—The American Constitution is written in Philadelphia.

MDCCLXXXIX
1789
—The French Revolution begins.

MDCCCLXI–MDCCCLXV
1861–1865
—The American Civil War.

MCMXIV–MCMXVIII
1914–1918
—World War I.

MCMXXXIX–MCMXLV
1939–1945
—World War II.

MCMLXIII
1963
—President John F. Kennedy is assassinated.

MCMLXIX
1969
—American astronauts Edwin E. Aldrin and Neil A. Armstrong land on the moon.

MCMLXXXIX
1989
—The Berlin Wall comes down.

LIST 271   NUMBERS AND SYMBOLISM

Since ancient times, many people have believed that some numbers are symbolic and possess special powers. Such people dabble in the pseudo-science of Numerology, which still has many believers.

1—As the beginning of the counting numbers, 1 is unique. Any number multiplied by 1 remains unchanged; any number divided by 1 remains unchanged, too. Geometrically, 1 is related to the point. The number symbolizes beginnings and often is thought to represent balance: male and female, good and bad, light and dark.

2—Unlike 1, the balanced point, 2, like the line which passes through 2 points and extends forever into space in opposite directions, represents contradictions. The ancients believed the number 2 symbolized truth and falsehood. We've all heard second opinions.

3—3 is symbolic of the triangle. In ancient mythology there were 3 Fates, 3 Graces, and 3 Furies. For Christians, 3 symbolizes the Holy Trinity: the Father, Son, and Holy Spirit. Peter denied Christ 3 times. Hindu priests represent their god with 3 heads.

4—The ancients believed the number 4 represented the 4 directions: North, East, West, and South. It also symbolized the ancient elements of Earth, Air, Fire, and Water. The 3 sides and 1 base of a pyramid equal 4, which is apparent in the cross and the square as well. The number also represents the 4 basic operations of mathematics: addition, subtraction, multiplication, and division.

5—The ancient Greeks used a 5-pointed star as a secret symbol. Even today a pentagram is considered by some to hold magical properties.

6—It was believed that God created the universe in 6 days. 6 represents two triangles and their bases, as well as the cube. It is a number associated with strength and harmony. The star of David, a 6-pointed star, is a symbol of the state of Israel.

7—7 appears often in the Book of Revelation in the New Testament. During the days preceding the end of the world 7 plays a prominent role: 7 stars, 7 churches of Asia, 7 spirits before God's throne, 7 horns, 7 vials, 7 plagues, a 7-headed monster, and the Lamb with 7 eyes. Scholars have been trying to figure out the meaning of the 7s for centuries. There were also Seven Wonders of the Ancient World; Shakespeare wrote about the 7 ages of man, and Seventh Heaven means complete joy. In Japan, according to folklore, there were 7 Gods of Luck.

9—Mystics believed that 9 symbolized wisdom and knowledge. 9 planets revolve around our sun, a fact that some astrologers find significant. 9 also possesses regenerative properties. Multiply 9 by any number and the sum of the digits of the answer will be 9. Example: $9 \times 61 = 549$; $5 + 4 = 9$; $9 + 9 = 18$; $1 + 8 = 9$.

LIST 271 (Continued)

12—Many numerologists believe 12 to have special qualities. After all, there are 12 signs of the Zodiac, 12 months in a year, and 12 hours in a day (the other 12 are night). There were also 12 knights of the Round Table. The Bible speaks of the 12 Tribes of Israel and, in the New Testament, the 12 Apostles.

13—In the minds of many 13 is the most unlucky of numbers. Much of the superstition comes from the beginnings of Christianity. 13 represents the number present during the Last Supper, Jesus and the 12 apostles.

40—This number appears throughout religion. The deluge reported in the Old Testament lasted 40 days, and another 40 passed before Noah opened the Ark. The Israelites spent 40 years wandering in the wilderness. Jesus spent 40 days and 40 nights in the wilderness where He was tempted by Satan.

666—According to Christians, this is the Number of the Beast as mentioned in the Book of Revelation. Some scholars believe that 666 referred to Nero, the mad Emperor who ruled Rome at about the time the Book of Revelation was written. They believe that the author of the text assigned number values to the Hebrew words that represented Nero and these equal 666. Perhaps fearing for his head should he be found out by the authorities, the author named Nero, who was certainly considered a beast for the brutality of his rule, by a secret number.

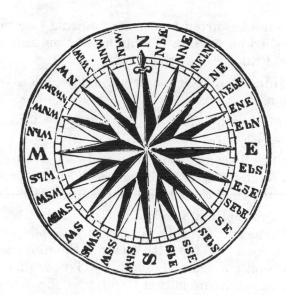

LIST 272   A NUMBER OF COINCIDENCES

One of the most fascinating things about numbers are coincidences—events that are linked numerically in some way. Some people are convinced that such occurrences are more than just coincidence; they believe that numbers have special properties and powers that we can only guess at. While that may be stretching reality a bit, after reading the following you'll need to have a cold, logical mind not to wonder—just a little—if numbers really are nothing more than numerical values.

- American presidents Abraham Lincoln and John F. Kennedy were both assassinated. Consider these numbers.

  —Lincoln was elected president in 1860; Kennedy in 1960.

  —Both men were assassinated on Friday, the 6th day of the week (assuming the week starts on Sunday).

  —Both Lincoln and Kennedy were succeeded by vice-presidents named Johnson. Andrew Johnson, Lincoln's successor was born in 1808, while Kennedy's successor, Lyndon Johnson, was born in 1908.

  —John Wilkes Booth, who assassinated Lincoln, was born in 1839 (according to most sources), and Lee Harvey Oswald, Kennedy's assassin, was born in 1939.

  —The names Lincoln and Kennedy have 7 letters each.

  —The names Andrew Johnson and Lyndon Johnson have 13 letters each.

  —The names John Wilkes Booth and Lee Harvey Oswald have 15 letters each.

- Raphael, the famous artist known for painting holy pictures was born on April 6 and died on April 6. His birth date and death date were both on Good Friday. Friday is the 6th day of the week.

- Harry Houdini, the master magician and escape artist, died on October 31, Halloween.

- The square of 13 is 169. Reverse 169 and you get 961. The square root of 961 is 31, which reversed comes to 13.

- Leo Tolstoy, the Russian author, believed 28 to be his special number. He was born on August 28, 1828, his son was born on June 28, and Tolstoy left his home for the final time, before his death, on October 28.

- The *Apollo 11* moon flight is related to the number 11. "Moon landing" has 11 letters. President Kennedy initiated the Apollo program, and his last name begins with "K," the 11th letter of the alphabet. The lunar lander touched down on the Sea of Tranquility. Tranquility has 11 letters. Neil Armstrong, an astronaut on that flight, was 38 years old; add the digits 3 and 8 and you get 11. Splashdown occurred in the Pacific Ocean, 11 miles from the recovery ship, the aircraft carrier, *U.S.S. Hornet*.

- Columbus discovered the New World in 1492. This opened a new age. In 1942, Enrico Fermi led a team that achieved a nuclear chain reaction. This

The Math Teacher's Book of Lists, © 1995 by Prentice Hall

LIST 272   (Continued)

began the atomic era, a new world. By switching the middle digits of 1942, you get 1492.

- Otto von Bismarck, the German Chancellor, was related to the number 3. He served under 3 emperors, had a role in 3 wars, signed 3 peace treaties, owned 3 estates, and fathered 3 children. Even the family crest was related to 3—"in trinity, strength." Trinity means 3.

- Three American presidents died on the Fourth of July —John Adams, James Monroe, and Thomas Jefferson.

- The composer Richard Wagner was related to the number 13. He was born in 1813. If you add the digits of the year, you'll find it equals 13. His name contains 13 letters. IIe wrote 13 great works of music. Wagner died on February 13, 1883. Drop the two 8s and you have 13.

Of course, the average, level-headed mathematician knows that these are all coincidences.

LIST 273   MATH AND SUPERSTITION

Over the years people have associated numbers with luck—good or bad. If you're the superstitious type, you need to know the following.

Do These and You'll Have Bad Luck—

Hang a calendar before January 1 . . .

Light three cigarettes on one match . . .

Plant seeds the last three days of March . . .

Give someone a gift of a knife unless you include a coin.

Start a trip or a project on Friday the 13th.

Break a mirror and suffer seven years of misfortune.

Do These and You'll Have Good Luck—

Find a four-leaf clover . . .

Carry a silver dollar . . .

Be the seventh child in a family (although you don't have much choice on this one) . . .

Eat cabbage on New Year's Day, January 1 . . .

Receive a coin with a hole in it . . .

LIST 274 MATHEMATICAL IDIOMS

Math is so important to our society that it has even found its way into common expressions. There are a lot here, but we're sure you can add more.

Two's company; three's a crowd . . .
It takes two to tango.
A penny for your thoughts.
Slap me five.
Take five.
Looking out for number one . . .
Don't be square.
Twenty-three skiddoo.
Second banana . . .
A third wheel . . .
Sixth sense . . .
Going in circles . . .
Ten-four . . .
Complete 180 . . .
Point of no return . . .
One-way ticket . . .
Murder one . . .
One and only one . . .
Simple as one, two, three . . .
Square meal . . .
Square deal . . .
Back to square one . . .
Divide and conquer . . .
Feel like you're ten feet tall . . .
Multiply like rabbits . . .
He (she) always gives 110%.
Another day another dollar . . .
A stitch in time saves nine.
An ounce of prevention is worth a pound of cure.
The eleventh hour . . .
Three cheers . . .
Fair and square . . .
The three R's . . .
A ten-gallon hat . . .
A love triangle . . .

Third rate . . .
Give him an inch and he'll take a mile.
One in a million . . .
One-way mirror . . .
One-way street . . .
Not a second too soon . . .
Dies a thousand deaths . . .
Forty winks . . .
Play second fiddle . . .
First class . . .
Put two and two together . . .
A bird in hand is worth two in the bush.
Don't count your chickens before they hatch.
Half a loaf is better than none.
Seventh heaven . . .
A penny saved is a penny earned.
One tree doesn't make a forest.
In the top ten . . .
Two wrongs don't make a right.
Two shakes of a lamb's tail . . .
Kill two birds with one stone . . .
Stand on your own two feet.
Two cents' worth . . .
Two heads are better than one.
Fool me once shame on you; fool me twice shame on me.
A picture is worth a thousand words.
First string . . .
Second string . . .
Third string . . .
Dressed to the nines . . .
As easy as one, two, three . . .
One for the book . . .
One-night stand . . .
One-two punch . . .

LIST 274   (Continued)

Just like adding two and two . . .

Three strikes and you're out.

Batting a thousand.

On cloud nine . . .

Fifty cents for one, a half dollar for the other . . .

A catch-22 . . .

Behind the eight ball . . .

My better half . . .

Once in a blue moon . . .

One-horse town . . .

One-man band . . .

Second childhood . . .

Second to none . . .

A hot number . . .

He (she) is number one.

One-track mind . . .

Seventh son . . .

Baker's dozen . . .

A square peg in a round hole . . .

The odds are a million to one.

One-armed bandit . . .

The Math Teacher's Book of Lists, © 1995 by Prentice Hall

LIST 275   NUMBERS IN NAMES AND EVENTS

Many names and events contain numbers. Some of them are included in the following list.

Battle of the Three Emperors—in 1805, the Battle of Austerlitz in which Napoleon (the French Emperor) defeated Francis I of Austria and Alexander I of Russia. During the battle, all three emperors were on the field.

Big Four—after World War II, the United States, Great Britain, France, and the Soviet Union.

Big Three—in 1919, Clemenceau, Lloyd George, and Wilson representing France, Great Britain, and the United States respectively at the Paris Peace Conference. In 1945, Churchill, Stalin, and Roosevelt representing Great Britain, Russia, and the United States respectively at Yalta to discuss the aftermath of World War II.

Chapter 11—a provision of the Federal Bankruptcy Act that permits debtors to transfer the ownership of their assets to new organizations owned by both the debtors and their creditors.

Eightfold Path—in Buddhism: 1) Right Understanding, 2) Right Thought, 3) Right Speech, 4) Right Action, 5) Right Livelihood, 6) Right Effort, 7) Right Mindfulness, 8) Right Concentration.

Fab Four—the vocal group, the Beatles, composed of John Lennon, Paul McCartney, George Harrison, and Ringo Starr.

Fifth Republic—the government of France since 1958.

First Cause—God as the Creator of all things.

First Empire—France under Napoleon, 1804–1814.

First Family—the family of the President of the United States. Also the family of a state governor.

First Lady—the wife of the President of the United States or a state governor.

First Republic—France after the overthrow of the monarchy, 1792–1804.

First Triumvirate—in 60 B.C. a coalition formed by Caesar, Pompey, and Crassus.

First World War—the great war between 1914–1918; the first war that involved much of the world.

Five Blessings—in Chinese art, the five bats that are symbols of longevity, wealth, serenity, virtue, and an easy death.

Five Pillars of Islam—the five most important obligations of believers: 1) Belief in one God, 2) Prayer five times each day facing Mecca, 3) Almsgiving, 4) Observance of the Ramadan fast, 5) The hadj, which is the pilgrimage to Mecca at least once during a person's life.

LIST 275   (Continued)

Formula One—a race car of specific size, weight and capacities.

Forty-Niner—someone who took part in the California gold rush of 1849.

4-F—an individual who is rejected for military service because of physical disability, mental instability, or moral deficiency.

Four-H Club—a club that encourages modern farming practices and good citizenship. The term "Four-H" comes from the idea of improving the "head, heart, hands, and health."

Four Horsemen—in 1924, the backfield of the University of Notre Dame: Harry Stuhldreher (quarterback), Don Miller and Jim Crowley (halfbacks), and Elmer Layden (fullback). Grantland Rice, a sportswriter for the *New York Herald Tribune,* is credited with first using the nickname.

Four Horsemen of the Apocalypse—as prophesied in Revelation of the New Testament, the personification of war, famine, pestilence, and death.

Four Nobel Truths—in Buddhism, 1) Life is suffering, 2) The cause of suffering is "birth sin," or craving and desire, 3) Only Nirvana can end suffering, 4) Nirvana can be attained by the Eightfold Path to Righteousness.

Fourth of July—Independence Day.

Fourth Republic—France's government from 1945–1958.

One in Three—in Christianity, a phrase describing the Holy Trinity.

Prime Mover—God.

Second Coalition—in 1799, an alliance between Britain, Austria, and Russia meant to drive the French out of Germany, Switzerland, and Italy.

Second Coming—the return of Jesus Christ, as prophesied in the New Testament.

Second Empire—France under Napoleon III from 1852–1870.

Second Republic—France from 1848–1852.

Second World War—the great war that involved most of the world's nations from 1939–1945.

Seven Wonders of the Ancient World—the Pyramids of Egypt, the Hanging Gardens of Babylon, Phidias' statue of Zeus at Olympia, the Temple of Artemis at Ephesus, the Mausoleum of Halicarnassus, the Colossus of Rhodes, the Lighthouse at Alexandria.

Six Day War—from June 5 to June 10, 1967, the war in which Israel defeated Egypt, Jordan, and Syria.

Ten Commandments—the ten obligations God requires of man, as given to Moses on Mount Sinai.

LIST 275   (Continued)

Third Reich—the Nazi dictatorship in Germany from 1933 to 1945.

Third Republic—France from 1870–1940.

Third World—the countries of Africa, Asia, and South America, often regarded as being underdeveloped.

Third World War—a hypothetical global war, generally assumed to be nuclear.

Thirty Years War—from 1618–1648, an extensive war between the Catholics of South Germany and the Protestants of North Germany.

Three Stooges—the U.S. comedians Moe Howard, Jerry Howard, and Larry Fine.

Three Wise Men—Melchior, Gaspar (also Caspar), and Balthazar, the three kings or Magi, who came from the East bearing gifts for the Christ child.

Triple Alliance—from 1882–1914, an alliance between Germany, Austria-Hungary, and Italy. In 1717, an alliance between France, the Netherlands, and Great Britain against Spain. In 1668, an alliance between Great Britain, the Netherlands, and Sweden against France.

Triple Crown—refers to three races: the Belmont Stakes, Kentucky Derby, and Preakness Stakes. The horse that wins all three is said to win the Triple Crown.

Triple Entente—from 1894–1907, an alliance between Great Britain, France, and Russia to counterbalance the Triple Alliance.

Twelve Tribes of Israel—the ancient name of the Israelites.

LIST 276   MATH WORDS USED EVERY DAY

Because many words have multiple meanings, many math words are used in language all the time.

acute	median
area	mode
average	natural
base	negative
check	null
chord	obtuse
complement	odd
complex	parallel
composite	parentheses
cone	point
coordinates	positive
cube	power
curve	prime
degree	product
difference	proper
double	rate
estimate	rational
even	ray
expression	real
extremes	remainder
factor	rod
formula	root
fraction	scale
function	segment
grand ($1,000)	series
grid	set
gross	similar
identity	simple
imaginary	slope
improper	square
increment	sum
index	supplement
interest	union
intersection	unlike
interval	variable
irrational	vertex
like	volume
line	whole
mean	

LIST 277   NUMBERS AND LANGUAGE

One of the ways anthropologists reconstruct the development of a people is through the group's cultural and linguistic heritage. On first glance, English seems as different from Greek as Greek is to French, but a review of the words that represent the numbers from 1 to 10 show clear linguistic similarities. In fact, the majority of modern European and Indian languages developed from an ancient language known as Indo-European and still show strong linguistic links. In some instances below the examples are striking.

English	German	French	Spanish	Greek	Latin
one	ein	un	uno	eîs	unus
two	zwei	deux	dos	dúo	duo
three	drei	trois	tres	treîs	tres
four	vier	quatre	cuatro	téssares	quattuor
five	fünf	cinq	cinco	pénte	quinque
six	sechs	six	seis	hex	sex
seven	sieben	sept	siete	heptá	septem
eight	acht	huit	ocho	októ	octo
nine	neun	neuf	nueve	ennéa	novem
ten	zehn	dix	diez	déka	decem

LIST 278   THE GREEK ALPHABET

Many formulas in mathematics use letters of the Greek alphabet as a constant or variable, for example, π which is equal to approximately 3.14. That we still use these symbols is a tribute to the ancient Greeks who did so much to further the understanding of mathematics. Below are the names and upper and lower cases of the Greek alphabet.

Name	Upper Case	Lower Case
alpha	A	α
beta	B	β
gamma	Γ	γ
delta	Δ	δ
epsilon	E	ε
zeta	Z	ζ
eta	H	η
theta	Θ	θ
iota	I	ι
kappa	K	κ
lambda	Λ	λ
mu	M	μ
nu	N	ν
xi	Ξ	ξ
omicron	O	o
pi	Π	π
rho	P	ρ
sigma	Σ	σ
tau	T	τ
upsilon	Υ	υ
phi	Φ	φ
chi	X	χ
psi	Ψ	ψ
omega	Ω	ω

The Math Teacher's Book of Lists, © 1995 by Prentice Hall

LISTS FOR TEACHER'S REFERENCES

LIST 279 THE MATH TEACHER'S RESPONSIBILITIES

Just as students have responsibilities that will help to ensure success in their classes, teachers must accept responsibilities, too. To be as effective as he or she can, every math teacher should:

- Prepare and present lessons that will enable students to learn the math skills and concepts contained in their curriculum.
- Offer clear directions, explanations, and deadlines for assignments.
- Develop and maintain a comfortable and orderly classroom atmosphere that will promote and support learning.
- Develop a clear set of classroom rules and procedures, and make certain that students understand and follow them.
- Provide a fair system of grading. Also make sure that students understand how their grades are determined.
- Encourage student questions, and strive to answer them.
- Be demanding of work, but also considerate of feelings.
- Help students learn problem-solving skills.
- Help students to see the importance of math in their everyday lives.
- Help students master technology such as calculators and computers.
- Be willing to listen to student concerns and problems.
- Applaud the efforts of students, and enjoy their individual growth.

LIST 280   UPGRADING YOUR MATHEMATICS CURRICULUM

The last few years have seen dramatic changes in the way mathematics are taught. Because of the widespread use of calculators and computers, and the increasing demands of our society that require high-level, problem-solving skills, the teaching of basic computation no longer enjoys the preeminence it once did. To adequately prepare students for the next century, math curriculums must evolve to offer students the skills that will enable them to be successful. Following is a summary of some changes you might consider to upgrade your math curriculum.

Grades 4–8

Greater Emphasis:

- Patterns and relationships.
- Relevant problems, in a variety of formats.
- Open-ended problems; written explanations of reasoning to find solutions.
- Group problem-solving.
- Applying mathematics to other subject areas.
- Incorporating various disciplines in problem-solving.
- Calculators and computers in problem-solving.
- Problems and situations that develop a sense of numbers.
- Estimation in problem-solving and checking for reasonable answers.
- Interpretation of graphs, tables, charts, etc.
- Inductive and deductive reasoning.
- Statistical methods.

Less Emphasis:

- Clue words to determine which operation to use in solving word problems.
- One-step word problems.
- Problems that use irrelevant situations which are of little interest to students.
- Drill.
- Skill development out of context.
- Memorization of formulas and facts.

Grades 9–12

Greater Emphasis:

- Problems that require investigation, either individually or in groups.
- Integrated math problems that tie into other disciplines.

The Math Teacher's Book of Lists, © 1995 by Prentice Hall

LIST 280 (Continued)

- Problems built upon real situations.
- Written explanations that detail reasoning.
- The use of calculators.
- The use of computers, particularly in problem-solving and to develop conceptual understanding.
- Inductive and deductive reasoning.
- Integration of various subjects and applications of mathematics.
- Modeling.

Less Emphasis:

- One-step word problems.
- Drill.
- Paper-and-pencil evaluations and solutions.
- Memorization.
- Paper-and-pencil graphing of equations.

LIST 281   MATERIALS EVERY MATH CLASSROOM SHOULD HAVE

It's tough teaching math with just a text. You need lots of materials and supplies. The following list provides the basics.

General Supplies

Calculators
Pens
Pencils
Paper
Colored Pencils
Rulers
Meter Sticks
Graph Paper
Scissors
Markers
Compasses
Protractors
Computers (and related equipment)

Tapes
Glue
Posters
Poster Paper
Grid Paper
Erasers
String
Overhead Projector
Erasable Markers
Math Dictionary
Resource Books
Various Templates
Software

Supplies You'll Need According to Topic

Stop Watch
Cuisenaire Rods
Decimal Squares
Fraction Squares
Fraction Circles
Algebra Tiles
Geoboard and Rubber Bands
Two Color Counters
Mirrors
Polyhedra Dice
3-D Geometric Models
Scales
Platform Spring Balance
Graduated Cylinder

Base 10 Blocks
Shape Tracers
Pattern Blocks
Spinners
Pentominoes
Tangrams
Snap Cubes
Color Tiles
Dice
Thermometers
Measuring Cups
Balance
Liter Cube
Mass Set

LIST 282 EXPANDING THE HORIZONS OF YOUR MATH CLASS

The learning environment of any math class can be enhanced by expanding its horizons and broadening its scope. Following are some suggestions.

- Keep your classroom bright and cheerful.
- Promote and foster fresh ideas, openness, and sharing.
- Encourage student creativity and discovery.
- Treat mathematics as a subject that can be learned by everyone—male, female, and any ethnic group.
- Encourage all of your students, all of the time.
- Remember that students are individuals and learn at their own pace.
- Demand an orderly classroom. Explain expectations and requirements so that students know what is expected of them. Model appropriate behavior.
- Move around the classroom and interact with your students. Become an encourager, guide, and nurturer as well as a giver of information.
- Be fair, consistent, and firm in your discipline.
- Encourage your students to consider and explain their reasoning during problem-solving.
- Use group work to foster the sharing of ideas.
- Incorporate other disciplines in your math class. Encourage writing. Show how math applies to science, social studies, and art whenever possible.
- Connect math to real-life problems and situations.
- Encourage the use of calculators and computers.
- Use manipulative materials.
- Use fair assessments that reflect the skills that have been taught.
- Remember that students will usually rise to your expectations. Maintaining high, realistic goals in a positive, nurturing environment will help your students to realize their greatest potential.

LIST 283   THE MATH TEACHER'S MANAGEMENT STRATEGIES

The following tips can help you run your day more effectively.

1. List and prioritize your tasks each day. Do the most important first.

2. Arrange your tasks according to times that are best for you. For example, if it is easier for you to grade papers at home, do your grading there rather than at school. Use your time in school for other tasks.

3. Try to stagger tests and projects so that you aren't swamped with a hundred papers to correct over one weekend. Get in the habit of taking one class's papers home each night.

4. Try to handle each paper only once.

5. Keep the papers of different classes separated. Use folders or large envelopes.

6. Keep your desk organized and your file cabinets in order. Few things are more aggravating than being unable to find something that is right in front of you, buried beneath the pile on your desk.

7. Remember that everyone has a limit. Don't take on extra tasks or responsibilities just because no one else will take them.

8. Set time limits to complete tasks and activities. Try to stick to them within reason.

9. Start meetings on schedule, and keep them focused on the agenda.

10. Whenever you need to wait for something—the dentist for example—take along plenty of reading materials. Use such times to catch up.

11. Enlist the help of students whenever possible.

12. Encourage students to work together and help each other in the solving of difficult problems.

13. At the beginning of the year, share your classroom rules with students and explain procedures. When students understand what is expected of them, they are more likely to act and behave appropriately. Once your rules are stated, be sure to enforce them.

14. When making phone calls, do them all in one sitting. When you can't reach a parent and must have that parent call you back, offer a time and a phone number (it's usually best to leave a school number) where you may be reached. This reduces the chances of conducting a conversation through answering machines or secretaries.

15. Learn to recognize when enough is enough. If you burn out today, tomorrow is lost.

The Math Teacher's Book of Lists, © 1995 by Prentice Hall

LIST 284   RUNNING AN EFFECTIVE MATH CLASS—PROBLEMS AND SOLUTIONS

You are indeed a rare teacher if your students never experience problems with discipline or motivation, or worse! While the following suggestions are by no means cure-alls, they can help.

Problem: Student does not complete assignments.

Possible Solutions: Speak to the student individually about finishing work on time. Perhaps the work is too difficult, and his class needs to be changed. Monitor his work closely. If there is no improvement, contact the student's parents or guardians and make arrangements for him to give up a free period or stay after school to complete the work. If necessary, consult a guidance counselor about the student. There may be an underlying problem.

Problem: Student is easily distracted.

Possible Solutions: Speak to this student about her behavior and stress the importance of remaining on task. Position her desk close to yours and seat her near quiet students who are less likely to distract her. When group work is required, be sure to place her with students who will remain focused on their assignment. Encourage her, and offer praise for appropriate behavior.

Problem: Student is disruptive or argumentative.

Possible Solutions: Address the unacceptable behavior quickly. Waiting for it to simply "go away" usually results in the problem growing bigger. Explain to the student why such behavior is not acceptable and will not be tolerated. You might try to draw the student out; ask him why he is misbehaving. An honest question from a caring adult often results in surprising openness. If that doesn't work, you may need to mention the consequences should the behavior continue. If it does, follow the standard disciplinary procedures of your school, which might include detention, a meeting with the vice-principal, or a conference with parents or guardians.

Problem: Several students aren't getting along.

Possible Solutions: The obvious first step is to separate the students. Speak to the students as a group and discuss the nature of the problem and how it might be solved. Offer strategies such as focusing on positive comments and actions, ignoring negatives, and keeping away from those with whom students can't settle disputes. In some cases, when the problem affects the entire class, it might be helpful to discuss the behavior—not necessarily the problem if it is personal—and seek constructive ways to cope with it. Students often can provide helpful suggestions. Try using mini-lessons and role-playing as methods of introducing social skills.

Problem: Student attempts to dominate groups of which he is a member.

Possible Solutions: Place this student in groups with equally strong personalities. Avoid putting him in a group that he can dominate. Speak to the student about appropriate behavior in a group setting, and sit in on groups of

LIST 284   (Continued)

which he is a part. Not only will you be able to closely monitor his behavior, but you will be able to model the appropriate behavior as well.

Problem: Student gives up easily.

Possible Solutions: Provide plenty of support and encouragement. Work with this student individually to make sure that she understands how to complete assignments. Offer praise for each small step forward. For group work, place this student with others who will provide her with support.

Problem: You feel that the student is copying homework.

Possible Solutions: Speak to the student individually about completing his own work. You may wish to address the entire class on this. Emphasize that only by doing their own work will they master the skills necessary to satisfactorily complete your course. You may need to contact the student's parent or guardian. Remember to be diplomatic here because you are on treacherous ground. You may be quite convinced that the student is cheating, but his mother and father may be equally convinced that he would never do such a thing. Be prepared to answer their questions. Noting how he always has his homework done perfectly, but then has trouble passing a quiz on the same material is a good way to prove your point. You can then discuss with the parents how important it is for their son to do his own work. Not only will he learn more, but he will gain satisfaction knowing that he is responsible for his good grades.

Problem: The student's work is suffering because of an undiagnosed learning disability.

Possible Solutions: Contact the student's guidance counselor, your school's child study team, or the administrator in charge of learning disabilities and recommend that the student be tested to discover if any learning problem exists. Consult with her previous and other current teachers to find out if they see some of the same problems you do. This can provide you with more anecdotal insight about the problem.

LIST 285   HOW TO RUN A COOPERATIVE MATH CLASS

Cooperative classrooms are based upon the belief that students can work together and help each other in the process of learning. The following points will help you to organize your math classes to take advantage of a cooperative atmosphere.

- Cooperative learning is based on teams.
  - —Pairs and groups of three or four work best in the elementary grades.
  - —In the middle school and high school, four to six generally work well.
  - —Mix abilities in your groups. Avoid having four top students in one group and four low students in another.
  - —Try to balance personalities. Form groups where students are likely to work well together. Don't put an overly dominate student with three shy, quiet ones.
  - —Mix ethnic groups and try to balance boys and girls.
  - —Change groups periodically.
- Explain the purpose of the groups fully. Unless they understand the structure, students may have trouble meeting your expectations.
- Assign roles to students, telling them that each student has an important part in the group. There are various roles you might assign, including:
  - —Leader, who keeps the group on task.
  - —Recorder, who writes down the team's ideas, conclusions, and results.
  - —Time Monitor, who keeps track of time.
  - —Materials Monitor, who is responsible for any materials the group might need.
  - —Checker, who reviews the group's work.

  In small groups, a student can assume more than one role.
- Arrange your classroom furniture to accommodate group work. You might utilize tables, or simply have students slide desks together to form tables.
- In the beginning of the year, do a practice run. Organize your groups, start them working on a task, and sit in on each group and model the appropriate behavior. Some students may not know how to work together. By assuming the various roles yourself, you will be showing them how to act.
- Set a time limit for group work, based upon the activity. Remember that work usually expands to fit the amount of time given to do it.
- Use a signal—flashing the lights on and off, a small bell, or clapping your hands—to gain your students' attention when you need to talk to the class or they become noisy.
- Allow a few weeks for students to become skilled at working in groups.

LIST 286   STUDENT GUIDELINES FOR
WORKING IN GROUPS

Many math activities and problems are ideal for group work. The following suggestions can help any group to work more effectively.

- Group members should be willing to cooperate.
- Each member should share his or her ideas.
- Members should refrain from attempting to dominate any discussion.
- Before speaking, members should carefully think about the points they wish to make. When they speak, they should try to state their ideas clearly.
- After speaking, individuals should give the floor to others.
- Members should remember that courtesy and politeness are essential to the smooth working of any group.
- The discussion should remain focused on math, particularly on the problem to be solved.
- Listeners should not interrupt speakers. They should note questions and ask them after the speaker is finished.
- When disagreements arise, they should be discussed calmly, without undue emotion. Everyone should be afforded the opportunity to speak and contribute.
- Comments should always be kept on the topic, and should always be constructive.
- If members are given specific roles to fulfill—for example, group leader, time monitor, or recorder—each should accept the responsibilities of that role.

The Math Teacher's Book of Lists, © 1995 by Prentice Hall

LIST 287   STEPS FOR CONDUCTING
EFFECTIVE CONFERENCES WITH STUDENTS

Conferences with your students over math often lead to increased motivation and achievement on the parts of students. A conference need not be lengthy or formal and may last only a minute or two. It may take place at your desk, at the student's desk, during a free period, or after school.

The purpose of any conference is to help your students improve their understanding of mathematics. During the conference, which may be initiated either by you or the student, you may offer praise for good work, encouragement, or explain a specific skill. No matter where or when they occur, your conferences will be more successful if you follow the guidelines below.

- Try to meet with all of your students periodically. You may be able to speak with only two or three from each class each day, but even that will give you the chance to meet with everyone regularly.

- Begin the conference by seeking the student's input. Ask him if he is having trouble with anything. If you know he is having problems with a particular skill, use that as your starting point.

- Keep the conference focused. Try to address only one or two skills, or one type of problem. Trying to do too much can overwhelm and frustrate students.

- Build an atmosphere of support and cooperation during the conference. Keep the tone upbeat.

- Tailor the conference to meet the individual needs of students.

- During the conference, be ready to assume one of several roles—cheerleader, encourager, nurturer, motivator, listener, giver of information, and guide.

- Be sincere with your praise. Students quickly realize when you're not.

- Offer positive comments, and always avoid negative or sarcastic remarks. The conference should be a time of support and help.

LIST 288   STEPS TO HELP STUDENTS DEVELOP PROBLEM-SOLVING SKILLS

There are many things you can do to help your students learn and use problem-solving skills. Such skills not only will help them in math class, but in life as well.

- Give students realistic, authentic problems that have meaning in their everyday lives.
- Give both numerical and non-numerical problems.
- Encourage students to make up their own problems and share them with classmates.
- Organize problem-solving groups of 4 to 5 students. Distribute problems to the groups, and let students work together and discuss possible methods for solution.
- Provide problems that have more than one answer.
- Give problems that have unnecessary information, or missing information. (Have students supply the missing data.)
- Give problems that can be solved using mental math.
- Encourage students to keep notes of their attempts to solve difficult problems.
- Provide problems that require estimation.
- Provide an assortment of high-level problems that require explanations in their solutions.
- Encourage the use of various problem-solving strategies.
- Suggest to students that they try to identify various ways to solve a problem and then choose the best one.
- Urge students to ask themselves questions as they solve problems.
- Consider beginning each class with a problem-of-the-day.
- Encourage students to review their progress in solving problems. They should adjust their plan as necessary.
- Stress to students that they should check their answers for logic. Answers should always "make sense."

LIST 289   A TEACHER'S PLAN FOR WRITING BETTER WORD PROBLEMS

While the vast majority of textbooks provide solid word problems for your students to solve, it's still likely that you can improve them, or at least tailor them for your class. Here are some suggestions.

1. Change the original question. Many word problems provide enough information so that you can easily change the question.

2. Add extra information to the problem. This forces students to find the necessary information and discard what's not needed.

3. Delete some information and have students identify the data needed to solve the problem.

4. Add some information and create multi-step problems out of one-step problems.

5. Provide students with data from word problems, and have them write the questions.

6. Offer hints to help students solve complicated or difficult problems.

7. Use graphs, charts, and tables in their textbooks for data from which students can write problems for each other.

8. Provide students with the answers to a few problems on a page of problems, and have them find the problems that match up with the given answers.

9. Mix problems that have different operations. This requires students to think carefully about which operation is necessary.

10. Ask students to write down the steps they use to solve problems.

LIST 290   SOURCES OF PROBLEMS-OF-THE-DAY

Many teachers find it useful to begin class with a problem-of-the-day. Unfortunately, it's sometimes a "problem" to come up with a problem-of-the-day. Following are some sources, as well as a few tips, for creating problems that will focus your students for your upcoming lesson.

Sources

- Newspapers, both local and national. You can find lots of good information that can be turned into relevant problems.
- Magazines. Consult news magazines, major monthlies, and the magazines that your students read.
- Almanacs. These provide plenty of interesting facts and statistics.
- Your math book. Many math books contain sections of "Extensions" or "Challenges" that you can use for problems-of-the-day.
- Books of math games and puzzles. If your school library doesn't have these, your local library will. There are countless titles from which you can find great information.
- Major events in school. As students scramble to come up with the cash for prom gowns and tuxedos, you might come up with problems that zero in on money.

Tips for Creating Problems-of-the-Day

1. Focus on a review skill. One of the best uses of a problem-of-the day is to keep students sharp with skills they've already learned.
2. Make the problems relevant. Tie the problems into a current event of interest to your students, or an issue or topic that affects them.
3. Create problems that have more than one step.

LIST 291 THE USE OF PORTFOLIOS IN YOUR CLASSES

A portfolio contains samples of a student's work that is collected over a given length of time. A good portfolio offers insights to a student's thinking, understanding, and mathematical problem-solving skills, and thus offers a picture of the student's progress in math. Following are some suggestions how you can incorporate the use of portfolios in your classroom.

- Explain to your students what a portfolio is, and how it will be used.
- Provide students with portfolio envelopes. They should be large enough to hold various kinds of work.
- Make sure that your students understand that they are to select their best work for their portfolios. Because one of the purposes of the portfolio is to show individual growth, all papers should be dated.
- Portfolios may be one of two kinds: an *assessment* portfolio that shows particular growth, or a *work* portfolio that contains various projects and activities. Generally, papers from the work portfolio are selected to go into the assessment portfolio.
- While you may guide students in their selection of material for their portfolios, they should be the judges of what actually goes in.
- The material that goes into a portfolio should help the teacher and others to understand how students see themselves in the learning of math.
- Many papers, activities, and projects are appropriate for inclusion in a portfolio. Following are some suggestions:
  —A table of contents.
  —Solutions to difficult problems that detail problem-solving abilities.
  —The use of mathematics in another discipline.
  —Problems created by the student.
  —An example of the student's group activity.
  —A written report on a major topic in math.
  —The student's written account of his or her growth in mathematics.
  —Responses to challenging questions and problems.
  —A written explanation of the contents of the portfolio.

LIST 292   HELPING STUDENTS PREPARE FOR MATH TESTS

Whether it's a unit assessment, an end-of-the-year exam, or a standardized test, there's much you can do to help your students prepare.

1. Be sure that students are familiar with the test's format. They should know how the test is organized, how many sections it contains, and if there are time limits.

2. Students should also be familiar with the types of problems they can expect. It's not fair for students to be given new or "trick" problems on the test.

3. Students should have plenty of practice with the types of problems they will have. If possible, give them a complete practice test.

4. Lead up to the test by beginning several classes with problems-of-the-day that are similar to problems that will be on the test. Such an on-going review will sharpen the skills of students.

5. If the test requires that students fill in responses on an answer sheet, they should have practice tests that have answer sheets.

6. Review the day before the test. Encourage students to come to this class with any questions that they might have about the test.

For additional material on test-taking strategies, see List 43, "Strategies for Taking Math Tests."

LIST 293   MATH BULLETIN BOARD IDEAS

There's nothing like a good bulletin board to stimulate your students' thinking about math. Ideally, your bulletin board should be located near your classroom or in a central location. While every teacher likes to have great bulletin boards, you're probably thinking you don't have the time to come up with ideas. Maybe the following suggestions will help.

- Names and photos of top math students. Students of the month are a good display.
- News about math. You might offer information about math contests, club meetings, conferences, scholarships, or post interesting articles clipped from newspapers and magazines.
- Challenging problems or puzzles. Perhaps offer a "Puzzle of the Week." Be sure to provide the answer for the previous puzzle.
- Top tests or projects.
- Career information about math. You might post various jobs, their descriptions, and their qualifications.
- Posters showing how mathematics is important to other fields and disciplines.
- Examples of mathematical ideas and principles.
- Brief biographical sketches about famous mathematicians.
- Computer-generated illustrations of mathematical concepts or ideas.
- A display of student essays titled, "Math and Me."
- A list of various colleges that are recognized for their mathematics departments.
- Illustrations or pictures highlighting various geometric shapes.

LIST 294   POSSIBLE MATH PROJECTS

Following are some suggestions for math projects.

- Create a booklet of original word problems. Produce the booklet via desk-top publishing software and distribute copies to your class.
- Create a packet of math problems derived from statistics, charts, and tables you find in newspapers and magazines. Distribute copies to your class.
- Write a report on a topic in mathematics. Select your own or consider one of these—
  —The History of Mathematics
  —Measurement in the Ancient World
  —Computers and Their Mathematical Applications
  —A Famous Mathematician
  —Math in Everyday Life
  —The Development of Numbers
  —The Increasing Role of Mathematics in a Technological World
  —The Mathematical Contributions of the Ancient Greeks
  —Mathematics and Architecture
  —Mathematical Principles in Nature
  —Math and Art
  —Math and Medicine
  —Inventions and the Use of Mathematics
  —Symmetry Patterns in Nature
  —Geometry and the City
- Choose your favorite sport. Consider how mathematics plays a part in its record keeping and statistics. Present an oral report to your class on the topic.
- Write a how-to manual for younger students, explaining how to use a calculator effectively.
- Create a collage of people using mathematics in their professions.
- Design and build models showing geometric shapes.
- Create a scale drawing of the floor plan of your home, or, if you are really ambitious, your school.
- Create charts and graphs detailing how the school day is broken down into periods and activities.
- Create a packet of cross-number puzzles, photocopy it, and distribute copies to the class.
- Design, create, and produce a newspaper or magazine about mathematics. Use desktop software to make high-quality copies.

LIST 294 (Continued)

- Collect magazine articles and newspaper clippings about mathematics and make a portfolio.

- Present an oral report about a famous mathematician.

- Organize a panel discussion on an interesting topic in mathematics. A good example—The Use of Calculators in Math Class. Another one—The Relevance of Mathematics Today.

LIST 295   HOW TO START A MATH MAGAZINE

Math magazines are an excellent way of sharing ideas and news about math. They may be rather simple productions—typed articles run off on old duplicators—or be the eye-catching result of the latest in desktop publishing. By far the best are written and produced by students. Following are several tips for producing quality math magazines.

- Although a math magazine can be a class effort, it is usually better to have the magazine produced by a math club. This permits more students from various classes and grade levels to participate.

- Students should assume most of the responsibility for producing the magazine. Students should act as editors, reporters, researchers, and proofreaders, as well as manage the overall production process.

- You might consider working together with the English teacher. He or she can help students with some of the finer points of writing while you focus on the mathematics.

- Your magazine should come out regularly. Decide whether it will be monthly or quarterly. More than monthly will be a tough pace to keep up; less than quarterly will make it hard to maintain continuity.

- With your students, decide on what types of articles your magazine will contain. You might focus on math topics and interests, news items regarding mathematics, contests, puzzles, reports of student projects, and interesting problems.

- Start collecting material for the magazine well in advance of deadlines. Set a deadline that will give you enough time for production.

- For typing, consider enlisting the aid of parent volunteers. If students have access to word processors, encourage them to type the articles. Desktop publishing software can be used to produce high-quality magazines.

- Illustrate your magazine, using computer software or line drawings. Remember that detailed illustrations may not reproduce well. To avoid ruining a finished page, cut out drawings and attach them to the page using white tape or paste.

- Before printing your magazine, have student proofreaders check every page carefully. Now is the time to catch any remaining mistakes.

- Producing the magazine on both sides of the paper results in an attractive appearance. Use a photocopier or duplicator to produce your magazine.

- Print enough copies of your magazine for students, faculty, administrators, and displays throughout your school.

LIST 296   HOW TO START A MATH CLUB

A math club provides an excellent forum for students and teachers to share ideas about mathematics, and listen to outside speakers or members reporting on special topics in math. If you are considering starting a math club in your school, keep the following points in mind.

- The typical math club is sponsored by a faculty member.
- The club's members may consist of faculty and students. Usually, students from various classes and grades may join.
- Many math clubs operate under a constitution that details the club's organization and bylaws.
- Meetings may be held whenever the members agree are appropriate times. However, most clubs meet either twice a month or monthly. Less than once a month makes it difficult to maintain the club's purpose; meeting more than twice a month may be a burden for some members.
- Meetings generally run a half-hour to forty-five minutes.
- Math clubs often select rather exotic names for themselves: the Euclidians, Pi Squares, The Circle are some.
- Many math clubs maintain math libraries that club members have access to.
- Many math clubs undertake various projects:
  —Maintaining a mathematics bulletin board.
  —Publishing a mathematics newspaper.
  —Sponsoring math contests in the school.
  —Providing a tutoring program for students who request help in math.
  —Providing reviews of mathematics books for the regular math classes.
  —Constructing models, diagrams, and posters highlighting topics in mathematics and distributing them throughout the school.
  —Providing a forum for recognizing student achievement in math.

LIST 297   IDEAS FOR MATH FIELD TRIPS

Following is a list of possible field trips for your math classes.

Museum—Look for exhibits that show how math is used in our lives.

Science Center—See how math is used in science.

Supermarket—See the ways numbers are used in pricing and calculating.

Accounting Firm—Learn how accountants work with numbers.

Engineering Firm—Learn how formulas are used in design.

Bank—Learn how interest rates and percents are used in banking.

Architectural Firm—See how architects use formulas in the design of buildings.

Insurance Office—Find out how insurance rates are determined.

Carpentry Shop—Learn how measurements are used in construction.

Toy Manufacturer—See how math is used in the design and manufacture of new toys.

Real Estate Office—Learn how commissions are determined as a percentage of the sale price of a new home.

Social Service Office—See how mathematical data are gathered and analyzed.

Lumber Yard—Find out how divisibility rules are used in cutting materials to produce the least amount of waste.

Sign Shop—See how geometry is used designing signs.

Print Shop—See how geometry is used in making posters and displays.

Retail Store—Learn how math is used in determining sales prices and discounts.

LIST 298   POSSIBLE GUEST SPEAKERS FOR YOUR MATH CLASS

Some students have trouble finding the relevance of math. They just don't see how important math is in their lives. Bringing guest speakers into your classes can often help students see that math is essential in our society. The list below suggests some people you might ask to speak to your classes.

Actuary—explaining how formulas are used to determine insurance rates.

Auto Mechanic—discussing the use of metric measurements in car repairs; or explaining how math is used in measuring liquid capacities for fuel, oil, power steering fluid, brake fluid, etc.

Bank Officer—speaking about savings, loans, and interest rates.

Stock Broker—explaining how stocks are bought and sold.

Architect—explaining how geometry is used to design buildings.

Computer Programmer/Operator—speaking about the use of spread sheets.

Advertising Agent—discussing how statistics are used in determining target audiences.

Builder/Contractor—speaking of how formulas are used in constructing buildings.

Engineer—discussing how formulas are used in determining the weight limit of bridges.

Astronomer—explaining scientific notation and light years for representing "astronomical" distances.

Accountant—discussing sales, income, and other taxes.

Newspaper Editor—explaining how statistics are gathered and used by newspapers in various articles.

Cook—talking about how fractions are used in baking.

Biologist—explaining how sampling can be used to determine animal or plant populations in a given area.

Interior Decorator—explaining how measurement plays a vital role in furnishing a room or a home.

Statistician—explaining how various types of data are gathered and analyzed.

Photographer—discussing shutter speeds on cameras.

Retail Sales Person—explaining how percents and discounts are determined.

LIST 299   STEPS FOR MAINTAINING POSITIVE RELATIONS WITH PARENTS

Enlisting the support of parents throughout the year can go a long way to helping students achieve their potential in your classes. The suggestions that follow can aid you in your efforts to enlist the support of parents.

- View parents as positive resources. While it's true that some parents are their children's biggest "problem," the great majority are truly interested in their children's education and want to help.

- Be available to parents. Be willing to return phone calls and answer notes promptly. At back-to-school night inform parents that you appreciate any support they can give to their children in the learning of math.

- Throughout the year, keep parents informed of their children's progress. Obviously, report cards and interim notices do this, but there are other means as well. When a student does exceptionally well on a test, drop a line home. If a student begins to slip, don't wait for the mid-marking notices—call or send a note. Most parents want to know about such changes in their children's performance.

- During conference time, be prepared to meet with parents. Take any notes, copies of tests, quizzes, and homework assignments that support what you need to say.

- Be specific in discussing the weaknesses and strengths of your students, and how parents can help their children.

- Be tactful when speaking with parents. Saying that Johnny "never does a lick of homework and is as sloppy as his old man" is unlikely to result in a positive or useful conference.

- Avoid sugarcoating. Don't tell a parent that if her daughter works exceptionally hard, she has a chance for a B when it's unlikely she will be able to get more than a D. Building false hopes only sets people up for a letdown.

- Share with parents your enthusiasm for mathematics, and educate them about the importance of learning mathematics.

The Math Teacher's Book of Lists, © 1995 by Prentice Hall

LIST 300   HOW PARENTS CAN HELP THEIR CHILDREN LEARN MATH

As their children advance through the grades, many parents begin to feel that they can no longer help them with their math. Either the math is becoming too complicated, they don't want to show their children the way "they" were taught, which might be different than the methods their children's teachers use, or they feel that by helping their children learn math they will be pushing into the teacher's space. Whatever the reason, when parents take a backseat, their children are denied a valuable resource. Following are some simple things all parents can do to help their children learn math.

- Become acquainted with the math teacher at back-to-school night and parent-teacher conferences.

- Let the math teacher know that you want to help your child at home. Ask what specific help you might provide. Most teachers will be glad to give suggestions.

- Encourage your child to complete his or her math neatly and accurately. This helps to minimize careless mistakes.

- Encourage your child to restate word problems, especially what information is given and what the question is.

- Practice estimation with your child. When you go to a convenience store to buy a few items, ask your child to estimate the cost.

- Practice measurement. Estimate the time necessary for trips, estimate the heights and weights of various objects. When you are measuring the windows for new curtains, encourage your child to help.

- Never tell your child that some people "just aren't good at math," or that you aren't good with math. Instead, emphasize that competency can be gained through hard work.

- Never think that girls can't do math as well as boys.

- Always reward your child with praise when he or she does well. That helps build confidence.

- At home talk about math in a positive manner. Point out the many practical tasks that require an understanding of mathematics—planning a home budget, calculating the grocery bills, setting enough money aside for a vacation.

- Whenever possible, use math at home in problem-solving. Encourage your child to work out the problem.

LIST 301   HOW TO HAVE A PARENTS' MATH NIGHT

Parents want their children to enjoy school and be successful. Most realize the importance of mathematics and would like to help their children with their work, but they aren't sure how. A parents' math night can show them some of the things they can do to support your efforts in the classroom, as well as emphasize the many ways mathematics affects our lives.

Plan in Advance

- Clear the idea of having a parents' math night with your principal or supervisor. Enlist his or her support.
- Decide on who your audience will be, for example parents of elementary, middle, or high school students. You might aim for the parents of a specific grade level. If you don't limit your audience, you risk not being able to present relevant activities. The needs of a 4th grade math student are quite different than those of a 10th grader.
- Decide on who will be invited. Just your school? The entire district? Will you include private and parochial schools?
- Decide on how many spaces will be available. If you will be working alone, more than 25 will be hard to manage, especially if your activities include manipulatives. You will be able to handle more if you have help, perhaps a colleague or student volunteers. Student council or math club members are usually good choices.
- Choose a date. Check your school calendar to make sure that there are no conflicts with sports events, concerts, or other programs. Generally, around major holidays, community activities, or near vacations are not good times. Perhaps tie your parents' math night to a general PTA meeting, which will add to your turnout.
- Obtain funds for supplies, promotions, and refreshments. Know how much you can spend and don't go over your budget.
- Publicize your parents' math night in district, school, and PTA newsletters and publications. List the date on the school calendar, announce it at any meetings you attend, and provide press releases to local newspapers. You should also send flyers home with students. If you are limiting the number of participants, be sure to inform parents that they must sign up in advance. Providing a confirmation slip on the flyer is an easy way to do this.
- Decide what activities you will provide. Ideally, activities should help parents to understand the math their children are learning, problems they might be encountering, and how they can support their children's efforts. Manipulatives provide hands-on experience while also illustrating concepts.

The Math Teacher's Book of Lists, © 1995 by Prentice Hall

LIST 301   (Continued)

The Big Night

- Arrive early and make sure that you're organized. Set up the refreshments at the back of the room. If a colleague or students will be helping you, meet with them and review what they are to do.

- Make any handouts available to parents as they enter. This eliminates the need for taking time to pass materials out during your presentation.

- To begin the session, introduce yourself and state your objectives. If the group is small enough, ask parents to introduce themselves.

- Briefly explain your math curriculum and how the activities you planned for this night will support the learning efforts of the parents' children.

- Move into the first part of your session as quickly and smoothly as possible. A parents' math night should be activity-oriented.

- Plan a break at about the halfway point. Encourage parents to help themselves to refreshments. During the break, make yourself available to parents. If many seem to have the same questions, address them in the second part. Limit the break to around 10 minutes.

- Provide time for parents' questions at the conclusion of the session. Hand out an evaluation form that asks parents how your math night might be improved.

- Provide followup as necessary. You'll likely find your parents' math night to be as enlightening to parents as it is rewarding to you.

LIST 302   PROFESSIONAL MATH ORGANIZATIONS

While there are many professional math organizations around, the following are likely to be of most interest to teachers and math supervisors.

American Mathematical Society
P.O. Box 6248
Providence, RI 02940-6248

Association for Women in Mathematics
4114 Computer and Math Sciences Building
University of Maryland
College Park, MD 20742-2461

Mathematics Association of America
1529 18th St., N.W.
Washington, DC 20036

National Council of Supervisors of Mathematics
P.O. Box 10667
Golden, CO 80401-0600

National Council of Teachers of Mathematics
1906 Association Drive
Reston, VA 22091-1593

School Science and Mathematics Association
Bloomsburg University
Bloomsburg, PA 17815

LIST 303 USEFUL ADDRESSES OF MANIPULATIVE AND SOFTWARE COMPANIES

If you are like us, we have catalogs for manipulatives and software everywhere. Unfortunately, we can never find the one we want when we need it. This list has been extremely useful for us. We trust it will be for you, too.

Manipulative Companies

- Creative Publications, Order Department, 5040 West 111th St., Oak Lawn, IL 60453. 800-624-0822.
- Cuisenaire Co. of America, Inc., P.O. Box 5026, White Plains, NY 10602-5062. 800-273-3142.
- Dale Seymour Publications, P.O. Box 10888, Palo Alto, CA 94303-0879. 800-827-110.
- Didax, Inc., Educational Resources, One Centennial Dr., Peabody, MA 01960. 800-458-0024.
- ETA, 620 Lakeview Parkway, Vernon Hills, IL 60061. 800-445-5985 or 708-816-5050.
- M^2 Solids, 24351 Condon, Oak Park, MI 48237. 810-399-9571.
- Tricon Publishing, Box 146, Mt. Pleasant, MI 48804. 517-772-2811.
- J. Weston Walch, P.O. Box 658, Portland, ME 04104. 207-772-2848.

Software Companies

- Gamco Industries, P.O. Box 1862W, Big Tree, TX 79721. 800-351-1404.
- IBM, 4111 Northside Pkwy., NW, P.O. Box 2150, Atlanta, GA 30055. 800-IBM-2468.
- MECC, 6160 Summit Drive North, Minneapolis, MN 55430-4003. 800-685-MECC.
- Scholastic, Inc., P.O. Box 7502, Jefferson City, MO 65102. 800-541-5513.
- Wings for Learning/Sunburst, 1600 Green Hills Road, P.O. Box 660002, Scotts Valley, CA 95067-0002. 800-321-7511.

LIST 304   BIBLIOGRAPHY

The following books offer a true treasure of ideas and practical activities.

Adler, Irving, and Adler, Ruth. *Numbers Old and New.* New York: The John Day Company, 1960.

Asimov, Isaac. *Realm of Numbers.* Cambridge: The Riverside Press, 1959.

Blocksma, Mary. *Reading the Numbers.* New York: Penguin Books, 1989.

Brandes, Louis Grant. *Math Can Be Fun.* Maine: J. Weston Walch, 1975.

Burns, Marilyn. *About Teaching Mathematics, a K–8 Resource.* USA: Math Solutions Publications, 1992.

Burns, Marilyn. *Math for Smarty Pants.* California: Yolla Bolly Press, 1982.

Burns, Marilyn. *The I Hate Mathematics! Book.* California: Yolla Bolly Press, 1975.

Coburn, Terrence. *How to Teach Mathematics Using a Calculator.* Reston, VA: NCTM, 1987.

Davidson, Neil, ed. *Cooperative Learning in Mathematics: A Handbook for Teachers.* Menlo Park, CA: Addison-Wesley, 1990.

Edwards, Edgar, ed. *Algebra for Everyone.* Reston, VA: NCTM, 1990.

Gardner, Martin. *Entertaining Mathematical Puzzles.* New York: Dover Publications, Inc., 1986.

Gardner, Martin. *Mathematical Carnival.* New York: Alfred A. Knopf, 1978.

Gardner, Martin. *Mathematical Circus.* New York: Alfred A. Knopf, 1979.

Gardner, Martin. *Mathematical Magic Show.* New York: Alfred A. Knopf, 1977.

Glatzer, David J., and Glatzer, Joyce. *Math Connections: Middle-School Activities.* Palo Alto, CA: Dale Seymour, 1988.

Grouws, Douglas A., Cooney, Thomas J., and Jones, Douglas. *Effective Mathematics Teaching.* Reston, VA: NCTM, 1988.

Gowar, Norman. *An Invitation to Mathematics.* Oxford: Oxford University Press, 1979.

Harnadek, Anita. *Algebra Word Problems.* Pacific Grove, CA: Midwest Publications, 1989.

Hiebert, James, and Behr, Merlyn. *Number Concepts and Operations in the Middle Grades.* Reston, VA: NCTM, 1988.

Hopkins, Nigel J., Mayne, John W., and Hudson, John R. *Go Figure! The Numbers You Need for Everyday Life.* Detroit: Visible Ink Press, 1992.

Johnson, Richard E., and Johnson, Cheryl G. *Algebra, The Language of Mathematics.* Menlo Park, CA: Addison-Wesley Publishing Co., Inc., 1975.

Jurgenson, Ray C., Maier, John E., and Donnelly, Alfred J. *Modern Basic Geometry.* Boston: Houghton Mifflin Co., 1976.

Kaplan, Andrew. *Careers for Number Lovers.* Connecticut: The Millbrook Press, 1991.

Kogelman, Stanley, and Heller, Barbara R. *The Only Math Book You'll Ever Need.* New York: Facts on File Publications, 1986.

Krause, Marina C. *Multicultural Mathematics Materials.* Reston, VA: NCTM, 1983.

Marcy, Steve, and Marcy, Janis. *Pre-Algebra with Pizzazz.* Palo Alto, CA: Creative Publications, 1978.

Meyer, Jerome, S. *Fun with Mathematics.* New York: The World Publishing Company, 1952.

National Council of Teachers of Mathematics. *Curriculum and Evaluation Standards for School Mathematics.* Reston, VA: NCTM, 1989.

LIST 304   (Continued)

National Council of Teachers of Mathematics. *Learning and Teaching Geometry, K–12, 1987 Yearbook.* Reston, VA: NCTM, 1987.

National Council of Teachers of Mathematics. *Professional Standards for Teaching Mathematics.* Reston, VA: NCTM, 1991.

Osen, Lynn, M. *Women in Mathematics.* Cambridge: The MIT Press, 1974.

Overholt, Dr. James, L. *Dr. Jim's Elementary Math Prescriptions.* Santa Monica: Goodyear Publishing Company, Inc., 1978.

Papert, Seymour. *Mindstorms: Children, Computers and Powerful Ideas.* New York: Basic Books, Inc., 1980.

Parson, Russel D. *Essentials of Mathematics.* New York: Wiley, 1989.

Peterson, Ivars. *The Mathematical Tourist: Snapshots of Modern Mathematics.* New York: W.H. Freeman and Company, 1988.

Room, Adrian. *The Guinness Book of Numbers.* Great Britain: Guinness Publishing Ltd., 1989.

Schlossberg, Edwin, and Brockman, John. *The Pocket Calculator Gamebook.* New York: William Morrow and Company, Inc., 1975.

Smoothey, Marion. *Let's Investigate Circles.* New York: Marshall Cavendish Corporation, 1993.

Smoothey, Marion. *Let's Investigate Number Patterns.* New York: Marshall Cavendish Corporation, 1993.

Sobel, M., and Maltsky, E. *Essentials of Mathematics with Consumer Applications.* Lexington, MA: Gunn and Co., 1977.

Thompson, Frances M. *Hands-on Math!: Ready-to-Use Games and Activities for Grades 4–8.* New York: The Center for Applied Research in Education, 1994.

Tobias, Sheila. *Succeed with Math: Every Student's Guide to Conquering Math Anxiety.* New York: The College Board, 1987.

Wooton, William, et. al. *Modern Trigonometry.* Boston: Houghton Mifflin Co., 1976.

Part II

Reproducibles

The reproducibles that follow are designed to support various programs and needs, and can be adapted to fit your lessons and teaching style. For example, "Number Lines" saves you the trouble of making number lines. Some of the samples on the sheet have been labeled, while others are not, allowing you to put in your own values. "Decimal Squares" shows your students the relationship between wholes, tenths, and hundredths. "Blank Checks" and "Blank Check Register" provide you with pre-made checks and a register that you can use to demonstrate to your students the proper way to write and record checks.

The other reproducibles can be just as helpful. In some cases you may wish to create transparencies to use with an overhead projector, or make your own manipulatives by cutting out the designs and laminating them.

Number Lines

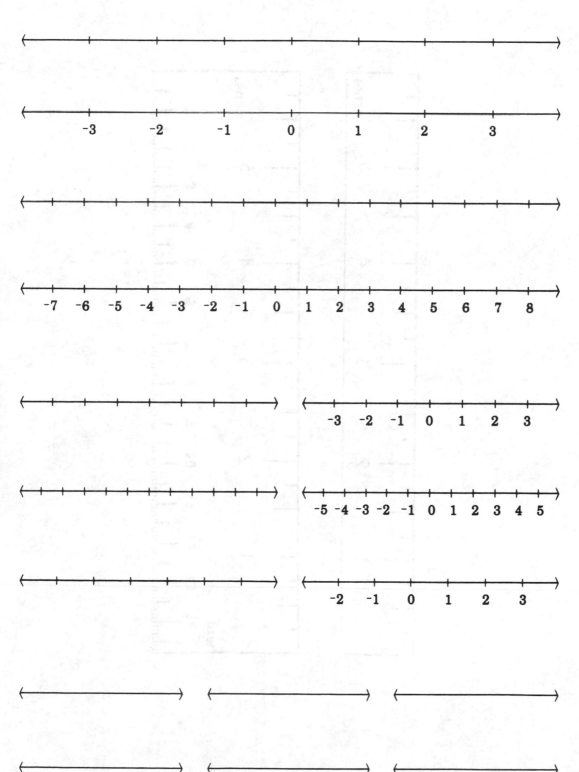

Rulers

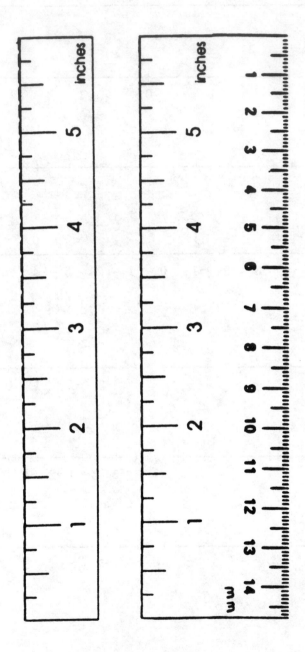

Rulers

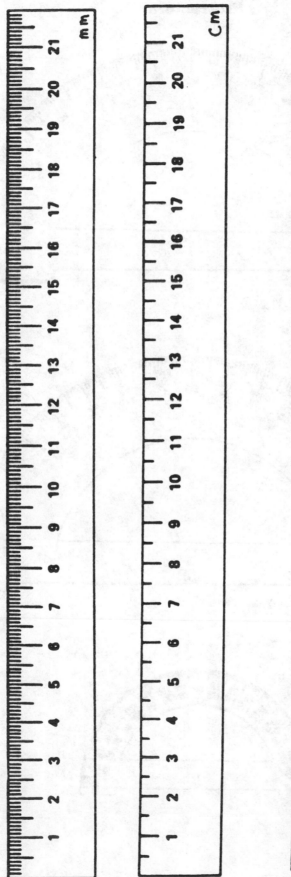
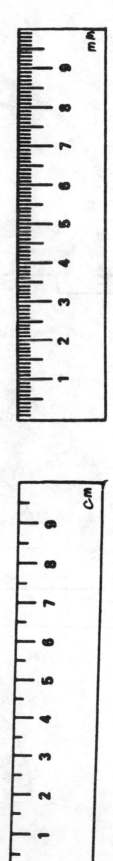

The Math Teacher's Book of Lists, © 1995 by Prentice Hall

Protractors

The Math Teacher's Book of Lists, © 1995 by Prentice Hall

Squares

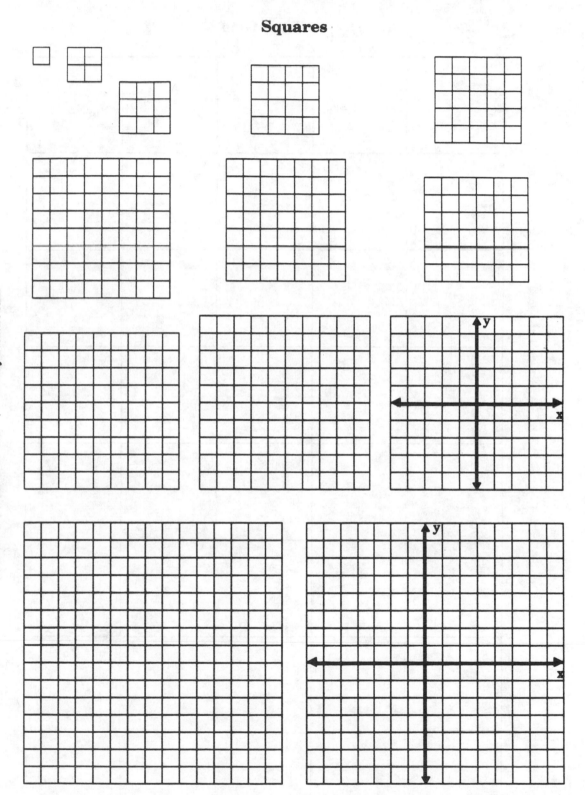

1 Inch Grid

½ Inch Grid

1 Cm Grid

The Math Teacher's Book of Lists, © 1995 by Prentice Hall

Isometric Dot Paper

Square Grid Dot Paper

The Math Teacher's Book of Lists, © 1995 by Prentice Hall

Decimal Squares

Fraction Strips

1											

$\frac{1}{2}$ $\frac{1}{2}$

$\frac{1}{3}$ $\frac{1}{3}$ $\frac{1}{3}$

$\frac{1}{4}$ $\frac{1}{4}$ $\frac{1}{4}$ $\frac{1}{4}$

$\frac{1}{5}$ $\frac{1}{5}$ $\frac{1}{5}$ $\frac{1}{5}$ $\frac{1}{5}$

$\frac{1}{6}$ $\frac{1}{6}$ $\frac{1}{6}$ $\frac{1}{6}$ $\frac{1}{6}$ $\frac{1}{6}$

$\frac{1}{8}$ $\frac{1}{8}$ $\frac{1}{8}$ $\frac{1}{8}$ $\frac{1}{8}$ $\frac{1}{8}$ $\frac{1}{8}$ $\frac{1}{8}$

$\frac{1}{9}$ $\frac{1}{9}$ $\frac{1}{9}$ $\frac{1}{9}$ $\frac{1}{9}$ $\frac{1}{9}$ $\frac{1}{9}$ $\frac{1}{9}$ $\frac{1}{9}$

$\frac{1}{10}$ $\frac{1}{10}$ $\frac{1}{10}$ $\frac{1}{10}$ $\frac{1}{10}$ $\frac{1}{10}$ $\frac{1}{10}$ $\frac{1}{10}$ $\frac{1}{10}$ $\frac{1}{10}$

$\frac{1}{12}$ $\frac{1}{12}$ $\frac{1}{12}$ $\frac{1}{12}$ $\frac{1}{12}$ $\frac{1}{12}$ $\frac{1}{12}$ $\frac{1}{12}$ $\frac{1}{12}$ $\frac{1}{12}$ $\frac{1}{12}$ $\frac{1}{12}$

Fraction Circles

Algebra Tiles

The Math Teacher's Book of Lists, © 1995 by Prentice Hall

Tangram

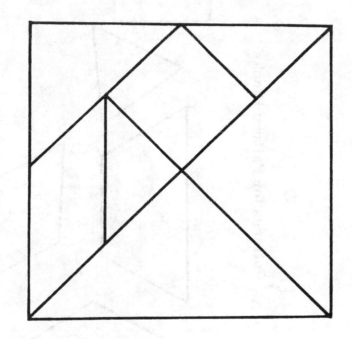

Patterns for Pattern Blocks

Patterns for Cuisenaire Rods

Net for Rectangular Prism

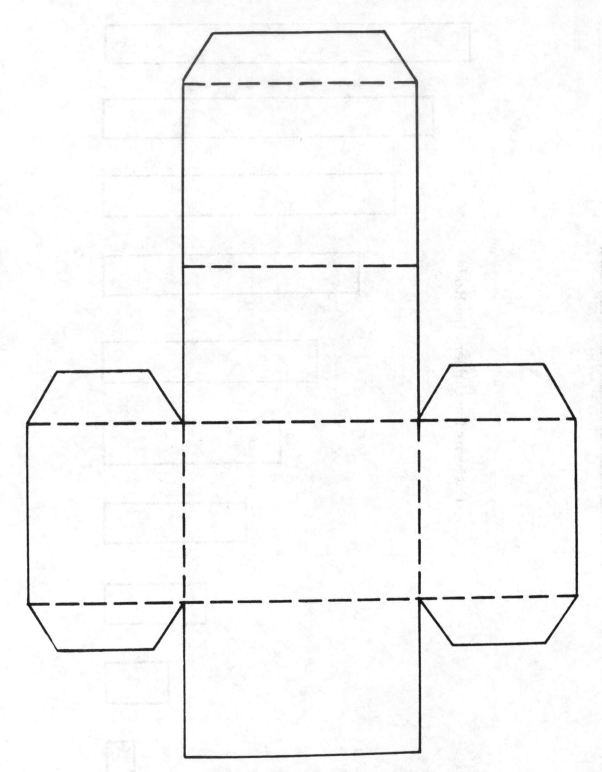

Net for Pyramid

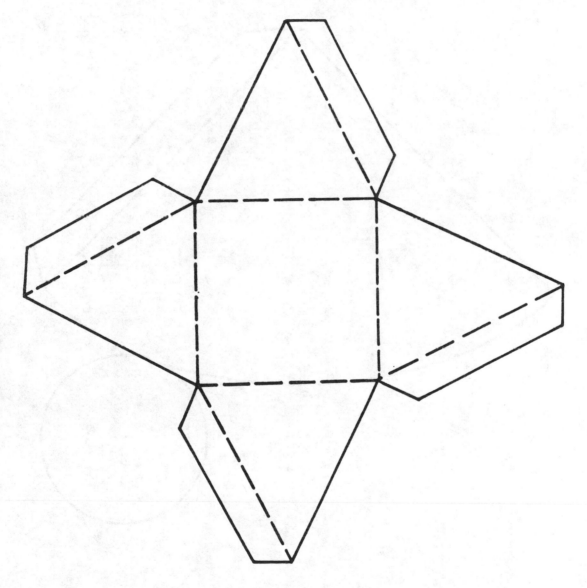

Net for Cone

The Math Teacher's Book of Lists, © 1995 by Prentice Hall

Net for Tetrahedron

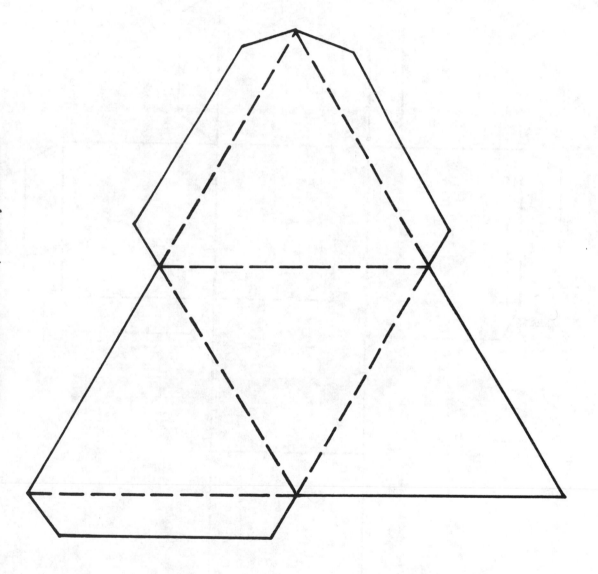

Net for Hexahedron (Cube)

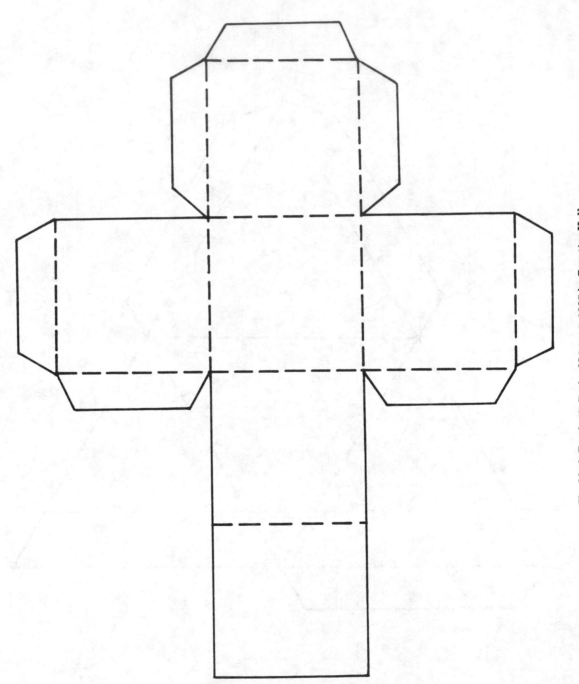

Net for Octahedron

Net for Dodecahedron

Net for Icosahedron

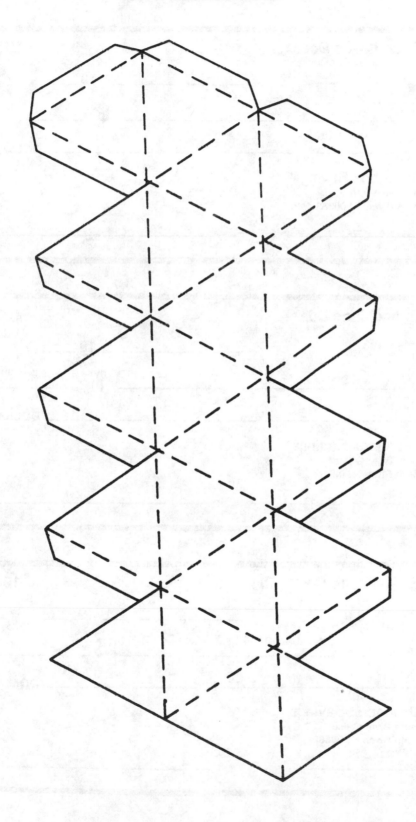

Blank Checks

John E. and Jane Doe   101

PAY
TO THE
ORDER OF _____ $ _____

_____ DOLLARS

Strongbox Savings
South River Office
South River, NJ 08882

FOR _____   _____

John E. and Jane Doe   102

PAY
TO THE
ORDER OF _____ $ _____

_____ DOLLARS

Strongbox Savings
South River Office
South River, NJ 08882

FOR _____   _____

John E. and Jane Doe   103

PAY
TO THE
ORDER OF _____ $ _____

_____ DOLLARS

Strongbox Savings
South River Office
South River, NJ 08882

FOR _____   _____

The Math Teacher's Book of Lists, © 1995 by Prentice Hall

Blank Check Register

The Math Teacher's Book of Lists, © 1995 by Prentice Hall

Check Number	Date	Description of Transaction	Payment Debit	✓	Deposit/ Credit	Balance